Financial
Words You
Should Know

Financial
Words You Should Know

Over **1,000** Essential Investment,
Accounting, Real Estate, and Tax Words

Michele Cagan, CPA and P.T. Shank

Aadamsmedia
Avon, Massachusetts

Copyright © 2009 by F+W Media, Inc.
All rights reserved.
This book, or parts thereof, may not be reproduced in any form without permission from the publisher; exceptions are made for brief excerpts used in published reviews.

Published by
Adams Media, a division of F+W Media, Inc.
57 Littlefield Street, Avon, MA 02322. U.S.A.
www.adamsmedia.com

ISBN 10: 1-60550-035-6
ISBN 13: 978-1-60550-035-5

Printed in the United States of America.

J I H G F E D C B A

Library of Congress Cataloging-in-Publication Data
is available from the publisher.

This publication is designed to provide accurate and authoritative information with regard to the subject matter covered. It is sold with the understanding that the publisher is not engaged in rendering legal, accounting, or other professional advice. If legal advice or other expert assistance is required, the services of a competent professional person should be sought.
—From a *Declaration of Principles* jointly adopted by a Committee of the American Bar Association and a Committee of Publishers and Associations

Many of the designations used by manufacturers and sellers to distinguish their product are claimed as trademarks. Where those designations appear in this book and Adams Media was aware of a trademark claim, the designations have been printed with initial capital letters.

Disclaimer: This book is not intended to take the place of professional financial advice. Please speak to a professional financial planner before making any decisions about your money.

This book is available at quantity discounts for bulk purchases.
For information, please call 1-800-289-0963.

*This book is dedicated to Yogi,
my best boy (my key grip).*
—MICHELE CAGAN

*This book is dedicated to David Willis . . .
for all the reasons it deserves to be.*
—P.T. SHANK

Contents

Introduction / xi

Financial Words You Should Know is categorized into the following sections:

Accounting / 2

Banking / 35

Bonds / 51

Economy / 69

Financial Planning / 90

Fund Investing / 115

Investing / 135

Real Estate / 177

Retirement / 192

Stocks / 201

Taxes / 223

Index / 239

Acknowledgments

I'd like to thank P. T. Shank, someONE I've really come to count on. Also, thanks to Jacky Sach, who's done so much for my career. And a big thanks to my ice cream supplier, without whom I would have had nothing to eat while writing this book.

—Michele Cagan

As with any book, there are people I must thank. First, Michele Cagan for one! One New Book! HAH-Hah-hah. Al Burgos, who taught me so much last time that I was able to use again this time. Heather McLean and Steve Tolle, for being such amazing cheerleaders from the very beginning. The usual suspects—Mitchell and Ed; Christine and Scott; Bridget and the Muppet; and Shanna—for just being there. Always. And, of course, Dr. C. Rex Mix and Betty Witt.

—P. T. Shank

Introduction

If you're over the age of eighteen, you either have a retirement account or know you'll need one. At some point in your life, you've probably at least thought about buying a house, a condo, or a car. And most of us understand the general idea of investing, managing our finances, and using our money to make more money. It's the details that sometimes bog us down.

For too many people, our retirement and savings planning is limited to the annual visit from the HR department where we work. They come in, talk about insurance, assets, retirement, and mutual funds . . . and it all goes straight over our heads. For those of us who are self-employed and have to wade through all the options without the benefit of a human resources representative, it can be even more daunting. Mutual funds, money market accounts, stocks, bonds, derivatives . . . sometimes it seems as if it would be easier to keep our money under our mattresses and hope for the best. But that's probably not an ideal solution and it makes your mattress very lumpy. So what to do?

That's where *Financial Words You Should Know* comes in. While this book won't, and shouldn't, replace sound financial advice, it will help you better understand the advice you're getting. It has more than 1,000 of the most commonly used financial words and phrases you are likely to come across.

Finances are important—too important not to understand. *Financial Words You Should Know* can help. And you won't need to sleep on a lumpy mattress.

Financial
Words You Should Know

ACCOUNTING

Accountant's opinion
A formal statement prepared by an independent certified public accountant (CPA) that spells out his judgment about the veracity and completeness of a set of financial statements prepared by company. When he believes those statements to be materially complete and accurate, his judgment will be "unqualified." A "qualified" judgment indicates that the statements may not be reliable sources of information, and that potential investors should beware.

See also: Annual report, CPA, Financial statements

Pete needed an **accountant's opinion** *before the bank would even consider his request for a business loan.*

Accounts payable (AP)
Short-term liabilities incurred by a business when it buys on credit from suppliers. Often associated with inventory purchases.

See also: Balance sheet, Liabilities

The flight school's bookkeeper kept track of the **accounts payable** *to ensure the school stayed in good standing with their vendors.*

Accounts receivable (AR)
An asset held by a business that measures the money still owed to them for their credit sales, but AR does not include credit card sales, unless the card is issued by that business, for instance, a department store card.

See also: Asset

The **accounts receivable** *office kept track of who owed the company money.*

Accrual
An accounting term used to describe revenue or expenses recognized although no cash has yet changed hands (for example, interest earned but not yet received).

See also: Accounts payable, Accounts receivable

The bookkeeper accounted for all the **accruals** *at the end of the period so the company's books would be accurate when the tax accountant arrived.*

Accrued interest
Money earned on an investment but not yet paid, typically occurring for investments (such as bonds) with fixed earnings and payout dates.

See also: Bond

Jack kept track of his **accrued interest** *so he knew approximately how much to expect when the check came.*

Accumulated depreciation
An accounting measure that holds the cumulative total of depreciation taken over the life of an asset.

See also: Asset, Depreciation

The **accumulated depreciation** *on the machinist's equipment made it appear worthless on the books, even though it was really worth thousands of dollars.*

Acid-test ratio
A measure of a company's ability to pay its short-term liabilities on time without having to sell off inventory. Calculated by dividing total short-term liabilities into the sum of cash, accounts receivable, and short-term investments. Results of 1.0 and higher indicate good liquidity. Also called the "quick ratio."

See also: Liabilities, Liquidity, Ratio analysis

Juanita always showed her clients the results of the **acid-test ratio** *before recommending an investment in a particular company.*

Acquisition cost
The total price paid to acquire an asset, including such things as sales tax, broker commissions, and delivery charges.

See also: Asset, Broker, Commission

The total **acquisition cost** *of 100 shares of stock came to $1,250 even though the market price was only $11 per share.*

Active income
Earnings derived from physical participation in a business activity. Active income includes earnings such as salary, wages, and profits from a business in which the owner actually works.

See also: Passive income, Portfolio income

Since Dan worked in the human services field, his **active income** *wasn't high, making his investments even more important.*

Adjusted cost basis
The full dollar amount paid for an investment, plus any fees paid (such as brokers' commissions). Can also be impacted by financial events, such as stock splits.

See also: Broker, Capital gains, Securities

After commissions and four stock splits, the **adjusted cost basis** *of Susan's Lion Joe shares bore almost no resemblance to the market price she'd paid for them.*

Aggressive accounting
Deceptive accounting practices used by companies to make their financial statements appear better than they are, especially when it comes to profits. Also called "cooking the books."

See also: Financial statements, Profit

The ethical CFO refused to work with companies that even considered **aggressive accounting.**

Annual report
A document prepared each year by a publicly held corporation or mutual fund to inform shareholders and potential investors about its financial performance, including audited financial statements covering the preceding year's activity.

See also: Financial statements, Mutual fund, Publicly held

Potential investors would do well to study a corporation's **annual report** *before investing large amounts of money.*

Appraisal
A professional valuation of an asset.

See also: Asset

The insurance company asked for an outside **appraisal** *of the woman's antiques before writing her policy.*

Asset
Anything of value, which may or may not have a physical form, owned by a person or other entity, such as a business or government office.

See also: Intangible asset

When money gets tight, people often forget that they may still have **assets** *that can be used to generate wealth or secure loans.*

Asset class
An investment category, such as stocks or real estate.
> See also: Asset

Marion's broker advised her to broaden her portfolio holdings because she was overloaded in a single **asset class**.

Asset coverage test
An accounting ratio that measures whether a company will be able to pay off its existing long-term debt obligations (such as bonds) with its existing assets after all current liabilities are met. This test is used to evaluate the risk of default on corporate bond issues. It is more effective when the market value, rather than the book value, of the assets is used in the equation.
> See also: Bond, Default risk, Ratio analysis

The CEO regularly insisted on an **asset coverage test** *to ensure the company was in solid financial shape.*

Asset turnover
A financial ratio that shows the dollar amount of sales generated per dollar of a company's assets, which is calculated by dividing revenue by total assets. This ratio shows how well a company is using its assets to produce sales; a higher result is better.
> See also: Fundamental analysis, Ratio analysis

The committee was charged with making the company's **asset turnover** *more efficient.*

Audit
Examination of financial records to verify their authenticity and accuracy.
> See also: IRS

Most Americans fear an IRS **audit** *even more than they fear a colonoscopy.*

Audited statements
Detailed financial reports that have been verified by an independent source, typically a reputable CPA firm.
> See also: CPA, Financial statements

Publicly traded corporations are required to present **audited statements** *to their shareholders and to the SEC.*

Average
A value calculated by adding all the numbers in a group, then dividing that sum by the number of numbers. For example, the average of 5, 7, 8 = (5+7+8)/3. Often used in quantitative analysis calculations and financial ratios.

See also: Weighted average

Brianna was happy as long as the day's **average** *share price was higher than what she'd paid for her stock.*

Average cost method
A way to calculate the basis of individual assets in a pool of like assets. Computed by dividing the total dollar value of the pool by the number of assets in the pool. Usually used to determine basis for stock or mutual fund shares when calculating capital gains or losses at tax time.

See also: Basis, FIFO, LIFO

When Veronica sold half of her mutual fund shares, she reported her gains on Schedule D using the **average cost method.**

Balance sheet
A financial statement that lays out the financial situation of a company on a specific date. This statement provides a summary of the company's total assets, liabilities, and equity.

See also: Asset, Equity, Liabilities

Joanne scrutinized the company's **balance sheet** *before deciding whether to invest in it.*

Basis
The full purchase price of a security, including any taxes, commissions, and fees paid. Also known as tax basis.

See also: Capital gains

Brenda's accountant made her keep track of the **basis** *for every investment she had so he wouldn't have to track down the information when she sold those investments years later.*

Big Four
The four biggest accounting firms in the United States often called upon by publicly traded corporations to issue official opinions on the companies' financial statements.

See also: Accountant's opinion, CPA

Between them, the **Big Four** *issued opinions on virtually every corporation listed on the New York Stock Exchange.*

Black knight
A company that attempts a hostile takeover on a target company
> See also: Hostile takeover
>
> *When Lion Joe Coffees heard the rumor of a* **black knight**, *the board immediately rallied to stave off the takeover.*

Board of directors
The governing body of a corporation, as elected by the corporation's shareholders.
> See also: Corporation, Voting rights
>
> *The* **board of directors** *voted to start dealing only with other organizations that upheld fair-trade practices.*

Book value
An accounting calculation that measures the net worth of a company by subtracting its outstanding liabilities from its total assets; also used to measure the net worth of individual assets by subtracting accumulated depreciation from the full cost of that asset.
> See also: Accumulated depreciation, Asset, Liabilities
>
> *Although the corporation appeared to be in good financial shape because of its high earnings, its* **book value** *told a different story.*

Capital lease
A lease agreement that conveys effective ownership of an asset, even though technically it is not owned by the lessee. Calls for special accounting treatment, where the asset is included on the balance sheet of the lessee.
> See also: Balance sheet, Operating lease
>
> *The ballet company had a* **capital lease** *through the convention center on the building they used for a rehearsal space and smaller productions.*

Capital loss
The amount by which the total purchase cost of an asset exceeds its selling price.
> See also: Capital gains
>
> *Dennis sold some stock for quick cash, but he suffered a* **capital loss** *on the sale.*

Capital structure
The methods a company uses to finance its assets, which typically include a combination of equity investment and short- and long-term debt.
> See also: Debt, Debt-to-equity ratio, Equity
>
> *Once the partners had their* **capital structure** *in place, they were able to open their new business.*

Carrying value

An accounting calculation used to measure a company's net worth, which is calculated by subtracting outstanding liabilities from total assets. Also known as "book value."

> See also: Accumulated depreciation, Asset, Liabilities

According to the **carrying value**, *the business wasn't doing as well financially as many investors believed.*

Cash flow

The movement of money into and out of a company, due to operating, financing, and investing activities.

> See also: Statement of cash flows

The software company ran into **cash flow** *issues when its latest upgrade didn't sell as well as expected.*

CEO (Chief executive officer)

The top executive of a company (often its president), who is responsible for overall decision-making for the company.

> See also: CFO

The new **CEO** *made it clear she would be taking the company in a new direction in order to keep the corporation modern.*

CFO (Chief financial officer)

The professional responsible for managing all the financial activities of a company. He sets the high-level financial policies for the company.

> See also: CEO

The **CFO** *was able to revitalize the corporation's budget and increase earnings in just two years.*

Churning and burning

The act, committed by unethical brokers, of excessively trading securities in a client account in order to increase commissions.

> See also: Boiler room, Fiduciary

The broker lost his reputation and most of his clients when it became public that he was **churning and burning.**

Commission

A service fee charged by brokers in exchange for their services, typically on a per-transaction basis. Rates vary widely by firm, but are usually highest for full-service brokers.

> See also: Broker, Discount broker, Full-service broker

Paying a **commission** *is usually a reasonable exchange for getting the wisdom and advice of a professional broker.*

Comparative statements
Financial reports for a single company from different time periods, which are formatted in the same manner and presented side-by-side to make it easy for investors to spot patterns and trends.

See also: Financial statements

Prior to making a large investment with a corporation, Bill liked to see the **comparative statements** *so he could draw his own conclusions.*

Conglomerate
A big company that has a controlling interest in several other, seemingly unrelated, smaller businesses.

See also: Wholly owned subsidiary

Laverne was shocked to learn that the company that made her child's playpen was owned by the same **conglomerate** *that owned a weapons manufacturer.*

Consolidation
The combination of two or more companies (or product lines) into a single new entity.

See also: Merger

The computer company and the software company realized that a **consolidation** *would increase efficiency for both of them.*

Controller
The top financial manager in a company, usually in charge of the accounting systems and related departments. In small companies, he may also be the CFO. Sometimes called the "comptroller."

See also: CFO

The **controller** *made all the financial decisions for the company, reporting only to the board of directors.*

Cook the books
Fraudulent accounting practices used by corporations to make their financial statements, particularly profits, look better than they are.

See also: Financial statements, Profit

The executives of the corporation faced charges when it came to light they had known about and approved of the plan to **cook the books**.

Corporate charter

A legal document that creates a corporation and sets the rules it follows. Information includes the name and purpose of the company, the number of shares authorized to be sold, and the names of the people creating the corporation. Filed with the state government where the corporation is based.

See also: Authorized shares, Corporation

The business partners celebrated the culmination of their dreams once the **corporate charter** *had been filed.*

Corporation

A company that operates as a separate legal "person," with its own legal rights and obligations. Owners, also known as "shareholders," bear no legal responsibility for the actions or financial obligations of the company. Ownership is measured in shares of the company, called "stock."

See also: Common stock, Limited liability

Lionel and Joe formed their **corporation** *in the hopes that one day it would be big enough to trade on the New York Stock Exchange.*

Cost of goods sold (COGS)

The amount originally paid for inventory items that have been sold to customers.

See also: Statement of profit and loss

Every company that sells goods has to show **costs of goods sold** *in their financial statements.*

Cost of sales

The original dollar amount paid to purchase the inventory items that have been sold to customers. More often called "cost of goods sold."

See also: Statement of profit and loss

The bookkeeper ensured the **cost of sales** *showed up on every one of the shop's financial reports.*

CPA (Certified public accountant)

A financial professional, licensed by the state in which she practices after fulfilling strict education requirements and passing a comprehensive series of exams.

See also: Broker, Certified financial planner

Molly hired a **CPA** *to do her annual tax returns and help with some financial planning.*

Credit cliff

When a company already struggling with debt problems faces additional troubles, which can cause a lowering of their credit rating. Companies with lowered credit ratings have to pay higher interest rates for their loans, increasing their costs of financing and cutting further into their cash.

See also: Credit rating, Default

The airline faced a **credit cliff** *when fuel prices skyrocketed and their vendors wouldn't extend any more credit.*

Current ratio

A mathematical measure of a company's ability to pay its short-term liabilities in a timely manner. Calculated by dividing total current assets by total current liabilities. A result of less than 1.0 indicates liquidity problems.

See also: Liquidity, Ratio analysis

James was concerned when the **current ratio** *on Lion Joe Corporation, his biggest investment, dropped below 1.0.*

Debt-to-equity ratio

A statistical measurement of a company's overall financial leverage, which is calculated by dividing the company's total outstanding long-term liabilities by its total outstanding common stock at book value. A result of more than 1.0 indicates a highly leveraged company, i.e., a company potentially drowning in debt.

See also: Book value, Common stock, Leverage

The board of directors considered replacing the CFO when they realized how high the company's **debt-to-equity ratio** *was getting.*

Debt-to-income ratio

This calculation is useful to figure out how much loan someone can afford, often used when trying to buy a house. Calculated by dividing total monthly debt payments by total monthly income, where a result of less than 35% is considered good.

See also: Credit rating, Mortgage

Danielle was pleased at the amount of house she was going to be able to afford based on her **debt-to-income ratio.**

Depreciation

An accounting calculation used to show an asset's loss of value (i.e., wear and tear) over time.

See also: Asset

The corporation's income statement showed $1 million in **depreciation** *expense the previous year.*

Divestiture
The act of getting rid of all or part of an investment or asset, which can happen in large chunks or in small pieces over a long time period.

See also: Asset

The woman demanded a rapid divestiture once she learned of the company's poor labor practices in its overseas factories.

Earnings
For an investor, a combination of capital gains, dividends, and interest produced by investments.

See also: Income, Profit

By the time she was fifty, Pauline was able to live off her investment earnings and use her paycheck for travel and spa sessions.

Earnings per share (EPS)
The net profit of a corporation divided by the total number of shares outstanding. Shows the portion of profits earned by a single share of stock.

See also: Dilution, Price-to-earnings ratio

When Lion Joe Corporation announced that its earnings per share had increased from last year, the stock price went up right away.

EBIT (Earnings before interest and taxes)
A company's profits before deductions are taken for interest expense related to long-term debt (meaning the interest that has to be paid on things such as bonds and mortgages) and income taxes. Also known as "operating income."

See also: Bond, Debt, Profit

The young company's EBIT was good, but needed to get better before their chief financial officer would be able to relax.

EBITDA (Earnings before interest, taxes, depreciation and amortization)
A company's profits before deductions are taken for interest expense related to long-term debt, income taxes, and depreciation and amortization expenses. Shows investors a truer picture of cash operations, particularly for companies with a large amount of fixed or intangible assets. Helps compare asset-heavy companies to other types of companies on a more level playing field.

See also: Amortization, Depreciation, Fixed assets, Intangible asset

Ethan's financial advisor told him to look at a company's EBITDA, as well as its cash flows and debt ratios before making any investment decisions.

Economies of scale
A per-unit cost advantage that comes with increased production levels. For example, if a company pays $1,000 rent for their factory and produces 100 units, the rent expense is $10 per unit. If they produce 500 items, the per-unit rent expense drops to just $2 per unit, thereby lowering the costs associated with each unit.

See also: Fixed expenses, Overhead

Often in manufacturing, the trick is to balance **economies of scale** *with quality workmanship without sacrificing either.*

Entrepreneur
A small business owner, usually of a unique or innovative business.

See also: Angel investor

The run-down building had stood empty until an **entrepreneur** *with vision realized it could be a lovely little tea shop.*

Equity
The portion of an asset or group of assets that is owned outright and not funded by debt.

See also: Debt

The couple had enough **equity** *in their house to borrow against it in order to remodel.*

Equity financing
Funding a company by selling ownership interest in the company, rather than by incurring debt.

See also: Debt, Equity

Since the computer techs didn't want to start out owing huge amounts of money, they used **equity financing** *to get their company up and running.*

Expense
The normal costs of trying to earn revenues.

See also: Profit

Many small business owners underestimate the actual **expense** *of starting up a new shop.*

Extraordinary item
A one-time business event (such as a flood loss) that substantially affects the net profits of a company. Reported separately on the statement of profit and loss to allow statement readers to see the extent of the impact.

See also: Statement of profit and loss

Vern knew to look for the **extraordinary item** *listing once he saw the report of the warehouse fire on the national news.*

Fair market value
The dollar amount an asset would sell for on the open market.

See also: Asset

The con man tried to get people to buy worthless stocks by claiming he was offering them well below **fair market value.**

Fat cat
Lingo for an excessively overpaid executive.

See also: CEO, CFO

After the merger, the new board of directors required the resignation of the **fat cat** *CEO who had been so ineffective for so long.*

FIFO (First in, first out)
A method for determining basis when selling a portion of an investment whose shares have been accumulated over time. The first shares that were purchased are considered the ones sold for purposes of determining capital gain or loss.

See also: Basis

Roni decided to use **FIFO** *to report her basis when she sold her shares in Lion Joe, because the first shares she bought had been at the highest price.*

Financial statements
The three reports—the Balance Sheet, Statement of Profit and Loss, and Statement of Cash Flows—that together detail the current financial strength of a company.

See also: 10-K, Annual report, Audited statements, Balance sheet, Statement of cash flows, Statement of profit and loss

Investors can learn more about a corporation's overall health by studying its **financial statements** *than by just reading the hype and looking at the pictures in the company's annual report.*

Fiscal year
The twelve-month period used for accounting purposes.

See also: Financial statements

The company had already met its goals by the time it was three-quarters through the **fiscal year.**

Fixed assets
A term for tangible property, including real property, which a business expects to used for at least one year.

See also: Balance sheet, Liquid assets

Todd's lawn mowers and trucks were some of the most important **fixed assets** *owned by his landscaping business.*

Fixed expenses
Business costs that remain stable regardless of sales or production. Examples include rent, property taxes, and interest expense.
  See also: Overhead

  The **fixed expenses** *were the easiest for the new business owners to plan into their budget.*

Forensic accounting
The investigation of a company's accounting information, providing information that can be used in court.
  See also: Cook the books

  News of the scandal broke when **forensic accounting** *uncovered an embezzlement scheme.*

Free cash flow
The amount of cash a company has on hand after paying all of its expenses, dividend payments, and making investments in assets. Indicative of a company's financial well-being.
  See also: Cash flow

  Tal encouraged his clients to look at a company's **free cash flow** *before making an investment decision.*

General partner
A person who owns an unincorporated business with at least one other person, yet bears personal financial responsibility for the entire enterprise.
  See also: Corporation, Limited partner

  Although the plumber's son was part owner of the company, the plumber himself was the sole **general partner.**

Godfather offer
A takeover bid made by an acquiring company that's so good it can't be refused by the company that's being bought (also known as the "target company"). Typically, it's an offer to pay well over market price for shares in the target company.
  See also: Acquisition

  Although Robert had never planned to sell his business, when the corporation made him a **godfather offer,** *he decided it was time to retire.*

Going concern
A company that has strong prospects for staying in business and staying solvent for the foreseeable future.
> See also: Bankruptcy, Insolvency, Liquidate

Investors were still comfortable buying the Lion Joe's stock because, despite temporary financial instability, they knew it was a **going concern**.

Golden handcuffs
Incentive benefits offered to employees to entice them into staying in their jobs.
> See also: Incentive stock option

Although the hours were long and her social life was almost nonexistent, the **golden handcuffs** *kept Jean at her firm.*

Golden parachute
Special generous benefits (such as stock options and sizable severance packages) promised to top employees of a company in the event the company is taken over. Considered protection against hostile takeover.
> See also: Hostile takeover, Stock options

Lion Joe Corporation had deep enough pockets that even the **golden parachutes** *offered by the target company weren't enough to prevent the takeover.*

Goodwill
A financial measure of a company's reputation, good name, and popularity. Equals the difference between fair market value of the company's actual assets and the excess amount someone would be willing to pay for those assets. Considered an intangible asset. Examples include name and brand recognition.
> See also: Fair market value, Intangible asset

The popular soda manufacturer included substantial **goodwill** *on its balance sheet, as its main product was a bestseller throughout the world.*

Gray knight
A second party that tries to muscle in on an ongoing takeover attempt, hoping to profit from discord between the target company and the original bidder.
> See also: Black knight, White knight

The **gray knight** *was able to purchase the company for a much better price than it had ever hoped for when the original takeover went bad.*

Growth rate
The percentage increase in a specific financial value between two periods. Usually measures the change in revenues, earnings, or dividends.
>See also: Dividend, Earnings, Revenue
>
>*Scott was pleased with the phenomenal* **growth rate** *on his Lion Joe stock.*

Holding company
A corporation that owns the controlling interest in other corporations, and therefore affects their management and operations.
>See also: Controlling interest
>
>*The off-beat clothing manufacturer hoped to remain independent and not under the control of a* **holding company**.

Hostile takeover
When one company acquires ownership of a second company against the express wishes of the second company's primary owners, management, or board of directors.
>See also: Board of directors, Merger
>
>*The two small firms merged in order to avoid the* **hostile takeover** *that was being threatened by an industry giant.*

Illiquid
Unable to be converted quickly into cash. Usually used in reference to fixed assets (including real estate) or securities for which there's no ready market.
>See also: Liquid
>
>*Although the man was asset-rich, he was* **illiquid**, *which made it difficult when he needed cash flow.*

Impaired asset
A company asset that's worth less on the open market than on the company's books, giving a distorted picture of the company's net worth. Often results in a write-down of the asset to the current market value.
>See also: Asset, Write-down
>
>*The warehouse would be an* **impaired asset** *to the company until it received serious rehabbing.*

In play
Industry lingo for a company that's up for sale and has received an initial bid.
>See also: Acquisition
>
>*No one was surprised that the corporation was* **in play** *so quickly considering its overall value.*

ACCOUNTING

In sight
When commodities underlying a futures contract are about to be delivered.

See also: Commodity, Futures

Investors breathed easier once the wheat had made it through the rainy season without being ruined and was **in sight***.*

Inflation-adjusted return
A way to measure investment returns after the impact of inflation. The simplest way to calculate this is to subtract the current inflation rate from the rate of return. This shows investors whether their investments are outpacing inflation.

See also: Inflation, Rate of return

Debbie was pleased that the **inflation-adjusted return** *on her portfolio showed her overall investments were growing much faster than inflation.*

Insider trading
A practice of buying and selling securities based on information known only to officers and high-level employees of a corporation. When done legally, the transactions are reported to the SEC. The illegal version involves a breach of fiduciary duty or unauthorized access to such nonpublic information resulting in an unreported transaction, and is prohibited under securities laws.

See also: Fiduciary, SEC, Securities law

A professional's morals and ethics must be strong in order to resist the understandable allure of **insider trading***.*

Intangible asset
An item of value which has no physical form, such as a copyright or patent.

See also: Amortization, Asset

With the advent of the Internet, the legalities of **intangible assets** *are becoming more important than ever for artists and musicians.*

Interest coverage ratio
A financial calculation that shows how well a company can handle its upcoming interest payments. Computed by dividing EBIT (earnings before interest and taxes) by interest expense for the same period. A result greater than 2 indicates the company can easily meet its interest obligations, while a result less than 1 shows that the company may not be able to make timely interest payments. Should be used by investors thinking about buying corporate bonds. Also called "times interest earned (TIE)."

See also: Corporate bonds, EBIT, Solvency

The **interest coverage ratio** *showed that the company was struggling to make interest payments, even though earnings were higher than last year.*

Internal rate of return (IRR)
The growth rate expected by a business for a project it plans to invest in. Used by companies for capital budgeting purposes, particularly when comparing potential projects. The project with the highest result has the best chance of adding to the company earnings.

See also: Growth rate

The company was willing to make less in its games division because their next piece of technology had an incredibly high **internal rate of return.**

Intrinsic value
The real worth of a company, based on things such as its assets and equity as well as other less measurable factors such as insightful management. May be completely unrelated to the current market value of the stock. Often looked at by value investors to find "bargain" stocks.

See also: Fundamental analysis, Value investing

The CEO's attitude toward employee and client relationships raised the company's **intrinsic value** *above that of its competitors.*

Joint venture
When two individuals or companies come together for a specific business project, agreeing to share profits (or losses) and control, without officially merging.

See also: Merger

The **joint venture** *between the Marion's farm stand and Howard's delivery service boosted earnings for both parties.*

Kicking the tires
Slang for due diligence, a thorough investigation of a potential investment.

See also: Fundamental analysis, Ratio analysis, Technical analysis

David appreciated his financial advisor because she was good at **kicking the tires** *before recommending any investments in new corporations.*

Leaseback
A business arrangement where one company sells a major asset to another company, then rents it back from them. A strategy used when a company needs a big cash infusion, but still needs to use their asset. Also called "sale and leaseback."

See also: Asset, Lease

The landscaping company entered into a **leaseback** *with the tractor retailer and managed to score enough cash to stay in business.*

Leverage
The use of debt, rather than equity, to finance assets or investments.

See also: Debt, Debt-to-equity ratio, Equity

The corporation had a solid equity position, so the CEO authorized using **leverage** *to expand the factory.*

Leveraged buyout (LBO)
When one company buys another with borrowed funds (usually 90%), such as bonds or loans, and uses the target company's assets as collateral. Considered a predatory takeover practice, often used with hostile takeovers.

See also: Hostile takeover, Target company, Leverage

Predators Inc. borrowed more than $8 billion to complete their **leveraged buyout** *of Lion Joe Corporation.*

Liabilities
Business debts, as reported on the company balance sheet.

See also: Asset, Balance sheet

When Alonzo considered buying corporate bonds, he always analyzed the company's other **liabilities**.

LIFO (Last in, first out)
A way to figure out the basis when selling just a portion of an investment whose shares have been accumulated over time (such as when investors reinvest mutual fund earnings in more shares of the fund instead of getting a cash payment). The most recent shares purchased are considered to be the ones sold for tax purposes, to determine the capital gain or loss. Most often used when share prices have been rising, since the last shares purchased would come with the highest price tag, and therefore minimize any taxable gains.

See also: Basis, Capital gains, Capital loss

When Bonita sold half of her mutual fund shares, she used the **LIFO** *method to report her gains on her Schedule D.*

Limited liability
A legal concept where a person cannot lose more than a predetermined amount, usually the amount he has invested in a company; the company's creditors cannot sue the owners/shareholders personally, but can only go after company assets. This means that shareholders can lose their entire investment, but not more than that. It is a key feature of corporations and limited liability companies (LLCs).

See also: Corporation, Liabilities

Limited liability *protected Tina and Max from personal financial disaster when their company had to file bankruptcy.*

Limited partner

A person who owns an unincorporated business with at least one other person, but takes absolutely no part in running or maintaining that business. Financial responsibility is confined to his investment. Also known as a "silent partner."

> See also: General partner, Limited partnership

The musician became a **limited partner** *in many small businesses located in New Orleans, with the hope that the added financing would help rejuvenate the city.*

Limited partnership

An unincorporated business owned by at least two people, with at least one general partner and at least one limited partner.

> See also: General partner, Limited partner

Since Craig wanted to run the company and Toby had the cash flow to get it started, a **limited partnership** *was the ideal solution.*

Liquid

Able to be immediately converted into cash.

> See also: Liquid assets, Liquidity risk

Scott needed to stay relatively **liquid** *so he kept his savings in a money market account.*

Liquid assets

Cash and other property that can be immediately converted to cash.

> See also: Fixed assets

Financial institutions hold more **liquid assets** *than fixed assets.*

Liquidate

Selling off assets (or an entire business) for immediate cash, transforming illiquid into liquid assets.

> See also: Insolvency, Liquid

In an attempt to stay in business, the furniture company **liquidated** *several of its stores and downsized its personnel.*

Liquidity

The ability to pay obligations as they come due.

> See also: Insolvency

George always invests in companies with strong **liquidity** *because it means they can pay their bills and cash dividends.*

Lobster trap
One way for target companies to avoid a hostile takeover is to pass a rule that disallows shareholders who own more than 10% of the equity from converting any convertible securities they hold (which keeps them from adding to their voting stock).

See also: Hostile takeover

The board's **lobster trap** *ended the larger company's attempt at a takeover.*

Lower of cost and market method (LCM)
A required accounting practice (in the United States) where inventory must be recorded on the books at its lowest value, whether it's the current book value or the current replacement cost.

See also: Impaired asset, Write-down

Although it would cost nearly double the amount to replace, the accountants were required by the **lower of cost and market method** *to list the machine's value at just under $10,000.*

Macaroni defense
A strategy used to prevent hostile takeover, where the target company issues special bonds that have to be redeemed for a lot of money in the event of a takeover. (The name comes from the fact that pasta expands when you cook it.)

See also: Hostile takeover

Hostile Inc. no longer had the cash to take over the Lion Joe Corporation once its board of directors instituted a **macaroni defense.**

Management buyout (MBO)
When a company's executives buy a controlling interest in the company.

See also: Controlling interest

Tired of where the board of directors was taking the corporation, the upper executives pooled their resources and staged a **management buyout.**

Mark to market
Logging the daily price (or value) of a security (or a portfolio or account). Done to track profits and losses, or to make sure minimum margin requirements are met.

See also: Margin account

After his account was **marked to market,** *Antonio got a margin call from his broker.*

Market value

The current publicly quoted price for which an investor can purchase or sell a security.

See also: Exchange

The **market value** *of a popular stock can change dramatically in one day's trading.*

Median

The center value of a group of numbers. For example, the median of (2, 3, 5, 6, 7) = 5 (but the average would be 23/5, or 4.6). The word is frequently used in discussions about the economy and economic indicators. For example, a decline in median home prices spells bad news for existing homeowners and mortgage lenders.

See also: Economic indicator

The **median** *trading price for Lion Joe Inc. today was $108.*

Merger

The combination of two or more businesses into one, usually through acquisition of a smaller company by a larger one. One of the companies is folded into the other, and the primary company remains in existence; no new company is formed by this action.

See also: Consolidation

After the **merger,** *the large corporation worked very hard to avoid layoffs, in spite of many duplicated positions.*

Mode

The most commonly occurring number in a set. For example, the mode of (2,2,2,3,5,5,6,7,7) would be 2. In investing, it is the price at which most shares of a security are traded.

See also: Technical analysis

Terry bought stocks in Lion Joe Inc. at just the right time and was able to get them for several dollars less than the **mode.**

Monte Carlo simulation

A way to figure out the probability of possible outcomes by running computer simulations. For example, this simulation may be used to figure out how likely it is for a stock to go up in price under a variety of different situations (if tax rates increase, if inflation increases, if the economy tanks, etc.)

See also: Quantitative analysis

The market timer ran a **Monte Carlo simulation** *before deciding if she should buy a stock or not.*

Net earnings
On an investment, the amount left over after investing expenses (such as commissions) are subtracted from capital gains, interest, and dividends.

See also: Capital gains, Dividend, Interest

Her **net earnings** *were less than she'd expected because of hidden fees.*

Net income
A company's earnings, calculated by subtracting expenses and cost of goods sold from revenues. Reported on the company's Statement of Profit and Loss. Also called "net profit."

See also: Cost of goods sold, Expense

Although the company was still struggling, the accountants were able to report its **net income** *was finally rising.*

Net profit
The periodic earnings of a company, which are determined by subtracting expenses and cost of sales from revenues. Also called "net income."

See also: Cost of sales, Expense

In spite of the weakening economy, Lion Joe Properties' **net profit** *continued to rise.*

Off-balance sheet financing
Use of leases and other similar arrangements to obtain assets without incurring long-term debt (through a loan or bond issue) or issuing additional equity shares (both of which would show up on the company's balance sheet). Allows a company to use necessary high-cost assets without changing its net worth.

See also: Balance sheet, Operating lease

The excavation company used **off-balance sheet financing** *to make sure they had enough equipment to get the job done without incurring too much debt.*

Operating expenses
The non-sale-related normal expenditures required to run a company.

See also: Net income, Selling expenses

Many new business owners have discovered their **operating expenses** *to be greater than originally estimated.*

Operating lease
A rental contract that allows a company to use an asset, but doesn't let that company exercise ownership–such as rights over the asset (for example, making modifications to the asset, or letting another company use it). Lease payments are treated as expenses on a company's books.

See also: Capital lease, Lease

According to the **operating lease**, *Lion Joe Bookkeeping Services had to get permission before they could sublet their extra office space.*

Opinion shopping
When a publicly held corporation searches for a CPA who will issue an unqualified opinion on its financial statements. A practice prohibited by the SEC.

See also: CPA, Qualified opinion, SEC

The young intern's suggestion that the company go **opinion shopping** *was met with stony silence.*

OPM (Other people's money)
Industry lingo for using borrowed funds to invest.

See also: Margin, Leverage

George bought all his shares on margin, because he liked to trade using **OPM**.

Overhead
Business costs that can't be specifically connected to production or sales. Examples include telephone expense and liability insurance.

See also: Fixed expenses, Insurance

Brandon was concerned about lagging sales that month because he wasn't sure they would be able to pay their **overhead** *expenses.*

Pac-Man defense
A strategy used to prevent a hostile takeover, where the original target turns the tables and tries to take over the acquiring company. (Named after the old video game where the Pac-Man character can chase ghosts after eating a power pellet.)

See also: Hostile takeover

The board of Lion Joe Inc. launched a **Pac-Man defense** *against Aggressive Company to repel their hostile takeover bid.*

Parent company
One company that holds a substantial portion of the voting stock in another company, enough to influence management decisions.

See also: Conglomerate, Wholly owned subsidiary

The **parent company** *was concerned enough about its own reputation that it voted down projects that might tarnish it, even if the projects would help the subsidiary.*

PEG ratio (price/earnings to growth)
A multiple that compares the current market price of a stock to the rate at which the company's earnings are expected to increase. A relatively low result may indicate an undervalued stock.

See also: Growth rate, Growth stock, Multiple

Frank searched out stocks with low **PEG ratios** *expecting their prices to rise as the public caught on to their true value.*

Poison pill
A strategy used to prevent a hostile takeover, where the target corporation takes steps to make its stock look less appealing. Basically, the target offers more shares to existing shareholders (except for the ones attempting the takeover) at very attractive discounts, which both dilutes the share value and offers shareholders instant gains without selling out to the acquirer.

See also: Hostile takeover

Current investors took advantage of the discounted stock price as the company tried to create a **poison pill.**

Price/book ratio
A calculation that lets investors compare a corporation's market value (what its stock is trading for) to its book value (what the company actually has, its tangible assets minus outstanding liabilities). Calculated by dividing the current share price by the book value per share (as reported in the company's most recent financial statements).

See also: Book value, Financial statements

As a value investor, Gina always considered a company's **price/book ratio** *before making a trade decision.*

Pro forma financial statements
A set of projected fiscal reports for a company, using estimates based on a combination of past performance, prevailing economic conditions, and management plans and expectations. Often used in business plans.

See also: Financial statements

Based on the **pro forma financial statements,** *Andrea decided to invest another $25,000 in the company.*

Profit
The excess of revenues over expenses.

See also: Expense, Revenue

Every business, from a small storefront to a major corporation, must earn **profits** *in order to survive.*

Qualified opinion
An accountant's report, written about a set of client-prepared financial statements, that casts doubt on the accuracy and veracity of those statements. Its purpose is to warn potential investors that the financial statements may contain material misstatements, and that they should not be relied upon when making investment decisions.

See also: Financial statements, Unqualified opinion

When her daughters learned there was a **qualified opinion** *attached to the new firm, they encouraged her to invest elsewhere.*

Quality of earnings
An assessment of the profits of a business, based on how they were achieved. Increased profits due to increased sales or cost-cutting measures are high quality, while changes in accounting methods or other (legal) on-paper manipulations are low quality.

See also: Due diligence, Profit

When the corporation went from floundering to thriving in one quarter, investors began wondering about the **quality of earnings.**

Quick ratio
A mathematical measure of a company's ability to meet its short-term debt obligations promptly without having to sell off inventory. Computed by dividing total short-term liabilities into total quick assets (which equal the sum of cash, accounts receivable, and short-term investments). Also called the "acid-test ratio."

See also: Liabilities, Liquidity, Ratio analysis

After running a **quick ratio** *on Lion Joe Aviation, Roark decided to invest.*

Ratio analysis
A mathematical way to evaluate financial statements for potential or existing investments. Also called "quantitative analysis." Used to compare different companies within an industry, as well as to evaluate changes in a single company over time. Can help assess a company's liquidity, debt load, and performance.

See also: Current ratio, Debt-to-equity ratio, Financial statements, Quick ratio

The **ratio analysis** *showed the company wasn't doing as well as it seemed.*

Research and Development (R&D)
The investigation of potential products and services, which includes analysis, experimentation, creation, testing, and enhancement. Frequently called R&D.

See also: Pure play

The young graduate was thrilled to be hired onto such a well-respected **research and development** *team.*

Residual value
The assigned amount a car is worth at the end of its lease period, for which the lessee can purchase the car.

See also: Lease

The young man had put so many miles on the car during the term of the lease that it was hardly worth the **residual value** *and he decided not to buy it outright.*

Return on assets (ROA)
A mathematical measure of how well a company's assets are being used to produce profits. Helps investors compare companies to one another when making investment decisions. Calculated by dividing the company's profits for the year by its total assets and usually shown as a percentage.

See also: Asset turnover, Ratio analysis

The consultant was able to use **ROA** *to show the board they could be more efficient with their assets.*

Return on sales
A measure of the amount of profit produced by every dollar of sales (revenue). Shows how well a company is managing its costs and expenses. Calculated by dividing the company's profits by its total sales for the same time period.

See also: Cost of goods sold, Profit, Ratio analysis

Whenever Gracie got an annual report, she calculated the company's **return on sales.**

Royalties
Payments to the owner of an intangible asset (such as a copyright or patent) for its use.

See also: Intangible asset

Merle was able to live on her **royalties** *when each of the books she wrote sold thousands of copies.*

Safe harbor
A legal theory that allows corporate management to make good-faith projections and estimates without fear of being sued. For example, the executive officers of Lion Joe Inc. posted pro forma financial statements that projected a 10% revenue increase, based on their historical growth trends. Then a tornado wipes out one of their factories, and revenues actually decrease by 2%. No lawsuit would be allowed because their original projection was made in good faith, regardless of the actual outcome.

See also: Pro forma financial statements

Investors simply took their losses after the fire in the warehouse because they knew the **safe harbor** *rule would protect the corporation.*

Sale and leaseback
A business agreement where one company sells a key asset to a second company, then leases it back from them. Sometimes just called "leaseback."

See also: Asset, Lease

Lion Joe Trucking had a mutually beneficial **sale and leaseback** *agreement with the warehouse.*

Salvage value
An accounting estimate used in depreciation calculation that places a value on the worth of an asset at the end of its useful life equal to the anticipated amount they could sell it for after using it. For example, a company that bought a computer for $3,500, estimated that at the end of its three-year useful life it could be sold for $500 (the salvage value).

See also: Depreciation, Fixed assets

In an attempt to raise cash quickly, Lion Joe Corporation sold unnecessary assets below **salvage value.**

Saturday night special
Industry lingo for an unexpected takeover bid. It is usually announced on the weekend when fewer people pay attention to the news.

See also: Hostile takeover

The conglomerate snuck in a **Saturday night special** *to bid for Lion Joe Toys, hoping to stay off the radar.*

Selling expenses
In a business, all costs directly associated with making sales (such as salesman's commissions and shopping bags). For investments, any fees associated with a security sale (such as redemption fees or broker commissions).

See also: Commission, Statement of profit and loss

Zach held onto his investments until the **selling expenses** *wouldn't be greater than his earnings.*

Series 6
An exam that's required for a financial professional to obtain a license to sell mutual funds and variable annuities.

See also: Annuity, Mutual fund

Al was thrilled when he passed his **Series 6**, *because he was able to offer a greater range of services to his clients.*

Shark repellent
Industry lingo for the measures a company can take to prevent a hostile takeover.

See also: Hostile takeover, Lobster trap, Pac-Man defense

The board of directors discussed the forms of **shark repellant** *available to them to stave off the takeover bid.*

Silent partner
A person (or company) who invests money in a company and participates in profits and losses but is not at all involved in the management of the company.

See also: Limited partner

The businessman preferred being a **silent partner** *because he made money while still enjoying his retirement.*

Sleeping beauty
A company with enormous profit potential that has not yet been taken over by a larger company, but is likely to be acquired. Shareholders at the time of acquisition are often able to sell their stock at a premium to current market value.

See also: Takeover bid

The capital corporation made its reputation on being able to identify **sleeping beauties** *and investing in them at the most opportune moment.*

Standard deviation
A statistical calculation that's used to quantify risk for a security. Measures the volatility of a specific stock over a defined time period. Shows how much variability there has been in the price of that stock.

See also: Technical analysis

The **standard deviation** *indicated Lion Joe Ltd. stock had become more volatile over the last six months.*

Statement of cash flows
An accounting report that shows the movement of money in and out of a business over a specific time period.

See also: Financial statements

The **statement of cash flows** *indicated the company didn't have as much actual cash coming in as it was spending.*

Statement of profit and loss (P&L)
An accounting report that shows the results of business activities for a set period of time. The report starts with revenue, then cost of goods sold and expenses are deducted to get to the net profit for the period.

See also: Cost of goods sold, Financial statements

The board of directors was pleased with the **statement of profit and loss** *because the net earnings were higher than predicted.*

Takeover bid
When a company tries to buy up the stock in another company by going to the existing shareholders and offering to buy their shares, usually at a higher price than current market price.

See also: Hostile takeover

Lion Joe Industries only approached stockholders who had never cast a vote during meetings in their **takeover bid** *of the tech firm.*

Tangible asset
Something of value that has physical form.

See also: Asset, Intangible asset

The breeder knew her prize-winning dachshunds, Lionel and Daisy, were her most valuable **tangible assets.**

Target company
A company that has been selected by another company for purchase, whether the company to be bought likes it or not.

See also: Hostile takeover, Takeover bid

The only reason Lion Joe Toys avoided a takeover was because its CEO heard rumors it was a **target company.**

Times interest earned (TIE)
A mathematical calculation that demonstrates a company's ability to handle upcoming interest payments; used to measure solvency. Calculated by dividing EBIT (earnings before interest and taxes) by interest expense. Should be considered by investors looking into corporate bonds. Also called "interest coverage ratio."

See also: Corporate bond, EBIT, Solvency

The **TIE** *reassured the board of directors that the company was comfortably solvent.*

Transaction
An arrangement between two parties (a buyer and a seller) to exchange an asset for payment.

See also: Trade

Ivan kept records of every **transaction** *he made, personally or through his broker, in a ledger and backed up on disk.*

Treasurer
The executive in charge of managing the overall financial activities of a company. Also called the "CFO."

See also: CEO

After the company realized the financial situation it was in, a new **treasurer** *was brought in to help bring them back into the black.*

Vertical analysis
A way to evaluate a set of financial statements by looking at each line item as a percentage of its category (for example, listing cash as 15% of assets in addition to its dollar value), which allows investors to see relative changes in the three major categories: assets, liabilities, and equity. The percentages also help investors more easily compare companies of different sizes or compare the same company's financials over a specific time period.

See also: Financial statements, Fundamental analysis

According to the **vertical analysis***, the corporation's assets were growing at a faster rate than their liabilities.*

Volatility
The uncertainty about the variability in the market price of a security, usually measured statistically with standard deviation. A higher result indicates wider, more dramatic price fluctuations and increased risk.

See also: Risk, Standard deviation

Risk-averse investors avoid **volatility***, but risk lovers prefer to go along for the wild ride.*

Weighted average

The average of a group of numbers that are each assigned weights (i.e., some values count more than others). For example, in a portfolio, the average stock price would be found by simply adding the current market price of each holding and dividing the sum by the number of holdings. But the weighted average stock price would be found by first multiplying the current market price of each holding by the number of shares held (the weight), then dividing by the total number of shares (the total weight). In the second example, larger holdings (by straight number of shares) would count more than smaller holdings.

See also: Average, Portfolio

The **weighted average** *share price in Judy's portfolio was much higher than its average because she held so many shares of Lion Joe Inc.*

White knight

A third-party (usually a company) that swoops in and stops a hostile takeover by launching a friendly takeover.

See also: Hostile takeover

Lion John Refreshments offered to act as a **white knight** *for the small restaurant chain in order to prevent the hostile takeover by the soft drink company.*

Wholly owned subsidiary

A company that is owned by another company that holds all of the first company's stock.

See also: Conglomerate

Few people realized that the cruise line was a **wholly owned subsidiary** *of Lion Joe Distributors.*

Working capital

A key measure of a company's immediate financial health. Calculated by subtracting current liabilities from current assets.

See also: Current ratio, Liquidity

The company's **working capital** *nearly doubled after the release of its latest game system.*

Write-down
Lowering an asset's value on the books due to a decline in market value.

See also: Impaired asset

If property values didn't rise soon, Lion Joe Inc. was going to have to do a **write-down** *on all the buildings on the site.*

Yellow knight
A company that originally attempted a hostile takeover, but ends up trying to merge with the target company. So-called because the acquiring company "chickened out" and stopped their hostile takeover bid.

See also: Hostile takeover, Merger

The board of Lion Joe Ltd. was insulted by the other company's attempt to be a **yellow knight** *when they couldn't pull off the takeover.*

BANKING

Add-on CD (Certificate of deposit)
A CD that allows the depositor to increase the balance in his account without altering other terms of the account agreement, particularly the interest rate.

See also: Certificate of deposit

When Yvonne came into some unexpected money, she put it into her **add-on CD** *so she could earn even more interest in the account.*

Adjusted balance method
A way to calculate interest or finance charges, based on the final account value at the end of a specified period after all transactions are accounted for. Normally used for bank savings accounts.

See also: Interest

Courtney used the **adjusted balance method** *at the end of every month to track the interest earned on her bank statement.*

American depository receipt (ADR)
A certificate issued by a U.S. bank that represents shares in a foreign corporation whose stock trades on a U.S. exchange. Certificates are valued in U.S. dollars. Makes it easier for Americans to invest in foreign companies, though it does not reduce the investment risks.

See also: Exchange, Stock

David was able to invest in some of the Japanese corporations that interested him the most by purchasing **ADR***s.*

Average daily balance method
A method for calculating finance charges, based on the average account balance each day. Beneficial for consumers because payments made during the period lower the daily balance. Often used by store credit cards.

See also: Credit card, Previous balance method

Angie loved the fact that her favorite store used the **average daily balance method** *on its card so she felt less guilty about charging her purchases.*

Balloon payment
Very large final installment due at the end of a loan period. Typically, balloon payments are associated with mortgage and car loans. The previous monthly payments are much smaller than they would be with a standard loan.

See also: 5-1 Hybrid ARM, Mortgage

Many borrowers have trouble making their **balloon payments** *in a depressed real estate market.*

Bank run

When an extremely large number of depositors try to get their money out of the bank all at once, it is more money than the bank has on hand. Typically the result of a widespread economic panic. Also known as a "run on the bank."

See also: Demand deposit

Several major companies tried to withdraw their funds quietly, in order to avoid causing a **bank run***, but they were unsuccessful when the media became aware of their attempts.*

Bridge financing

A form of short-term debt funding used when cash inflows are anticipated but not yet received. Used to get people and companies through a cash flow gap.

See also: Debt financing

Lion Joe Toys needed **bridge financing** *to get them through the January slump, because they didn't expect customers to pay their December bills until February.*

Bump-up CD

A time deposit account that offers the holder the opportunity to take advantage of rising interest rates one time during the contract term without terminating that contract.

See also: Certificate of deposit, Interest rate, Time deposit

Since interest rates looked as if they would be rising within the next six months, Sarah put her money into a **bump-up CD***.*

Cap

A firm limit on the periodic or lifetime adjustment amount for an interest rate or mortgage payment under an ARM agreement.

See also: Adjustable-rate mortgage, Payment cap, Rate cap

A **cap** *does not guarantee an ARM will not rise to a level that makes it difficult to pay in full every month.*

Certificate of deposit (CD)

A financial product, usually offered by a bank, where funds are held in an account for a specified time period to earn a special interest rate. Earned interest may be forfeited if the original funds are withdrawn before the time period ends.

See also: Money market account, Time deposit

Joan put her money in a six-month **CD** *because she would get a higher interest rate than she would with her regular savings account.*

Collateral
Assets pledged to creditors to guarantee loan repayment. Ownership of those assets may transfer to the creditor should scheduled loan payments not be made.

See also: Asset, Creditor

Brandon was so sure the store would eventually succeed that he put his house up as **collateral** *for the loan to keep the business afloat for another year.*

Commercial paper
A short-term corporate debt security, not secured by collateral, issued by corporations at a discount to face value to return prevailing market interest rates. Usually matures in nine months or less. Issued in $100,000 increments.

See also: Collateral, Par value

Individuals can invest in **commercial paper** *through money market funds.*

Compensating balance
A minimum deposit required by and held by a bank in an account that earns no interest, maintained to offset an unpaid loan balance or to gain free bank services.

See also: Home equity line, Revolving debt

The bank's required **compensating balance** *was low enough that it was worth it to her to open the account in order to get the overdraft coverage on her main checking account.*

Compound interest
Earnings paid on a total account balance, rather than just on the original principal investment. Calculated using specified time periods, such as daily or semiannually, where shorter calculation periods translate to greater earnings. Current earnings are computed by multiplying the current total account balance (including original balance plus all accumulated earnings) by the interest rate divided by the specified time period.

See also: Interest, Simple interest

Brad's savings account grew more quickly with its **compound interest** *feature.*

Credit bureau
An agency that gathers, analyzes, and sells information about the ability of individuals and companies to pay their debt obligations on a timely basis.

See also: Credit rating, Equifax, Experian, Fair Isaac & Co., Transunion

Before applying for their first mortgage, the young couple got their report from the **credit bureau** *to make sure they would find no surprises during the bank's credit check.*

Credit card
A way for consumers to finance their everyday purchases, through an agreement with a financing company. Such borrowing is meant to be short-term, and it comes with very high interest rates and required minimum monthly payments.
> See also: Debt
>
> *Teenagers are often swamped with* **credit card** *offers following their eighteenth birthdays.*

Credit history
A listing and analysis of an individual's (or business's) borrowing and repayment habits.
> See also: Credit rating, Credit report
>
> *Most rental management companies will check an applicant's* **credit history** *before the official lease signing.*

Credit rating
A numerical score given to a person or company that measures his (or its) likelihood to pay debts in full and on time.
> See also: Credit bureau, Credit report
>
> *College students need to make sure they pay their credit card bills on time so they don't damage their* **credit rating** *early.*

Credit report
A detailed account of the debt repayment ability of an individual or a company. Information includes credit rating, current outstanding debt, debt repayment history, employment history, current and former addresses, and personal identifying information (such as birth date and social security number). Created by a credit bureau, and used by companies intending to lend money.
> See also: Credit bureau, Credit rating
>
> *The rental company checked all applicants'* **credit reports** *before agreeing to lease an apartment.*

Credit score
A number grade assigned to an individual or a business that measures the probability that he (or it) will pay debts in full and on time. Sometimes called "credit rating."
> See also: Credit bureau, Credit report
>
> *The young woman was concerned about her* **credit score** *so she paid off all her bills on time.*

Creditor
Someone to whom money is owed.
> See also: Debtor
>
> *She worked very hard to pay her bills on time so as to not get into trouble with her* **creditors**.

Currencies
Units of money used throughout the world. Often traded to capitalize on slight variations in exchange rates.
> See also: Currency basket, Exchange rate
>
> *Jeanine often invested in foreign* **currencies** *when the dollar was weak.*

Debt
A legal obligation to pay another individual or company with cash or other assets.
> See also: Credit card, Debt securities
>
> *While she graduated with a degree, she was several thousand dollars in* **debt** *due to student loans.*

Debt consolidation
Exchanging multiple liabilities for a single loan, meant to help people with credit problems pay off their obligations more easily. The single loan usually has a lower interest rate and a longer payoff period than the replaced loans.
> See also: Bankruptcy, Credit rating, Debt
>
> *The couple worked with a credit counselor to arrange for* **debt consolidation** *once they realized they were in over their heads financially.*

Debt financing
Funding company assets through loans and other borrowed funds (such as notes or bonds).
> See also: Bond, Debt
>
> *The manufacturing company used* **debt financing** *to ensure it had the equipment and raw materials it needed at all times.*

Debt-equity swap
A deal where a debt holder cancels a company's outstanding debt in exchange for an ownership (equity) position in the company.
> See also: Debt, Equity
>
> *The* **debt-equity swap** *helped Lion Joe Party Foods avoid bankruptcy, because they no longer had to make high-interest loan payments.*

Debtor
Someone who owes money.

See also: Creditor

Some lenders are willing to work with a troubled **debtor** *in order to recoup most of a loan, if not all of it.*

Default
Failure to pay a debt.

See also: Debt

When he **defaulted** *on one credit card, other lenders became concerned about his ability to live within his means and pay them back.*

Default risk
The chance that an individual or company won't pay a debt.

See also: Debt

Since she was currently unemployed, her **default risk** *was high enough that she was unable to get a loan for a new car.*

Demand account
Money held in a bank or other financial institution that is available to the depositor whenever he wants to make a withdrawal.

See also: Time deposit

Basic checking and savings accounts are **demand accounts.**

Demand deposit
An account (such as a standard savings or checking account) where the money can be taken out at any time without restrictions.

See also: Certificate of deposit, Time deposit

Most people have **demand deposit** *accounts for paying their regular bills.*

Demand note
A loan without a fixed maturity or repayment schedule called in by the lender whenever he wants as long as he has made the agreed-upon notification.

See also: Debt, Maturity

Bobbi's father gave her a **demand note** *for her business startup loan, so she wouldn't have to make payments until the company started making money.*

Discount rate
The interest percentage used in the formula that determines the present value of a future cash flow.

See also: Discounting

Stacey and Randi argued about what to use for the **discount rate** *when trying to figure out how much money they would need for a luxurious retirement.*

Discounting

The mathematical process of determining the present value of a future cash flow; determines how much a specific amount of money some time in the future is worth in the present.

See also: Discount rate

After winning the lottery, Claire used **discounting** *to decide if she wanted a lump-sum payment now or if she should take the yearly payout for the next thirty years.*

Early withdrawal

The removal of funds from a time deposit before it matures, which may result in financial penalties.

See also: Time deposit

After the car accident, Krystal was willing to accept **early withdrawal** *fees in order to have the cash she needed for bills.*

Equifax

One of the three major credit reporting agencies that compile credit histories and assign credit scores to individuals and companies seeking loans using unique calculations.

See also: Credit history, Credit rating, Credit report

Before applying for the loan, Madelyn checked her credit score through **Equifax** *to ensure she was in good standing.*

Experian

One of the three major credit reporting agencies that compile credit histories and assign credit scores to individuals and companies seeking loans using their proprietary PLUS Score method.

See also: Credit history, Credit rating, Credit report

According to **Experian,** *Joseph's potential tenants had never had a late payment on a credit card.*

Fair Isaac & Co.

Creator of the FICO score model, which is used to assess the creditworthiness of individuals and companies attempting to secure debt financing.

See also: Credit score, Credit report

Fair Isaac & Co. *made it possible for banks to approve loans based on more than just the applicant's word and reputation.*

FDIC (Federal Deposit Insurance Corporation)
A U.S. government institution that guarantees certain consumer deposits of up to $100,000 per person per institution.

See also: Certificate of Deposit, Jumbo CD

Most people assume that money market mutual funds are covered by **FDIC** *but they're not.*

Federal funds rate
The interest percentage charged by banks to lend money held at the Federal Reserve to other banks, typically overnight.

See also: Federal Reserve

Financial experts look at the **federal funds rate** *for guidance about the direction of commercial interest rates.*

Federal Reserve
The United States' central banking system. Also known as "The Fed," this agency manipulates the national money supply by adjusting interest rates.

See also: Interest rate

The **Federal Reserve** *will often lower or raise interest rates as a way to stabilize the economy.*

FICO score
A numerical rating given to an individual or a company that represents the likelihood that he (or it) will pay debts in full and on time. Also known as "credit rating."

See also: Credit bureau, Credit report

Zay was able to get a loan because his **FICO score** *was strong.*

Fixed interest rate
A flat percentage charged as a fee for borrowing capital; the percentage does not change over the life of the loan.

See also: Interest rate

A **fixed interest rate** *makes planning a long-term budget easier because the payments will stay the same until the loan is paid off.*

Float time
The lag between the day a person writes a check and the day funds are removed from his account. Typically just one business day now.

See also: Demand account, Rubber check

The young woman hoped the **float time** *would be enough for her deposit to clear so she didn't bounce a check.*

Floating interest rate
A variable percentage charged as a fee for borrowing capital. The percentage varies based on a specified formula, tied to an easily determined factor (such as "prime rate plus 1%"). Also called an "adjustable rate."
> See also: Interest rate, Prime rate

He hadn't realized his loan payments would vary as much as they did when he originally agreed to the **floating** interest rate.

Inactivity fee
A charge on a brokerage account when an investor does not make the minimum number of trades.
> See also: Fee schedule

Less active investors would do well to work with a firm that doesn't charge **inactivity** fees.

In-house financing
A loan from a product or service seller. A prime example is getting a car loan from a car dealer, rather than from a bank.
> See also: Loan

The furniture store offered **in-house financing** *with twelve months interest free.*

Insurance score
A computation performed by insurance companies to help them figure out which clients are likely to file the most claims. A high score can translate to lower premiums. Often linked with credit score.
> See also: Credit score, Premium (insurance)

Some companies have begun to offer incentives to customers who maintain a high **insurance** score.

Interest
A fee paid on borrowed funds; the cost of borrowing.
> See also: Compound interest, Loan, Simple interest

Paying loan principal faster than scheduled could save you thousands of dollars in **interest** *expense.*

Interest rate
The fee for borrowing capital, expressed as a percentage of the loan amount. Can be fixed or floating.
> See also: Fixed interest rate, Variable interest rate

It is important to know the **interest rate** *on a credit card before using it.*

Jumbo CD
A very large time deposit, usually with a minimum balance of $100,000, which can earn the depositor higher than average interest rates. May not be wholly FDIC-insured.

>See also: Certificate of deposit, FDIC, Time deposit
>
>*Madelyn took half of her inheritance and bought a* **jumbo CD**, *while investing the rest in blue-chip stocks.*

KYC rules (Know your client)
A requirement that demands detailed standard forms be filled out by bank and financial institution customers.

>See also: Broker, Demand deposit
>
>*It took Arianna over an hour to fill out all the forms her broker needed to satisfy the* **KYC rules.**

LIBOR (London Interbank Offered Rate)
The interest percentage, set each day by the British Banker's Association, charged by a British financial institution when lending money to another British financial institution. Often used as a base percentage for calculating the interest charged on adjustable-rate loans.

>See also: Federal funds rate, Federal Reserve
>
>*The interest rate on Jim and Susan's adjustable-rate mortgage is based on* **LIBOR.**

Lifetime cap
The maximum interest rate that can ever be used during the full term of an adjustable-rate mortgage.

>See also: Adjustable-rate mortgage, Rate cap
>
>*The couple took comfort in the fact that no matter how high interest rates got, the rate on their mortgage could never go higher than the* **lifetime cap.**

Loan
A binding agreement where one party borrows money from another party, and promises to pay that money back at a specific time or on demand. The agreement may also provide for scheduled payments, interest, and collateral for the borrowed funds.

>See also: Debt, Interest
>
>*Valene took out a* **loan** *to open the salon she'd been dreaming of since she was a little girl.*

Money market account
A limited-access savings plan that usually earns higher interest rates than a regular open-access savings plan. Withdrawal type transactions (such as checks or transfers) are typically limited to six per month. Carries FDIC insurance just like any other form of bank savings.

See also: FDIC, Money market fund

The young woman put her emergency funds into a **money market account** *because she wanted assurance that money would be there when she needed it.*

Negotiable instrument
A signed document that promises to pay money to the holder. May be transferred from one person to another (by endorsing a check over to someone else with "pay to the order of"). Examples include checks and notes.

See also: Demand note

Lucinda didn't realize that every check she wrote was considered a **negotiable instrument.**

Payback period
The estimated amount of time it will take an investment to pay for itself. Usually used by businesses to figure out how soon a prospective project will pay off. Shorter payback periods are better.

See also: Internal rate of return

The **payback period** *was short enough for the board to approve the new project, although some members thought it would take too long to reap the rewards.*

Payment cap
The maximum allowable monthly remittance for an adjustable-rate mortgage, regardless of the remittance calculated by formula and regardless of the prevailing interest rate.

See also: Adjustable-rate mortgage, Negative amortization

Even though interest rates soared, Nancy's mortgage payments only increased by $150, due to the **payment cap** *in her ARM agreement.*

Payment formula
The mathematical calculation that determines the amount due for the next installment on an adjustable-rate mortgage. Based on the terms of the mortgage contract, the payment may be recalculated monthly, semiannually or annually.

See also: Adjustable-rate mortgage, Cap, Floor, Rate formula

The mortgage company always notified Billy and Sue about upcoming changes based on their **payment formula.**

Predatory lending
A practice of pushing unqualified borrowers into loans they cannot reasonably be expected to be able to pay back. Also convinces borrowers to accept high-fee, high-rate, or negative-equity loans. Done by unscrupulous loan brokers to keep their own numbers up, with no regard for the financial well-being of the borrower.

See also: Negative equity, Subprime mortgage

Skip and Amy were stuck with mortgage payments they couldn't afford because they'd been manipulated with **predatory lending** *practices.*

Present value
The current worth of cash to be received in the future, either as a series of payments or as a lump sum. Calculated with a standard mathematical formula using an estimated discount rate.

See also: Discount rate, Discounting

Chris and Missy considered the **present value** *when deciding whether to take their lottery winnings as a cash payout or an annuity.*

Previous balance method
A way to calculate finance charges, based on the closing balance from the last period. Typically used by credit card companies.

See also: Average daily balance method, Credit card

Katja recalculated interest charges using the **previous balance method** *in order to verify the printout on her monthly credit card bill.*

Prime rate
The interest percentage charged by commercial banks when lending funds to their most creditworthy clients (usually large corporations).

See also: LIBOR

After years of growth and strong credit, the company finally qualified for **prime rate** *loans.*

Rate cap
The maximum interest percentage that may be applied to an adjustable-rate mortgage, regardless of the percentage calculated by the rate formula.

See also: Adjustable-rate mortgage, Negative amortization, Rate floor, Rate formula

The **rate cap** *ensures there is a set limit on the interest on an ARM, no matter how high market interest rates climb.*

Rate floor
The minimum interest percentage that may be applied to an adjustable-rate mortgage, regardless of the percentage calculated by the rate formula.

See also: Adjustable-rate mortgage, Negative amortization, Rate cap, Rate formula

Edward was frustrated when the interest percentage on fixed mortgages dropped below the **rate floor** *he had to pay on his ARM.*

Rate formula
The mathematical equation that determines the new interest percentage for an adjustable-rate mortgage. which may look something like this: The interest equals LIBOR plus 0.25%, not to exceed 8.5% or go below 5%. So, for example, if LIBOR was at 5.5%, the adjusted rate on this mortgage would be 5.75%.

See also: Adjustable-rate mortgage, LIBOR, Rate cap, Rate floor

Max asked his CPA to look over the **rate formula** *on his mortgage before he signed the papers.*

Rate of return
The total amount earned or lost on a security, expressed as a percentage of its original purchase price.

See also: Capital gains, Capital loss, Dividend, Interest

Phyllis bought more of the corporation's stock because she expected a high **rate of return** *in the long run.*

Rate step-up
The amount by which an interest percentage increases over time, common to adjustable-rate mortgages and some coupon bonds.

See also: Adjustable-rate mortgage, Bond

Adjustable-rate mortgage holders are often unpleasantly surprised by their first **rate step-up.**

Rate trigger
A substantial drop in prevailing interest rates that sets off (or "triggers") a rash of bond calling. Bondholders often get paid a premium (an amount more than the par value) for this type of call.

See also: Callable bond

Although the **rate trigger** *caught some people by surprise, Toby wasn't shocked based on the way interest rates had been moving.*

Reference rate
The benchmark interest rate used to calculate a variable interest rate, such as in an adjustable-rate mortgage.

See also: Adjustable-rate mortgage, Benchmark

Since the **reference rate** *itself went up, the payments on adjustable-rate mortgages had to as well.*

Revolving debt
Loans that grow through increased borrowing and decrease through payments. Have no set balance and no fixed maturity date. Examples include credit lines and credit cards.

See also: Credit card, Loan

Many personal bankruptcies are caused when people lose control of their **revolving debt.**

Rubber check
A bounced check, returned to the payee by the bank due to the check writer's insufficient funds.

See also: Insolvency

After the third **rubber check,** *Megan's landlord started eviction proceedings.*

Sallie Mae (Student Loan Marketing Association)
The largest student loan provider in the United States, they are a publicly traded company (no government ownership) that makes direct loans to students, buys student loans from other lenders (to provide those lenders with additional lending capital), and offers financing for state-sponsored student loans.

See also: 529 plan

Marion was amused when she received **Sallie Mae** *stock for her college graduation because they were the company that held her student loans.*

Secured credit card
A revolving borrowing account directly linked with the holder's savings account, which may be seized if regular payments are not made. Often used to develop or improve a credit history.

See also: Debt, Default

After filing for bankruptcy, Randy was grateful to get a **secured credit card** *in order to start building up his good credit rating again.*

Simple interest
Earnings are paid only on an initial investment balance, regardless of other earnings. Usually calculated annually, by multiplying the original investment by the stated rate.

See also: Compound interest, Interest rate

Jenna invested in a CD paying only **simple interest**, *but at a higher than average rate.*

Solvency
A company's ability to meet its long-term financial obligations and achieve its long-range plans. A state of good financial health.

See also: Insolvency

Lion Joe Construction was one of the few companies in the industry that maintained **solvency** *during the recession.*

Surrender charge
A fee incurred by an investor for terminating a time-related investment (such as a CD) before its maturity date.

See also: Annuity, Certificate of deposit, Maturity

The **surrender charge** *on the CD was high enough that Janie decided to forgo cashing out early and to find another way to pay for her vacation.*

Sweep account
A special bank account that transfers "unused" money out at the end of every day, into an account with higher earnings potential. For example, a checking account with remaining balance after all checks are cashed against it, where that balance gets "swept" into an investment account at the end of the day. The next day, the checking account is replenished from the investment account.

See also: Demand account

The shop owners opened a **sweep account** *to help make the small store a little extra money.*

Teaser rate
A very low initial interest rate charged on debt instruments (such as credit cards or mortgages) to attract customers. At the end of the period, the interest rate climbs, often dramatically, to market levels.

See also: Adjustable-rate mortgage, Payment shock

Elaine got a new credit card with a 1.2% **teaser rate***; she was shocked when that rate changed to 12% after thirty days.*

Time deposit
An account (such as a CD or certain savings accounts) where money may not be withdrawn at will, but rather is committed to the account for a certain time period. In some cases, funds may only be withdrawn after notice is given. Penalties may be charged if any funds are removed before the commitment period is up or without appropriate notification.

See also: Demand deposit

Her cash flow was stable, so Ashley kept her savings in a **time deposit** *account.*

Time value of money
The financial assumption that a dollar owned today is worth more than a dollar in the future.

See also: Present value

Due to the **time value of money**, *lottery winners opt for a lump-sum payment.*

Transunion
One of the three major credit reporting agencies that compiles credit histories and assigns credit scores to individuals and companies seeking loans using a distinct scoring equation.

See also: Credit history, Credit rating, Credit report

The nonprofit ran credit histories through **Transunion** *to help them decide which entrepreneurs could best pay back any loans.*

Undercapitalized
When a company doesn't have enough money to operate or pay the bills. This often happens with small startup companies whose owners underestimated the amount of money they'd need to get their business up and running.

See also: Insolvency

Edith was heartbroken when she realized her little boutique was **undercapitalized** *and would have to close if she was unable to increase sales.*

Unsecured debt
A loan made with no collateral to back it up in case of nonpayment.

See also: Collateral

Credit cards are the largest piece of **unsecured debt** *in the United States.*

Variable interest rate
A periodically changing percentage fee charged for borrowing capital. The percentage is linked to a publicly published factor (such as "prime rate plus 1%"). Also called an "adjustable rate" or a "floating interest rate."

See also: Interest rate, Prime rate

Juan actually expected his rates to fluctuate more than they did after agreeing to a **variable interest rate.**

BONDS

Accrual bond
A unique type of bond that appears often in CMO issues. The bondholder receives no payments until every other bond in the series has been paid off. The interest payments, that should have been paid over the life but weren't, get added to the balance of the bond. The next "would-be" interest payment is calculated using that increased bond balance. Also called a "Z-bond" or a "Z-tranche."

See also: CMO, Zero-coupon bond

Since Toby suspected rates would be going up, he invested in **accrual bonds**.

Asset-backed security
A bond that is backed by loans, leases, accounts receivable, or other debt originally created for the purchase of personal property assets. Cash inflows from the underlying loans, leases, debts, or receivables are distributed to investors. Similar to mortgage-backed securities except that they involve no real estate.

See also: Accounts receivable, Mortgage-backed securities, Personal property

Madison put a small amount of money into **asset-backed securities** *to cash in on their high returns while not exposing her portfolio to too much risk.*

Average coupon
The mean interest rate earned on a portfolio of bonds.

See also: Bond, Interest rate

Jim was pleased with the **average coupon** *on his client's portfolio because it was higher than most.*

Baby bond
A debt security issued with a par value of less than $1,000 (the standard par value).

See also: Bond

As his first investment, the high school student decided to invest in a **baby bond**.

Basis point
A unit of measure for changes in financial instruments, where 100 basis points equals a 1% change. For example, if a bond has 10% yield and the yield increases to 11%, that's a change of 100 basis points. Used in regard to fixed-income securities to mark changes in things such as interest rates and yields. Also used in regard to interest rate changes, such as when the Federal Reserve raises or lowers rates (i.e., the Fed raised rates by 25 basis points, from 3.25% to 3.50%).

See also: Fixed-income securities, Interest rate, Yield

When rates dropped by 2 **basis points***, Michaela knew it was time to refinance her mortgage.*

Bearer bond
A negotiable debt instrument, for which ownership information is not stored anywhere, which allows for principal and interest to be paid to whomever is holding it, regardless of the original owner.

See also: Bond, Negotiable instrument

Since **bearer bonds** *are untraceable, stories about their theft have made for great summer blockbusters.*

Bond
A noncollateralized debt instrument issued by an entity (often a corporation or government) to raise funds. Typically issued in increments of $1,000 with loan terms of at least ten years. Often traded in a secondary market.

See also: Debt instruments

Many people buy **bonds** *when their children are born to help pay for college when the time comes.*

Bond indenture agreement
The contract between a bondholder and a bond issuer, which details the terms of their agreement. Specific terms include interest rate, maturity, and par value. Also referred to as an "indenture."

See also: Bond, Interest rate, Maturity, Par value

The **bond indenture agreement** *indicated the bonds would mature about the time the couple was ready to retire.*

Bond laddering
An investment strategy designed to minimize risk and ensure a steady income flow in a bond portfolio, achieved by holding bonds of differing maturities.

See also: Bond, Maturity

Since her primary income came from her portfolio, Elsa knew **bond laddering** *would be a good choice for her.*

Bond rating
A system that grades long-term debt securities based on their default risk. U.S. government debt securities are considered no-risk, and come with the highest grade; other debt securities are ranked relative to that. Grades may differ by agency.
> See also: Investment grade, Junk bond, Moody's ratings, Rating agency

Judith's grandfather bought her a bond every year for her birthday, but only those with the investment-grade **bond ratings.**

Call date
The defined day upon which a bond can be redeemed by its issuer before the stated maturity date.
> See also: Call provision

Joseph knew his bonds would be called on their **call date** *because interest rates had dropped so substantially.*

Call protection
A condition where a security cannot be redeemed by its issuer for a specified time period, even though it is allowed to be redeemed before maturity after that period has passed.
> See also: Callable bond, Call provision, Call risk

To make them a more attractive purchase, the bonds were issued with **call protection.**

Call provision
A covenant in a bond agreement that allows the issuer to redeem the bond issue before its stated maturity date.
> See also: Bond, Maturity date

Ben tried to avoid buying bonds with **call provisions** *because he didn't like sudden changes in his monthly income.*

Call risk
The possibility that a bond will be redeemed before its maturity date, resulting in a negative investment situation for the bondholder. Call risk usually occurs when market interest rates have fallen.
> See also: Bond, Call provision

Bond investors should always take **call risk** *into account, especially when interest rates are volatile.*

Callable bond
A long-term debt security that can be redeemed by the issuer (the company or government entity that created and sold the bond) before its stated maturity date (such as an early loan payoff). In other words, an issuer can demand that all its bonds be turned in for cash before they're supposed to be redeemed.

See also: Bond, Call risk, Maturity date

*Joan suspected all her **callable bonds** would be redeemed early because the Fed had just lowered interest rates again.*

CBO (Collateralized bond obligation)
An investment-grade debt security, which is supported by a diverse pool of junk bonds. Receives a higher rating than the individual underlying securities because the pool offers enough diversity to offset some of the default risk.

See also: Bond rating, Junk bond

*In spite of people's reassurances that a **CBO** was safer than junk bonds alone, Marion was hesitant to invest.*

CMO (Collateralized mortgage obligation)
A debt security backed by a pool of home loans issued in pieces called "tranches," where each tranche has unique payout characteristics. Investors can buy whichever tranches they want, based on what would fit best in their portfolios. Payments on these debt securities are dependent on payments on the underlying home loans. Though these tranches come with maturities, those maturities are based on all the loan holders paying their loans as scheduled, so the tranches can be paid off much earlier when a lot of loan holders refinance and payoff their original loans earlier than expected. Often purchased by institutional investors, such as mutual funds and banks.

See also: Companion bonds, Mortgage-backed securities, PAC bond

*The bond fund manager bought several of the more stable **CMO** tranches to try to boost returns on the fund.*

Commodity-backed bond
A debt instrument whose interest (and sometimes principal) payments are linked with the price of a tradable physical good (such as gold).

See also: Bond, Commodity

*Daisy was pleased to see the price of gold rise because she had just recently bought several **commodity-backed bonds**.*

Companion bonds

A special class of debt instruments issued as part of a collateralized mortgage obligation series. Used to help limit volatility and stabilize payments for PAC bonds in the series by absorbing prepayments. The inherent volatility in this class is typically offset with higher coupon rates.

See also: CMO, PAC bond, Prepayment, Volatility

Miko bought several **companion bonds** *when she invested in the collateralized mortgage obligation fund because she loved high risk and high returns.*

Convertible bond

A debt security that can be traded for shares of stock in the same company. The security holder has the right, but not the obligation, to make the exchange. If the stock goes up, the bondholder can convert and enjoy the growth along with the other shareholders. If the stock does not perform well, she just holds on to her bond, collects interest, and redeems it for full value at maturity. Allows an unsure investor a safer way to get involved with a company, with an opportunity to participate in growth while limiting downside risk.

See also: Bond, Stock, Maturity

Sidney was interested in Lion Joe Technology, so she purchased their **convertible bonds** *hoping to cash in on future growth.*

Corporate bonds

Long-term debt securities issued by publicly held companies with no specified collateral to back them. They typically pay higher coupon rates than government debt securities to make up for the added default risk. Risk ratings are assigned to these securities by independent rating agencies, such as Standard & Poor's.

See also: Coupon rate, Default, Moody's ratings, S&P ratings

Santos invested in **corporate bonds** *with the money he had left after investing in more secure blue-chip stocks.*

Coupon bond

A debt instrument that pays out interest periodically, typically quarterly or semiannually, some of which have actual slips attached that must be redeemed to receive the interest.

See also: Zero-coupon bond

The family's budget included the income from the quarterly **coupon bond** *payments so she had to make sure she redeemed the slips in a timely manner.*

Coupon rate
The stated interest rate on a bond.
See also: Bond

Susan preferred to buy bonds with high **coupon rates**, *even though they cost more.*

Covenant
A provision in a legal agreement, usually a bond indenture agreement.
See also: Bond, Indenture

Noah liked to invest in bonds with **covenants** *that promised the company would maintain a special account to ensure timely interest payouts.*

Credit risk
The chance that timely or any payments (including return of principal) due on a bond or other debt investment will not be made.
See also: Bond

Laura bought junk bonds despite their high **credit risk** *because they offered potentially tremendous returns.*

Debenture
Bonds issued without collateral to back them up, but rather just the reputation of the issuer. May be issued by government entities or corporations.
See also: Bond, Government bond

Lion County issued **debentures** *to raise money for its new skate park project.*

Debt instruments
A financial arrangement between a lender (creditor) and a borrower (debtor) that details the terms of their agreement, including the original loan amount (face value), loan term, maturity date, repayment schedule, and interest rate.
See also: Creditor, Debtor, Investment grade, Par value

Treasury bills and municipal bonds are among the most common **debt instruments** *found in conservative investors' portfolios.*

Debt securities
Investments that represent a loan made by the investor to the issuer, in exchange for the promise of repayment plus interest. Includes such securities as bonds.
See also: Bond

As Marina got older, she invested in more **debt securities** *to help reduce the volatility in her portfolio.*

Debt service
The principal and interest payments made over time to repay monies owed. Typically used in reference to bond payments.

See also: Bond, Interest

Lion Joe Corporation always made their monthly **debt service** *payments, even when cash was tight.*

Default premium
Additional compensation offered to a lender (such as a bank giving a loan or an investor buying bonds) to offset a high default risk. This compensation is usually in the form of a higher-than-average interest rate.

See also: Bond rating, Default, Junk bond

Lion Joe's corporate bonds came with a hefty **default premium** *because they had a mediocre credit history.*

Downgrade
When a rating agency lowers the rating on a bond due to an increased default risk.

See also: Bond rating, Default, Rating agency

Moody's decided to **downgrade** *the bonds when the company took on even more debt.*

Dwarfs
Industry lingo used to describe a pool of FNMA-issued mortgage-backed securities with a fifteen-year maturity (the standard is thirty years).

See also: Fannie Mae, Mortgage-backed securities, Maturity

When Simon was looking for a mid-length investment, he bought into **dwarfs** *instead of standard mortgage-backed securities.*

Effective yield
The percentage returns on a bond if the interest payments are reinvested.

See also: Interest, Returns, Yield

The **effective yield** *on Bailey's investments was almost double what she would have made if she'd spent her interest payments instead of using them to buy more mutual fund shares.*

Fannie Mae (FNMA)

The nickname for the private corporation, Federal National Mortgage Association (FNMA), sponsored by the federal government that was created to buy specific private mortgages from lenders and resell them in the form of mortgage-backed securities. Its chief mandate is to keep money flowing through the mortgage market. FNMA has been around since 1938, and helps provide funding so that low- and middle-income families can secure home loans.

See also: Mortgage-backed securities, Pass-through security

The couple applied for assistance through **Fannie Mae** *to help secure their home loan.*

Ginnie Mae (GNMA)

The nickname for the U.S. government corporation, Government National Mortgage Association (GNMA), that guarantees payment on those mortgage-backed securities that hold pools of federally guaranteed or insured mortgages. These mortgage pools fall into two categories (GNMA I and GNMA II); GNMA I pools hold homogeneous loans in terms of interest rate and duration, while GNMA II pools may hold more diverse loans. GNMA bonds are the only mortgage-backed securities backed by the full faith and credit of the federal government.

See also: Mortgage-backed securities, Pass-through security

Wilbur preferred to buy **Ginnie Mae** *bonds because they are guaranteed by the U.S. government.*

GNMA I

A mortgage-backed securities program that uses uniform mortgage pools, primarily including single-family home loans from a single loan issuer. Only mortgages with specific loan maturities and interest rates are allowed to be included in the pool. Separate principal and interest payments are made to investors on the fifteenth day of each month.

See also: Ginnie Mae, GNMA II, Mortgage-backed securities

The retiree was heavily invested in **GNMA I** *pools, because he liked the combination of mid-month payments and higher returns than Treasury bonds.*

GNMA II
A mortgage-backed securities program that includes nonuniform mortgage pools, primarily including single-family home loans, which may come from a variety of loan issuers. The characteristics of the underlying loans may vary somewhat: for example, interest rates on every loan must fall within a 1% range of the pool stated rate. Combined principal and interest payments are made to investors on the twentieth day of each month.

See also: Ginnie Mae, GNMA I, Mortgage-backed securities

A mortgage-backed security from a **GNMA II** *pool offers investors better returns than other U.S. government bonds.*

GNMA midget
Unofficial industry lingo used to describe a pool of GNMA mortgage-backed securities with a fifteen-year maturity (the standard is thirty years).

See also: Ginnie Mae, Maturity, Mortgage-backed securities

GNMA midgets *are rarely issued, because fifteen-year mortgages are not very common.*

Gold bond
A debt security issued by a precious metal mining company with the precious metal as collateral. Interest rates vary, and are tied to the current price of the metal.

See also: Bond, Interest rate

Shortly after hitting a new vein, the mining company issued another series of **gold bonds.**

Government bond
A long-term debt obligation issued by a government entity.

See also: Municipal bond, Treasury bond

During WWII, many Americans chose to support "the cause" by purchasing **government bonds.**

Government securities
An umbrella term that covers all debt instruments (such as bonds or notes) issued by a public authority as a way to raise funds for specific expenditures.

See also: Municipal bond, T-bill, Treasury bond, Treasury note

During wartime, **government securities** *become an important way to bring money into the defense budget.*

High-yield bond
A debt security issued by a company with an elevated credit risk rating. They typically pay greater-than-average interest to compensate for the additional default risk borne by the holder. Also called "junk bonds."

See also: Bond, Risk

Investing in **high-yield bonds** *may sound like a good idea because of the potential returns but the losses can be even greater.*

Hybrid security
An investment vehicle that has properties of both debt and equity securities, such as a convertible bond.

See also: Convertible bond

Ethan went for the **hybrid security,** *so he could collect interest on the bonds until the company's growth was strong enough for him to invest in its stock.*

Imputed interest
Earnings on debt instruments that are taxable even though they haven't been paid yet. This situation normally occurs with securities such as zero-coupon bonds.

See also: Interest, Zero-coupon bond

Mark didn't understand why he had to pay tax on **imputed interest** *until he talked with his accountant.*

Indenture
The legal contract between a bond issuer and a bondholder, spelling out the terms of their agreement. Terms include interest rate, maturity, and par value.

See also: Bond, Interest rate, Maturity, Par value

According to the **indenture,** *the bonds would mature in thirty years.*

Interest-only (IO) strips
A slice of bond where the holder is entitled only to receive the interest payments on the bond, but never any principal payments (i.e., the face value of the bond, which normally is paid back like a loan). IO strips typically come from collateralized mortgage obligations (CMOs). The holder of this security will receive interest payments as long as the principal portion of the bond (which has been sold to other parties) remains outstanding. Investors earn more when these bonds are outstanding longer (as, for example, twenty years of interest payments deliver more than sixteen years of interest payments).

See also: CMO, Interest, Principal-only (PO) strips

Clara's financial advisor told her to include some **IO strips** *in her fixed-income portfolio to boost her returns.*

Interest-rate risk

The chance that an investment will decline in value as a result of a change in the prevailing cost of borrowing. Typically affects bonds (and other debt securities) more than stocks.

See also: Interest rate, Risk

Most investors who buy bonds are willing to accept the **interest-rate risk** *in exchange for the steady payment stream they receive.*

Investment grade

A bond rating of BBB or higher by Moody's. The lowest rating for a bond to be considered likely to be paid in full at maturity.

See also: Bond, Default, Moody's ratings

Her grandmother preferred to buy bonds but always made sure they were **investment grade** *or better.*

Junk bond

A high-risk, high-yield corporate debt instrument with a poor rating and higher than normal chance of default. Also referred to as "non–investment grade."

See also: Bond, Default, Bond rating

Juana was a savvy enough investor to simply avoid **junk bonds**, *even though her broker encouraged her to buy them.*

Maturity

The amount of time that will elapse before a debt instrument must be repaid.

See also: Bond, Debt instrument

When Jeanine got pregnant, she and her husband bought bonds with a twenty-year **maturity**, *to help with their child's future college costs.*

Maturity date

The day on which a debt instrument comes due, and the principal must be paid to the holder.

See also: Debt instruments, Principal

The couple was thrilled when they paid off their mortgage a full year before the **maturity date.**

Moody's ratings

A ranking system created by Moody's Investor Services to indicate relative credit risk among bonds.

See also: Bond, Bond rating, Credit risk

Whenever a client asked him about a potential bond investment, Al automatically checked **Moody's ratings** *before making a recommendation.*

Mortgage pool
A collection of home loans used as collateral for a mortgage-backed security.
   See also: Mortgage-backed securities
   The investors were lucky because the **mortgage pool** *supporting their securities stayed stable even during the housing dip.*

Mortgage-backed securities (MBS)
Bonds backed by a pool of home loans. The bond issuer collects the payments from all of the mortgages in the pool, then passes along (a large portion of those) principal and interest payments to the bondholders. Unlike regular bonds, MBS usually pay principal and interest monthly (just such as what they'd collect from the underlying mortgages), so the bonds pay down over time rather than in one lump sum at maturity.
   See also: Freddie Mac, Fannie Mae, Ginnie Mae, Mortgage, Pass-through security
   Nelli's financial planner advised her to buy **mortgage-backed securities** *to balance her portfolio.*

Municipal bond
A debt instrument issued by a state or local government entity to raise funds. The interest income earned on these instruments is exempt from federal income tax, and often state and local income tax as well. Sometimes referred to as "munis" (pronounced "myoo-nees"); only issued by government agencies and are usually tax-preferred, which other bonds are not.
   See also: Bond
   Financially savvy investors can live off the tax-free interest on their **municipal bonds** *for years.*

Original issue discount (OID)
The difference between a price lower than par value for which a newly issued bond is sold and its par value (which is also its maturity value). Normally occurs when interest rates rise between the time a bond offering is made but before it's actually issued. Usually counts as interest income for tax purposes.
   See also: Bond, Par value
   Ben always got confused about how to report the **OID** *on his bonds when he did his taxes, so he left that to his CPA.*

Original maturity
The initial term of a contract. Usually talked about in references to bonds, mortgages, and mortgage-backed securities.
   See also: Bonds, Maturity, Mortgage-backed securities
   Patricia was miffed when her 8% bonds were called in long before their **original maturity** *date.*

PAC bond (Planned amortization class)
A priority class of debt securities in a collateralized mortgage obligation series. Designed to stabilize and minimize potential prepayment volatility, which allows investors a better idea of their cash inflow schedule as long as prepayment activity remains in an expected range. The decreased prepayment risk typically comes with a lower coupon rate than other classes within the series.

See also: CMO, Companion bonds, Prepayment

Freddie invested in **PAC bonds** *because he was willing to accept slightly lower returns in exchange for a more reliable payment schedule.*

Pass-through rate
The interest rate on a mortgage-backed security that is given to, or "passed through" to, the bondholders. Based on the average interest rate on the underlying mortgages, less servicing and guarantee fees.

See also: Mortgage-backed securities, Weighted average coupon

Zoe only invested in securities that promised a **pass-through rate** *of at least 6.5%.*

Pass-through security
An investment pool made up of fixed-income assets (such as coupon bonds or mortgages), where the income earned on those underlying investments are given directly to pool shareholders, minus a pool management fee.

See also: Coupon bond, Derivatives, Mortgage-backed security

Edna's income from **pass-through securities** *helped supplement her monthly social security check.*

Premium (bond)
The excess over par value paid for an interest-bearing debt security (such as a bond) due to a prevailing interest rate drop. Here's how it works: A bond issued April 1 has par value $1,000 and pays 3% interest. On May 1, the interest rate dropped to 2%. So a bond buyer in May would pay more for an old 3% bond than a newly issued 2% bond.

See also: Bond, Interest rate

Lena had to pay a **premium** *to buy a 5% bond, which she needed because her budget called for $500 a year in interest payments.*

Prepayment
Early redemption of debt or debt securities. Examples include refinancing a mortgage and paying off the old mortgage and calling a bond before its maturity date.

See also: Callable bond, Debt securities, Mortgage

People who count on fixed-income investments worry about bond **prepayment**.

Prepayment risk
The chance that a debt security will be redeemed before its maturity. Common with callable bonds and mortgage-backed securities, including collateralized mortgage obligations. Happens when interest rates go down. With callable bonds, the bondholder cannot replace interest income from his called bond at the same rate for the same risk level. With MBS, this happens when homeowners refinance their mortgages to cash in on lower rates, paying off their old higher-rate mortgages in full, which decreases the remaining principal and cash flows on the MBS.

See also: Callable bond, Mortgage-backed securities

Harriet didn't fully understand the **prepayment risk** *that came with her 10% coupon bond until rates started going down.*

Principal-only (PO) strips
A bond, usually part of a CMO issue, that pays only the principal portion of the underlying mortgages to the holder. Usually sold for a deep discount (i.e., less than the face value of the bond). Bondholders benefit from more rapid paydowns, unlike most bondholders (who receive interest payments).

See also: CMO, Interest-only (IO) strips

Evelyn always bought **PO strips** *when she expected mortgage interest rates to go down.*

Pure discount instrument
A debt security that offers no formal interest payments, where the holder derives income by paying less for the security than its face value. No payments are received until the lump sum at maturity.

See also: Zero-coupon bond

Pure discount instruments *made up a large portion of baby Elliot's college fund.*

Rating agency
A company that assigns default risk scores to bonds.

See also: Bond rating, Moody's ratings

Before buying a new bond, Tim always checked a **rating agency's** *report.*

Residual interest
The interest leftover after the higher priority tranches of a REMIC have been paid their required share, which is then paid out to lower priority tranches.

See also: REMIC, Tranche

Clare's **residual interest** *payments fluctuated widely, so she used them for shopping sprees instead of rent payments.*

S&P ratings (Standard & Poor's ratings)
A system for evaluating and ranking the risk that bond issuers will default.

See also: Bond, Bond rating, Moody's ratings

Brokers pay close attention to the **S&P ratings** *in order to advise their clients appropriately and well.*

Savings bonds
Debt securities sold by the United States government that can be redeemed but not resold. These securities enjoy special federal tax treatment; they remain tax-deferred until redeemed, and can be tax-free when the proceeds are used to pay tuition expenses.

See also: Bond, Series EE bond, Series I bond

The young woman's grandmother presented her with a **savings bond** *every year for her birthday and at holidays.*

Securitize
To create a security using an underlying pool of financial assets (such as mortgage loans) that provide steady payment streams.

See also: Asset-backed security, Mortgage-backed securities

Lion Joe Construction decided to **securitize** *several of its largest housing developments.*

Senior debt
Debt (often bonds) that has the right to be paid off first, before any other debts of the issuer.

See also: Bond, Debt

When Stu bought corporate bonds, he always looked for **senior debt** *to offset some of the default risk.*

Serial bond
A bond issue where groups of bonds mature at different times, even though they were issued at the same time.

See also: Bond, Maturity

June bought **serial bonds** *so she would always have plenty of cash on hand once she retired.*

Series EE bond
A fixed-rate U.S. savings bond that is guaranteed to double in value by maturity, which is typically twenty years.

See also: Savings bond, Series I bond

Wilbur bought several **Series EE bonds** *when his granddaughter was born, knowing they would be available to help her with her college costs.*

Series I bond
A U.S. savings bond that offers a two-part interest rate: a fixed portion and an adjustable portion that adjusts twice a year based on inflation.

See also: Savings bond, Series EE bond

Although Jack wasn't thrilled with the rising inflation rates, he took some comfort knowing it was increasing the worth of his **Series I bonds.**

Sinker
A bond for which principal and interest payments are made from a specially segregated pool of money (called a "sinking fund"). Preferred by fixed-income investors because of the lower default risk.

See also: Bond

Once Madge retired, she chose to invest in **sinkers** *because she knew she didn't have time to recoup major losses.*

TIPS (Treasury Inflation-Protected Securities)
Long-term bonds issued by the U.S. government with a unique redemption feature: the maturity principal may adjust over time based on the economic climate. When the economy is experiencing inflation, the bond principal increases proportionately; in periods of deflation, the principal decreases. Though the coupon rate is fixed, semiannual interest payments may not be, as the fixed rate is applied to the current adjusted principal balance.

See also: Deflation, Inflation, Treasury bond

In an attempt to protect his investment against the fluctuations of the economy, George preferred to invest heavily in **TIPS**.

Tranche
A portion of a bond deal, characterized by a unique feature within the deal. Though all of the bonds are issued at once by a single issuer (and usually backed by mortgages or loans on other assets), each portion carries its own repayment terms, including interest rate and expected maturity.

See also: Asset-backed security, CMO

Jan bought **tranches** *with varying maturity dates in order to spread out her earnings and payments.*

Treasuries
A term used to describe all debt instruments issued by the U.S. government.

See also: Treasury bill, Treasury bond, Treasury note

Treasuries *are good investments for anyone looking for fixed income.*

Treasury bill (T-bill)
Short-term debt instruments issued by the U.S. government and sold at deep discount to their $1,000 face value. No interest is paid on these instruments, and maturities range from three months to one year
   See also: Discounting, Treasury bond, Treasury note, U.S. Treasury

Rhonda's granddad had been investing in **T-bills** *since he was 18 years old.*

Treasury bond
Long-term debt instruments issued by the U.S. government in $1,000 increments, carrying fixed interest rates and maturing in no fewer than ten years.
   See also: Bond, Treasury bill, Treasury note, U.S. Treasury

Since Joanna was heavily invested in the stock market, her financial planner suggested rounding out her portfolio with **Treasury bonds.**

Treasury note
Medium-term debt instruments issued by the U.S. government in $1,000 increments, carrying fixed interest rates and maturing within two to ten years of issue.
   See also: Discount, Treasury bond, Treasury bill, U.S. Treasury

Brian's parents invested in **Treasury notes** *that would come due the year he graduated from college to ensure he had some money to start off with.*

Upgrade
When a security rating goes up a grade, meaning it's a less risky investment.
   See also: Bond rating

It only took a year after the new CEO of Lion Joe Industries took over for their corporate bonds to experience an **upgrade.**

Vanilla issue
A new security that has only standard features—no bells and whistles; the most basic version of a security. Usually used in reference to bonds and derivative securities.
   See also: Bond, Derivatives

Since the current bonds were **vanilla issue,** *they went on the market without much fanfare.*

Weighted average coupon (WAC)
The weighted average of the interest rates of the mortgages making up a mortgage pool at the time they were securitized. Used in describing and analyzing mortgage-backed securities.
   See also: Mortgage-backed securities, Pass-through rate, Weighted average

The current weighted average of the pool was a full point lower than the original **weighted average coupon.**

Yellow sheets
A daily bulletin that provides current bid and ask prices and other information for over-the-counter corporate bonds.

See also: Ask price, Bid price, Corporate bond

Many day traders check the **yellow sheets** *every morning before making their investment decisions.*

Yield to call
The earnings an investor would receive on a bond if it is held until the first date upon which the issuer can demand redemption.

See also: Yield to maturity

Bev hoped her bonds would not be redeemed because their **yield to call** *was still very low.*

Yield to maturity (YTM)
The total return expected on a bond if it is held until its original stated redemption date. A complex calculation that includes coupon and prevailing interest rates, remaining bond term, par value, and current market price.

See also: Coupon rate, Maturity, Par value, Yield

Edward was so impressed with the **YTM** *on the bonds that he bought some for each of his grandchildren and put them away in a safety deposit box so the temptation to sell them wasn't even there.*

Zero-coupon bond
Debt instruments that make no periodic interest payments, and are sold for far less than their redemption value but redeemed for full value at maturity.

See also: Bond, Debt instruments, Discount, Interest, Maturity

Zero-coupon bonds *fit nicely into Lee's college fund portfolio.*

Z-tranche
A special type of bond often included in CMO issues. This bond receives no payments until all of the other bonds in the series have been paid off. The skipped interest payments (that it should have received but didn't) get added to the balance of the bond. The next "would-be" interest payment is based on that higher bond balance. Also called a "Z-bond" or an "accrual bond."

See also: CMO, Zero-coupon bond

Miki invested in **Z-tranches** *because she expected rates to start going up, and she knew it would be outstanding for a very long time.*

ECONOMY

Agflation
Rising food prices that come on when demand exceeds supply (agricultural inflation). Occurs when food products (such as corn or soy) are diverted for another use such as alternative fuels instead of for food.
See also: Inflation

The rising demand for ethanol created **agflation** *within the corn sector.*

Aspirin count theory
A belief that the stock market and aspirin production move in opposite directions; i.e., when the market goes up, aspirin production goes down. Based on the idea that people take more aspirin when the market is in decline.
See also: Stock market

Due to the **aspirin count theory**, *pharmaceutical companies expected higher sales as the economy started to slow.*

Bailout
When a failing business receives emergency funding from an outside source (often the government) in order to prevent a full business failure.
See also: Bankruptcy, Insolvency

Congress debated the pros and cons of giving the airline industry another **bailout** *before finally deciding to do so.*

Bandwagon effect
When individual investors follow and imitate the trades of the masses, i.e., sell because "everyone else" is selling.
See also: Panic buying, Panic selling

When word hit the street that the philanthropist was selling his shares of Lion Joe Ltd., it created a **bandwagon effect** *that nearly sunk the stock.*

Bear market
A time period during which securities prices consistently drop, typically accompanied by an economic recession and rising inflation.
See also: Bull market

When stock prices start declining, a **bear market** *may be right around the corner.*

Big Three
The largest car manufacturers in the United States: Ford, Chrysler, and GM.

See also: Bellwether

Tracking the movements of the **Big Three** *is one way to gauge the overall health and stability of the market.*

Breadth indicator
A type of measure used in technical analysis to determine overall market movement (whether prices are going up or down) and participation (based on volume or how many trades are made).

See also: Absolute breadth index, Advance/decline index, Technical analysis

When an investor wants solid information about which way the market is going, she can count on **breadth indicators.**

Breadth of the market
An analytical theory that looks at the number of advancing and declining issues as a way to determine overall market strength.

See also: Advance/decline line, Technical analysis, Stock market

Although certain sectors were weakening, the **breadth of the market** *indicated solid growth.*

Break
A sudden severe decline in the futures market. Usually brought on by unpredictable natural occurrences (such as wildfires and earthquakes) that impact the underlying commodities.

See also: Commodity, Futures

The traders worried that if the pilots didn't get the fires out in time, it could cause a **break** *in the citrus futures market.*

Bubble theory
A phenomenon where securities' market prices rise dramatically above their true value, usually followed by an equally dramatic decline.

See also: Echo bubble, Panic buying

Many investors are caught by surprise when what they thought was realistic growth drops suddenly due to the **bubble theory.**

Bull market
A period of time characterized by stock market growth, often driven by a strong economy and thriving corporate profits.

See also: Bear market

Gina's portfolio grew by 300% during the last **bull market.**

Bureau of Labor Statistics
A federal agency that collects and reports on data pertinent to the U.S. economy, such as the unemployment rate and the Consumer Price Index.

See also: Economic indicator

Analysts look to the **Bureau of Labor Statistics** *to help identify if the economy is in a recession or just going through a slump.*

Business cycle
A standard economic pattern of predictable ups and downs in financial activity for a defined time period.

See also: Peak, Trough

Business cycles *are less predictable than most people realize, and can last twelve months or twelve years.*

Calendar effect
The theoretical impact on the securities market of certain days or periods during the year, where investors believe those times are good or bad for investing.

See also: January effect, Monday effect, October effect, Weekend effect

Many brokers swore that day traders working without the advice of financial professionals had increased the **calendar effect.**

Circuit breaker
A group of steps that can be taken to prevent a market crash due to a bout of panic selling. Such steps include a trading halt or restricted trading.

See also: Crash, Panic selling

The NYSE activated a two-hour **circuit breaker** *when the market plunged.*

CNN effect
A temporary change in consumer buying habits that comes on because of riveting news (such as the run on duct tape when consumers feared chemical attacks).

See also: Bank run, Eva Longoria stock index

The **CNN effect** *caused sales of bottled water to skyrocket after concerns about water processing plants were reported.*

Consumer Confidence Index
A measure of the way Americans feel about the economy, both now and about their expectations for the near future.

See also: Leading indicator

In spite of pundits' reassurances that the economy was fine, the **Consumer Confidence Index** *was steadily dropping.*

Consumer Price Index (CPI)
A benchmark number that tracks the change in a select collection of normal household expenditures, such as food, electricity, housing, and transportation. Measures changes in the cost of living.

See also: Benchmark, Economic indicator

According to the **Consumer Price Index**, *the costs of life's necessities in the United States have been climbing steadily for over a decade.*

Correction
A temporary security price decrease that breaks up a prevailing uptrend. An official correction is a decline of at least 10%. (Theoretically, a correction can be a temporary price spike during a prevailing downtrend.)

See also: Uptrend

The **correction** *in the housing market caught many sellers by surprise and they were unable to get the prices they originally asked for.*

Cost-of-Living Adjustment (COLA)
A yearly modification of social security payments and wages based on changes in the Consumer Price Index (CPI). Meant to help defray declines in consumer purchasing power.

See also: Consumer Price Index, Purchasing power

The company made sure its employees received **COLA** *raises, even in the years when that was the most it could offer.*

Crash
A substantial, sustained overall drop in a financial market. Technically, a 20% decline in the total value of a prevailing market index.

See also: Bear market, Break, Depression

Whenever there is a **crash**, *it renews fears of another Great Depression.*

Debt bomb
A disruption in the global financial system caused by the default on enormous liability obligations by a major multinational financial institution (though this level of disturbance can also be caused by a widespread default on individual consumer liabilities).

See also: Default

The **debt bomb** *that was created when the country defaulted on its loans rocked economies throughout the world.*

Deer market
A period of time characterized by lack of investment activity, due to wary, overly cautious investors employing "wait and see" strategies.
   See also: Bear market, Bull market
   Since the pundits couldn't seem to agree about the strength of the economy, the public responded by creating a **deer market**.

Deflation
An overall decline in the prices of consumer goods. Can be brought on by a lack of spending and credit use or a decrease in the general money supply.
   See also: Inflation, Stagflation
   By mid-June, travelers were pleased to realize the **deflation** *in auto prices from the previous spring would allow them to buy a brand new car for next to nothing.*

Depression
A substantial, prolonged economic decline.
   See also: Recession
   Irving had already lived through a **depression**, *so he always made sure to keep a lot of cash hidden in his house.*

Devaluation
A huge drop in the value of a currency, either in relation to other currencies or to gold.
   See also: Currency risk, Exchange rate
   After the **devaluation** *of the small country's currency, people flocked there to take advantage of cheap vacation packages.*

Domini 400 Social Index
A measure of the weighted market value of a collection of 400 stocks whose companies meet strict ethical and environmental standards. A yardstick for measuring socially responsible investment portfolios.
   See also: Green investing, Index, Socially responsible fund
   Since Zoe respected her clients' decision to invest responsibly, she worked very hard to ensure their portfolios did at least as well as the **Domini 400 Social Index**.

Dot-com
A company that primarily does business on the Internet (such as Amazon .com).
   See also: Click and mortar
   Tiffany preferred clothes shopping through her favorite **dot-coms** *because her work schedule rarely allowed her the time she needed to go to stores.*

Dove
An economic advisor who aims to keep interest rates low, and believes that inflation has a minimal impact on society. Low interest rates lead to increased consumer borrowing and spending, which can lead to inflation.

See also: Economic indicator, Hawk, Inflation

The **doves** *fought to keep interest rates low, claiming it would help the economy pick up more quickly.*

Dow Jones Industrial Average (DJIA)
A financial index used to measure the current success or failure of the stock market. Consists of thirty very large and widely held public corporations. The weighted average share prices are combined to calculate the daily index value. Also called the "Dow" or the "Dow 30."

See also: Index, Index fund, S&P 500 Index

A decline in the **Dow Jones Industrial Average** *doesn't bode well for the U.S. economy.*

Dow Jones Transportation Average (DJT)
A commonly tracked stock index consisting of a weighted average of the prices of the twenty largest transportation stocks in the United States.

See also: Dow Jones Industrial Average, Index, Weighted average

Investors were wary—but not surprised—when the **DJT** *declined after months of rising fuel prices.*

Dow Theory
The idea that the overall stock market will follow uptrends and downtrends of the DJIA and DJT moving together in the same direction (i.e., they increase or decrease at the same time instead of one increasing while the other declines).

See also: Dow Jones Industrial Average, Dow Jones Transportation Average, Downtrend, Uptrend

According to the **Dow Theory,** *the stock market was going into a downtrend.*

Durables
Long-lasting consumer goods, such as refrigerators and hammers, that people expect to have for a long time without replacing.

See also: Commodity, Economic indicator

When new home sales decline, so do orders for **durables.**

Echo bubble
A small, less pronounced rally that comes on the heels of a period where security (or other asset) prices rise considerably above their actual value.

See also: Bubble theory, Rally

The real estate market experienced an **echo bubble** *when home prices began to rebound slightly following an unreasonable dip.*

Economic indicator
A quantifiable factor that impacts or is impacted by the overall economy. Examples include the unemployment rate, the Consumer Price Index (CPI), and housing starts.

See also: Lagging indicator, Leading indicator

Although most consumers were still concerned about the economy, the **economic indicators** *showed things were starting to get better.*

Emerging markets
Stock exchanges in countries that are just beginning to stabilize financially. Typically considered risky for investors due to volatile political, economic, and currency markets within those countries or their regions.

See also: Global fund, MSCI Emerging Markets Index

After the fall of the Soviet Union, many investors saw the potential of the **emerging markets** *that would evolve.*

Employee buyout
When a company's employees buy a controlling interest in the company, usually as a result of restructuring. Often done via an ESOP.

See also: ESOP, Controlling interest

The travel industry as a whole was shaken up when the airline underwent an **employee buyout** *and raised the standards of customer service.*

Energy sector
A category of securities related to energy production and supplies, from drilling companies to gas stations.

See also: Sector

Hardy invested in the **energy sector** *just as a wind farm bill passed in the legislature so he ended up making even more money than he'd expected.*

Equilibrium
The point where supply and demand intersect, stabilizing prices.

See also: Bid-Ask spread

It wasn't until after the holidays that the demand and the supply for the new video game reached **equilibrium**.

Eva Longoria Stock Index
A hypothetical stock portfolio consisting of shares in companies with ties to Eva Longoria (the *Desperate Housewives* actress). Based on the idea that her popularity can influence product sales enough to impact share prices.

See also: Index

The **Eva Longoria Stock Index** *could rise whenever the actress appeared in a commercial, as fans would buy whatever product she was plugging.*

Exchange
A marketplace created for the purpose of trading securities, commodities, or derivatives.

See also: Commodity, Derivatives, Securities

Although the NYSE may be the most easily recognized **exchange***, there are several throughout the world.*

Exchange rate
The value of one country's currency compared to another country's currency. Also called "foreign exchange rate."

See also: Currencies

Fiona preferred to cross the Canadian border and shop in the United States in order to take advantage of the favorable **exchange rate***.*

Fiscal policy
Government financial practices that influence and direct the overall economy. Examples include setting interest rates and redefining tax rates.

See also: Federal funds rate, Federal Reserve

The presidential candidates both promised to address and make changes in the country's **fiscal policy** *as a way of trying to connect with working-class voters.*

Fungibles
Interchangeable assets, where it would make no difference if one were substituted for another. Examples include raw metals, shares of common stock, bonds from the same issue, and commodities.

See also: Commodity

Since the apples from her orchard were **fungibles***, it didn't matter which ones Sarah delivered to the produce buyer.*

Gold fixing
A posted, quoted price set twice a day in London for bullion, allowing for universal pricing of the precious metal, especially for bulk sales.

See also: Gold bullion

The first **gold fixing** *took place in 1919, and has occurred every trading day since.*

Gross domestic product (GDP)
The entire market value of goods and services produced in a country for a specific time period (usually one year). Calculated by adding consumer spending, government spending, and total investment, then adding to that the value of exports minus imports. More important than this measurement itself is its relative growth, which can measure a country's economic health.

See also: Gross national product

As the country began to move out of recession, its **GDP** *slowly began to rise again.*

Gross national product (GNP)
The sum of the gross domestic product and the international income earned by U.S. residents minus the U.S. income earned by people living in other countries.

See also: Gross domestic product

Many economic strategists believe that increases in **GNP** *signify a higher standard of living.*

Hawk
An economic advisor who takes a negative view toward inflation, and sets policy to control it, usually through interest rate increases. Believes that inflation has an overall negative impact on the public. Also called an "inflation hawk."

See also: Dove, Economic indicator, Inflation

The economist received his placement in the administration because his **hawk** *views almost guaranteed he would agree with the President's policy goals.*

Health-care sector
An industry group that includes companies with a link to medical goods and services. Examples include pharmaceutical companies, medical labs, and health-care providers.

See also: Sector

The recent drug breakthrough caused a jump in share prices across the entire **health-care sector.**

Heavy industry
A group of companies that depend on large investments in assets such as factories, equipment, and machinery. May also mean a labor-intensive industry. Examples include automotive and mining.

See also: Fixed assets

When yet another plant announced layoffs, Eleanor seriously considered selling her **heavy industry** *stocks.*

Housing bubble
A quick, widespread increase in home prices, which usually cannot be sustained over the long term. Rising interest rates, a glut of properties, or more strict lending practices can cause those inflated prices to quickly drop (bursting the bubble).

See also: Bubble theory

Many homeowners took advantage of the **housing bubble** *and were able to sell at much higher prices than expected.*

Housing starts
The number of new residential housing projects that begin construction during any given month. A key economic indicator, as more people buy new houses when the economy is strong.

See also: Economic indicator

The number of **housing starts** *increased steadily during the administration's second term.*

Index
A specific set of securities used as a benchmark to measure market activity and growth. Some of the most widely known include the S&P 500 and the Dow Jones Industrial Average.

See also: Dow Jones Industrial Average, S&P 500 Index

Consumers will often change their investing habits based on **index** *reports because the reports cause them to have more or less faith in the markets.*

Inflation
An overall increase in the price of goods and services which drives a decline in purchasing power. Numerically expressed as a percentage.

See also: Deflation, Stagflation

Although salaries have gone up, paychecks don't go as far as they used to due to **inflation**.

Inflation risk
The chance that the relative returns on an investment will be lessened by a general increase in prices and a corresponding decrease in purchasing power.

See also: Risk, Inflation, Purchasing power

There is a certain amount of **inflation risk** *with any long-term investment since the cost of living usually rises over time.*

Initial claims
A measure of the new unemployment (or jobless) claims filed with state agencies. When this number increases, it's usually a sign of a weakening economy.
   See also: Economic indicator

After five straight quarters of rising unemployment, **initial claims** *finally began to level out.*

International stock markets
Forums for trading equity shares outside the United States.
   See also: NASDAQ, New York Stock Exchange, Stock market

As the Internet and global infrastructure has made the world more accessible, investors have greater access to **international stock markets** *as well.*

Lagging indicator
A quantifiable economic factor that changes after a change in the overall economy. Often used to confirm economic trends.
   See also: Leading indicator

The rising unemployment rate, a **lagging indicator,** *confirmed that the economy was indeed heading toward a recession.*

Leading indicator
A quantifiable economic factor that changes, followed by a change in the overall economy. Used by analysts to predict economic changes.
   See also: Lagging indicator

When the Consumer Price Index, a key **leading indicator,** *was up two months in a row, Rodrigo knew it was time to re-examine his fixed-income portfolio.*

Leading lipstick indicator
An oddly accurate economic indicator based on the idea that when the economy is weak, people tend to splurge on small luxuries, such as lipsticks.
   See also: Economic indicator

Analysts familiar with the **leading lipstick indicator** *weren't surprised when cosmetics sales went through the roof after the 9/11 attacks.*

Lehman Aggregate Bond Index
A financial benchmark created by one of Wall Street's major trading houses to measure activity in the overall debt securities market. Includes all forms of debt securities (i.e., Treasury, mortgage-backed, corporate) with maturities greater than twelve months.
   See also: Bond, Index, Maturity

Pundits were predicting a slowing of the economy in part due to the downward trend in the **Lehman Aggregate Bond Index.**

Lipper indexes
A group of financial benchmarks that each follow the performance of a specific class of mutual funds, based on their designated investment style. For example, there are indexes covering large-cap, aggressive growth, and biotechnology funds. Lets investors compare a single fund's performance to the whole pack of similar funds. Owned by Reuters.

See also: Investing style, Mutual fund, Reuters

Before Talia invested in any mutual fund, she always checked the applicable **Lipper index** *to see how its performance stacked up.*

Macroeconomics
The study of the economy as a whole, a big-picture view. Focuses on national factors, such as federal interest rates and gross domestic product.

See also: Economic indicator, Gross domestic product

One must first understand **macroeconomics** *before being able to grasp the subtleties of the stock market.*

Market
A forum for securities transactions.

See also: Stock market

Karl rushed to buy the stock he wanted before the **market** *closed.*

Market breadth
A method of analysis used to determine overall market movement and momentum.

See also: Absolute breadth index, Advance/decline index

Although several popular stocks were rising, the **market breadth** *showed a gradual decline.*

Market jitters
General uneasiness about the current investing environment. May be brought on by things such as an increase in housing foreclosures, interest rate changes, economic uncertainty, or poor corporate performance.

See also: Economic indicator, Panic selling

Current economic conditions are causing **market jitters** *for most investors.*

Market profile
An analysis of the behavior of all investors, which impacts a single investor's trading strategy.

See also: Bandwagon effect

The current **market profile** *scared Daniel into selling all his shares in financial services companies.*

Market risk
The chance that the value of a specific security will drop because of an overall decline.

See also: Liquidity risk, Risk, Stock market

Chuck was willing to bear the **market risk** *and buy Lion Joe shares anyway, expecting their new technology to cause its prices to rise again, even if the market kept going down.*

Microeconomics
A little-picture view of small pieces of the economy, such as individual people or companies, to see how and why they participate in the economy. Looks at factors such as who makes purchase decisions and price-setting of specific products.

See also: Macroeconomics

Although the big picture still looked good, analysts looking at the **microeconomic** *view were beginning to become concerned about the economy's overall health.*

Misery index
A measure of the current state of the economy. Equals the unemployment rate plus the inflation rate. When the sum is rising, the economy is worsening.

See also: Inflation

After yet another corporation announced layoffs, even the most optimistic analysts had to admit the **misery index** *would continue rising.*

Monday effect
The idea that stock market price movements on Mondays will follow the prevailing trends from the Friday before.

See also: Calendar effect

Alberto assured his client that there was no reason to rush into the week after moderate trading on Friday because of the **Monday effect.**

Morgan Stanley EAFE Index (Europe, Australasia and Far East)
A benchmark measure of foreign (i.e., not U.S. or Canadian) stock performance. Calculated by summing weighted average (based on market capitalization) share prices, and used to track the overall health of foreign stock markets.

See also: Index, Stock market

Although the **Morgan Stanley EAFE Index** *was declining, Joseph took a chance and invested in Chinese companies, because he thought China would be the next hot economy.*

MSCI Emerging Markets Index
A financial benchmark created by Morgan Stanley to track overall stock performance in up-and-coming countries around the world.

See also: Emerging markets, Index, Morgan Stanley

Investors are showing an interest in Latin American countries due to positive reports from the **MSCI Emerging Markets Index.**

Multinational corporation (MNC)
A company that has holdings in more than one country.

See also: Corporation, NAFTA

Before investing in any **multinational corporation**, *Stephanie made sure to research its overseas business practices.*

NAFTA (North American Free Trade Agreement)
A policy instituted in 1994 by the United States, Canada, and Mexico to promote free trade among them by eliminating financial barriers (such as tariffs and fees normally placed on international trading).

See also: Multinational corporation

The success or failure of **NAFTA** *is one of the most hotly debated issues that came from the late twentieth century.*

NASDAQ 100 Index
A financial benchmark that measures the activity of the 100 biggest and most frequently traded stocks—excluding financial industry companies—on the NASDAQ Exchange.

See also: Index, NASDAQ

The **NASDAQ 100** *posted big gains, despite investors' fears that the markets would go down.*

New home sales
An economic indicator that quantifies sales of just-built homes.

See also: Lagging indicator

Rising **new home sales** *indicated that the real estate market was picking up again.*

New York Mercantile Exchange (NYMEX)
The world's largest commodities futures exchange. Often referred to as "the Merc," as in "Mercantile."

See also: Commodity, Futures

Everyone kept an eye on the **NYMEX** *because they were concerned about oil futures.*

October effect
The idea that stock prices will go down during October, which causes some investor anxiety, even though there's no real statistical basis for the theory. It is primarily based on the fact that some of the biggest crashes happened during October: Black Monday in 1929, which was followed by the Great Depression; October 19, 1987, when the DJIA dropped by more than 22% in a day.

See also: Calendar effect

Some financial professionals approach autumn somewhat cautiously because of the **October effect***, even though they realize they are mostly just being superstitious.*

OPEC (Organization of Petroleum Exporting Countries)
A group of oil-producing nations that got together in 1960 to jointly manage their sales and shipments to outside nations. Because they can substantially influence oil production levels, they can also significantly influence oil prices.

See also: Commodity

A large portion of the oil consumed by the United States is produced by **OPEC***.*

Panic buying
When a lot of people start buying a security simply because its price has increased.

See also: Due diligence, Painting the tape

The sudden jump in Lion Joe's share price set off a spate of **panic buying***.*

Panic selling
When a lot of people start selling a security as a reaction to a price dip, regardless of the value of the security.

See also: Circuit breaker, Stop loss

Even though the storm only damaged one plant, **panic selling** *started shortly after that quarterly drop was announced.*

Peak
The highest point reached by economic expansion in a business cycle before things start going downhill.

See also: Business cycle, Trough

A savvy financial professional can recognize **peaks** *and get their clients out of the industry before losses become too great.*

Purchasing power
The amount of goods or services that can be bought with $1, which changes based on inflation.

See also: Inflation

The high-end department store had to drop its prices drastically because consumers simply didn't have the **purchasing power** *they had the year before.*

Rally
A time period characterized by steady increases in overall market prices (stocks or bonds), usually following a period of flat or declining prices. Often caused by new cash influxes.

See also: Bear market, Bull market, Selloff

Economists hoped for a **rally** *after several weeks of poor market performance.*

Recession
A sustained period of economic decline, defined by a drop in national gross domestic product (GDP) that lasts for at least six months.

See also: Depression, Inflation

Consumers curbed their spending habits as fears of a **recession** *loomed.*

Ripple
A brief market trend.

See also: Wave

Leora's financial advisor told her to ignore **ripples**, *and focus on long-term success.*

Russell 1000 Index
A benchmark measure of the large-cap portion of the United States stock market. Tracks the market value of around 1,000 of the largest securities, based primarily on their market capitalization.

See also: Index, Large-cap stock, Russell 3000 Index, Russell 2000 Index

The **Russell 1000 Index** *indicated a slowing trend among the securities it measured.*

Russell 2000 Index
A financial index that measures the overall performance of the small-cap securities market.

See also: Index, Small-cap stock

According to the **Russell 2000 Index**, *investing in the startup technology corporation was an excellent idea.*

Russell 2500 Index
A benchmark measure of the performance of about 2,500 small and mid-cap stocks, put out by Russell Investments. A subset of the Russell 3000 Index. Sometimes called the "smid cap" index.

See also: Mid-cap stock, Russell 3000 Index, Small-cap stock

Tabby kept an eye on the **Russell 2500 Index** *because she was heavily invested in small-cap stocks.*

Russell 3000 Index
A financial index that tracks the performance of approximately 98% of the total U.S. stock market.

See also: Index, Stock market

The professor assigned tracking the **Russell 3000 Index** *to his econ students so they could see how the market changed over the course of the semester.*

Russell Top 50 Index
A benchmark measure that tracks the performance of a theoretical portfolio consisting of the fifty largest stocks (by market capitalization, i.e., large-cap stocks) included in the Russell 3000 Index. The combined value of these fifty stocks accounts for about 40% of the total Russell 3000 universe.

See also: Blue chip, Large-cap stock

Professor Nessel had his Intro to Economics class follow the **Russell Top 50 Index** *as a good example of how the major stocks were moving.*

S&P 500 Index (Standard & Poor's 500)
A stock market index that tracks the movement of 500 stocks considered to be representative of the total market. Covers approximately 70% of the market capitalization for the U.S. stock market.

See also: Index, Market capitalization, Stock market

The young day trader lost a lot of money by trying to outdo the **S&P 500**.

Salary freeze
When a company officially stops giving raises. Usually done when its financial picture is bleak, and then is reversed when things pick up.

See also: Insolvency

Lion Joe University instituted a **salary freeze** *in an attempt to forestall layoffs at the end of the school year.*

Santa Claus rally
An overall increase in the price of stocks that almost always happens during the week between Christmas and New Year's.

See also: Calendar effect

Many companies depend on the **Santa Claus rally** *to make their yearly projections.*

SEC (Securities and Exchange Commission)
The U.S. government agency that administers and enforces the laws regarding the public trade of investments.

See also: Exchange, Securities

The **SEC** *must approve all public corporation sales.*

Sector
A specific economic segment or industry, such as energy or insurance.

See also: Sector fund

The strength or weakness of certain **sectors** *can be indicative of the overall health of the economy.*

Selloff
A sudden market-wide rush to get rid of (divest of) securities, which leads to rapid price drops in those securities.

See also: Rally, Securities

The dot-com bubble burst in the 1990s due to the massive **selloff** *of Internet stocks.*

Shock absorber
A short-term restriction on the trade of index futures (a kind of derivative investment), normally due to substantial declines in the value of the underlying index during the day.

See also: Circuit breaker, Index futures

The **shock absorber** *kicked in when the S&P 500 dropped fifty points in a matter of hours.*

Sideways market
When market prices remain stable, and the market as a whole moves neither up nor down.

See also: Bear market, Bull market

No one makes money in a **sideways market.**

Sideways trend
Indicates steady security prices over a time period, with no significant up or down movement. Also called "horizontal trend."
See also: Downtrend, Uptrend

Sluggish earnings coupled with upcoming product launches put Lion Joe shares in a **sideways trend** *as investors waited to see what came next.*

Silicon Valley
The Northern California area where a lot of computer-based companies (including Internet companies) are headquartered. So-called because silicon is a key component of computer chips.
See also: Dot-com, Research and Development

Silicon Valley *became the unofficial capital of the technology world during the 1990s.*

Slump
A period of economic weakness; a general slowdown of business activity.
See also: Recession

Consumers and businesses alike hoped that the holidays would help end the **slump** *that had been happening since summer.*

Stagflation
An economic condition characterized by a slow- or nongrowing economy and high unemployment rates mixed with rising prices.
See also: Deflation, Inflation

Consumers were concerned about **stagflation** *due to the current economic trends.*

Sticky deal
An impending security offering where the issuing company is suddenly plagued by bad news (either company-specific, industry-specific, or about the economy as a whole), making it less likely that there will be a good response to the offering. May result in the offering being canceled or postponed, or the offering price being lowered.
See also: IPO, Subsequent offering

The CEO realized that the scandal around the research department would immediately turn their highly anticipated launch into a **sticky deal.**

Super Bowl indicator
An unexpectedly accurate stock market predictor, based on the winner of the Super Bowl. The theory is this: If an AFC team wins, the market will decline over the coming year, and if an NFC team wins the market will go up during the year.

See also: Calendar effect

When the Dallas Cowboys beat the Denver Broncos in the Super Bowl, Rex bought stock because the **Super Bowl indicator** *predicted the market would rise.*

Top-down investing
A big-picture analysis style that first concentrates on the direction of the economy and prevailing financial conditions, then narrows focus to specific sectors before looking into individual securities.

See also: Bottom-up investing

Judy decided on her financial advisor because she liked his **top-down investing** *style.*

Trading volume
The number of shares bought or sold during a specific time period.

See also: Advance/decline line, Average daily volume

Although the day's **trading volume** *wasn't high, the stock market still rose several points.*

Trough
The phase of the business cycle that indicates the end of decreasing activity and the beginning of a period of expansion.

See also: Business cycle, Peak, Slump

Sadly, the declaration of war often results in a **trough**.

U.S. Treasury
The federal agency responsible for overseeing revenue collection and issuing government debt securities. Its authority includes managing the IRS and the U.S. Mint, and overseeing all the U.S. banks.

See also: IRS, Treasury bill, Treasury bond, Treasury note

The **U.S. Treasury** *is one of the most powerful agencies in the country.*

Unemployment rate
The percentage of U.S. civilians (nongovernment workers) who are able to work but are currently jobless.

See also: Lagging indicator

The President won re-election based largely on the fact that **unemployment rates** *were lower than they had been in nearly twenty years.*

Volatility Index (VIX)
A measure of the expected variability of the market over the next thirty days; quantifies market risk. Gauges investor comfort (or discomfort). High values (more than thirty) indicate fear and uncertainty (discomfort), and higher price variability.

See also: Market risk, Volatility

Shortly after the country went to war, the **Volatility Index** *skyrocketed.*

Wave
A day of market activity that goes against the trend of the week. For example, if the market closes higher on Monday through Wednesday, then dips on Thursday, and closes higher again on Friday, Thursday's activity would constitute a wave.

See also: Ripple

Heidi learned to ride market **waves** *after a few losing selling experiences.*

Weekend effect
A phenomenon where financial market returns are almost always lower on a Monday than they were on the preceding Friday. Possibly caused by the fact that many corporations release bad news statements on Fridays, or by investor excitement cooling down over the nontrading days in between.

See also: Calendar effect

Louie always avoided trading on Mondays, because he believed in the power of the **weekend effect.**

Yield curve
A graphical presentation of the mathematical relationship between interest rates and maturity dates on debt issued by the U.S. government, where the norm is for higher interest rates to correspond with longer maturity dates.

See also: Maturity, Treasuries, Yield

Economists have certain expectations when reading a **yield curve;** *they will take notice when there are unexpected changes on the graph.*

Zigzag indicator
Shows trend analysts whether a change is a true reversal or just a momentary blip. Typically used to confirm a trend reversal rather than to predict the next one.

See also: Trend reversal pattern

The financial advisor used a **zigzag indicator** *to prove to his client that public interest in the stock was waning and now was not the time to open a long position.*

FINANCIAL PLANNING

529 plan
A qualified state tuition program, named after its section in the United States tax code, which allows tuition savings and their earnings to grow tax-free.

See also: Tax-free

George and Mary opened up a **529 plan** *to save for college tuition as soon as their son was born.*

Above water
1. When a person or company is able to stay out of financial trouble. 2. When the market value of a company's assets is much higher than their recorded book value (which is the value that must appear on financial statements).

See also: (1) Bankruptcy, Insolvency, (2) Book value, Financial statements

1. The small shop owners were hoping they would be able to keep their business **above water** *during the recession. 2. Due to skyrocketing real estate prices in Colorado, the ski resort property was* **above water**, *and REIT investors were seeing substantial gains.*

Amortization
The reduction of a loan balance through regular principal payments.

See also: Amortization schedule

Most mortgage loans use **amortization** *to create payment schedules.*

Amortization schedule
A listing of all regular payments due on a loan, along with their due dates. Each line typically includes the total payment, the principal portion of the payment, the interest portion of the payment, and the remaining loan balance due after payment.

See also: Amortization

Gina got a copy of her **mortgage amortization** *schedule from the bank.*

Annuity
A fixed sum of money paid regularly to a named individual.

See also: Immediate annuity, Joint and survivor annuity, Variable annuity

He saved his quarterly **annuity checks** *from his grandfather's estate in order to take a vacation at the end of the year.*

Automatic reinvestment

A program that allows securities holders (usually mutual fund holders) to direct that their earnings (such as dividends and capital gains) routinely be used to purchase additional shares rather than being paid out. Though not paid directly to shareholders, these distributions are still taxable.

> See also: Capital gains, Dividend, Mutual fund

In order to help her investments grow faster, Lynn set up an **automatic reinvestment** *program with her financial advisor.*

Bankruptcy

A legal action that stops creditors from trying to collect debts from an individual or company.

> See also: Debt, Insolvency

Stacy filed for **bankruptcy** *when she realized her debts were insurmountable, in spite of her best efforts to pay them off.*

Barbell strategy

A strategy used with fixed-income portfolios, where one group of investments within the portfolio matures very soon and another matures far in the future. In between the two maturity lumps comes a steady stream of graduated mid-term maturities. Used to provide major cash influx at two fixed points.

> See also: Fixed-income securities, Maturity, Portfolio

Harriet decided on a **barbell strategy** *so that her first large payment would come at retirement and the next when she expected to move into a retirement home.*

Beneficiary

A person or other entity, such as a charitable organization, identified in a legal document as the recipient of goods, gifts, or assets.

> See also: Life insurance, Trust, Stretch IRA

Insurance companies require their clients to name a **beneficiary** *to the policies.*

Bequest

A gift left to a named person or other entity, such as a charitable organization, through a provision in a will.

> See also: Beneficiary, Probate

The college counted on **bequests** *from its alumni to help keep its scholarship funds available to students.*

Budget
A complete listing of income and expenses for a specific time period. Can be historical or prospective.

See also: Expense, Income

Dan and Mary made a household **budget** *to help them get a better handle on their cash.*

Cash position
The highly liquid portion of a portfolio, including short-term securities with maturities shorter than ninety days and demand accounts (such as money market funds).

See also: Demand account, Liquid, Money market fund

Ben maintained a large **cash position** *so he could take advantage of lucrative investment opportunities as they arose.*

Cash surrender value
The amount of cash a person can get when he cancels a whole life insurance policy.

See also: Whole life insurance

She canceled the secondary insurance policy because the **cash surrender value** *was good.*

Cash-value life insurance
An insurance contract that combines the death benefits of a term policy with an investment component. A part of the premium paid is applied to the death benefits guarantee, and the rest goes into an investment reserve; as the policy holder gets older, a greater portion of the premium is used for benefits, and less for investment. Often called "whole life insurance."

See also: Premium (insurance), Term life insurance

Andrea bought **cash-value life insurance** *as a way to protect her beneficiaries while investing for her own old age at the same time.*

Certified financial planner (CFP)
A licensed professional who specializes in designing investment strategies for individuals.

See also: Broker, CPA

Linda saw a **certified financial planner** *to help her figure out her financial goals and design a winning investment portfolio.*

Charitable lead trust

An irrevocable legal arrangement where money or property is donated to an account for the benefit of two parties: an income beneficiary, which must be a tax-exempt charitable organization, and a final beneficiary. The arrangement states the amount of income the organization will receive for a specified time period. At the end of that period, all remaining assets are turned over to the final beneficiary (which can be the trust creator or a family member). The donor receives tax benefits as soon as the arrangement is created, and over the next several years.

See also: Charitable remainder trust, Irrevocable trust

When Martha set off on her journey around the world, she set up a **charitable lead trust** *so her favorite food bank would be fully funded for eight years, until her granddaughter turned twenty-one.*

Charitable remainder trust

An irrevocable legal arrangement where money or property is donated to an account for the benefit of two parties: an income beneficiary and a final beneficiary, which must be a tax-exempt charitable organization. The arrangement states the amount of income the income beneficiary (and there may be more than one) will receive during his life. Upon the death of the income beneficiary, all leftover assets are given to the final beneficiary. Once the arrangement is made, the donor receives tax benefits in the form of tax deductions for several years.

See also: Charitable lead trust, Irrevocable trust

The man set up a **charitable remainder trust** *to ensure that his wife was taken care of until her death and yet he could also show support for the organization that had done so much for him during his life.*

Chartered financial consultant (ChFC)

A title offered by the insurance industry to professionals who pass all required exams on finance and investing and meet a three-year minimum industry experience requirement.

See also: CPA, Certified financial planner

Jim was so loyal to his clients that he maintained even the smallest accounts once he received his **chartered financial consultant** *standing.*

Cluster analysis
A method for determining portfolio diversification that groups securities based on the correlation between their returns. Can help investors eliminate doubling up so their portfolios are really as diversified as they want them to be.

See also: Diversification

Jan and Chris referred to the **cluster analysis** *in order to ensure neither one bought into a sector the other one had already loaded up on.*

COBRA (Consolidated Omnibus Reconciliation Act)
Refers to employer-provided health insurance coverage that can remain in effect for a specified time period after loss of employment. Premiums are paid wholly by the former employee, but at the group rate which is typically much lower than one could normally spend for an individual policy. Allows for continuation of group health coverage so the individual can avoid a temporary lapse in coverage between jobs.

See also: Health insurance, Premium (insurance)

Pauline was able to keep her **COBRA** *for eighteen months after quitting her job, while she was waiting for the royalties from her first book to come in.*

Community property
Assets owned or acquired by a married person during his marriage that become legally half-owned by each spouse. This determination is established by state law. Also called "marital property."

See also: Joint tenancy with rights of survivorship

Currently, only nine states have **community property** *laws, and those laws vary widely.*

Correlation
A measure of how two securities perform relative to one another. Knowing this information can help with portfolio diversification, to make sure all holdings don't perform in the same way.

See also: Diversification, Portfolio

Bobbi looked at the **correlation** *between the stocks she already owned and the ones she was considering to ensure they would be a smart purchase.*

Correlation coefficient

A numerical score that shows how securities perform compared to one another, on a scale of +1 to –1. A score of +1 means they are perfectly correlated, and will perform exactly the same under a given set of circumstances. A –1 indicates negative correlation, where the securities will perform exactly opposite under a given set of circumstances.

See also: Correlation, Technical analysis

The **correlation coefficient** *indicated Rosa's stocks would perform differently enough to give her some stability in her income, regardless of the circumstances.*

Coverdell educational savings account (ESA)

A tax-advantaged plan that allows families to put aside up to $2,000 per child per year for tuition and similar expenses, where the money can grow tax-deferred. Formerly know as the Education IRA.

See also: 529 plan

With three children in the family, it was important for the parents to take advantage of a **Coverdell educational saving account.**

Credit shelter trust

A formal legal arrangement used by married couples to greatly reduce or possibly eliminate federal estate taxes when the second spouse dies. Also called "AB trust" or "bypass trust."

See also: Estate tax, Trust

Vivian and Benjamin set up a **credit shelter trust** *so that their heirs wouldn't have to pay hefty taxes on their estate.*

Decedent

A person who has died.

See also: Probate, Testamentary trust

A hearing was held when the will was contested in order to interpret the **decedent's** *true wishes for her estate.*

Deductible (noun)

The preset amount an insured person must pay before insurance benefits will be paid.

See also: Insurance

The **deductible** *on Zoe's car insurance was $500 per incident.*

Disability insurance
A financial safety net that replaces income lost due to sustained illness or injury that prevents work.

See also: Insurance

Katja bought **disability insurance** *because she was her family's sole breadwinner.*

Discretionary income
The amount of money a person has left to spend on luxury items after all necessities are bought, all the bills and taxes are paid, and savings or investment deposits are made.

See also: Disposable income, Income

The couple's goal was to have enough **discretionary income** *to be able to tour a different country every year.*

Disposable income
The amount of money a person has left after his taxes are paid.

See also: Discretionary income, Income

After Marc's raise, he had enough **disposable income** *to pay all his bills and start saving.*

Diversification
Including a wide variety of securities in a portfolio to reduce its overall risk. Presumes that different types of investments behave differently under the same set of economic conditions.

See also: Asset allocation, Correlation, Volatility

Although Al's client wanted to invest heavily in the gas and oil industry, he recommended greater **diversification.**

Donee
A person or other entity, such as a charitable foundation, who receives a gift.

See also: Donor

The philanthropist was always on the lookout for a worthy **donee** *he could assist with funding.*

Donor
A person or other entity, such as a corporation, who gives a gift.

See also: Donee

Every year, the opera held a special performance for their major **donors.**

Double indemnity
A special provision found in some life insurance policies that allows for twice the contracted death benefit in the case of accidental death.

See also: Life insurance

Because of the dangers inherent in his job as a firefighter, Ken's insurance policy did not have a **double indemnity** *clause.*

Education IRA
A special tax-advantaged plan created to help families pay for college by putting aside a maximum of $2,000 per child per year for tuition and related expenses, where the money can grow tax-deferred. Now more commonly known as a "Coverdell ESA."

See also: 529 plan

The parents opened an **education IRA** *when their children were young.*

Estate
All property, real and personal, owned by a person at the time of his death.

See also: Estate tax

Since Emilio had limited cash in the bank, his heirs were surprised to discover his **estate** *was quite large.*

Executor
The person named in a will to manage all aspects of the deceased person's estate; the duties include paying estate taxes, distributing the decedent's assets as specified by him, and paying all outstanding debts of the decedent.

See also: Decedent

The **executor** *of an estate should be knowledgeable and trustworthy.*

Expected return
The estimated income and gains that will be produced by an investment.

See also: Capital gains, Returns

As high as the **expected returns** *were for the fund, the actual income was even greater.*

Family limited partnership (FLP)
Financial lingo for a specially structured family business, where one or two members (usually the parents) act as general (managing) partners and the others (usually children and grandchildren) act as limited (silent) partners. Used primarily for estate planning and asset protection purposes.

See also: Estate planning, General partner, Limited partnership

The family elders agreed setting up the business as an **FLP** *from the beginning was a good idea, especially because the parents wouldn't be retiring for many years.*

Fiduciary
A company or a person who holds assets for another company or person (who will benefit from the assets), generally with the legal obligation and authority to make financial decisions regarding those assets. Legally required to act in the best interests of the beneficiary.

See also: Assets, Trust

The dictates of the will only allowed Derrick to be the **fiduciary** *of his nephew's trust fund.*

First dollar coverage
A special insurance policy that offers reimbursement for the full amount of a loss with no deductible. Normally costs more than policies that do call for a deductible payment.

See also: Insurance, Premium (insurance)

He was willing to pay extra for a **first dollar coverage** *policy on the antiques he had collected for years.*

Fixed-income assets
Securities that provide steady interest or dividend payments to investors.

See also: Blue chip, Bond, Dividend, Interest

After her retirement, Blanche relied on her **fixed-income assets** *to help keep her budget in the black.*

Fixed-income securities
Investments that offer definite periodic payments to holders. Usually in the form of regular dividends (on preferred stock) and interest (on bonds and other debt instruments). Since they usually don't increase in value, they are a poor choice for investors looking for growth.

See also: Bond, Preferred stock

Maude included some **fixed-income securities** *in her portfolio to add stability, as the rest of her investments were much more risky.*

Gap insurance
A special auto insurance policy used when standard loss coverage is less than the amount still due on the car loan, which happens when the car's book value is less than the remaining loan balance.

See also: Insurance

Bonnie still owed a few thousand dollars on her old Jeep, so she bought **gap insurance** *to cover her in case her car got totaled.*

Generation-skipping trust
A legal arrangement where grandparents place assets into an account for the benefit of their children and grandchildren. The children receive income from the trust assets, and the assets themselves are eventually distributed to the grandchildren (upon the death of the children), thereby passing over (or "skipping") one level of estate tax.
> See also: Estate tax, Generation-skipping tax, Trust

As an attorney, he knew the wisdom of setting up a **generation-skipping trust** *so his children and grandchildren would all be cared for properly.*

Gift splitting
A tax rule that allows a married couple to divide a large gift between them, turning it into two separate gifts for tax purposes.
> See also: Gift tax

When her grandparents gave her $24,000 to beef up the down payment on her dream house, the couple opted for **gift splitting** *so the money wouldn't be subject to taxes.*

Grantor-retained income trust (GRIT)
An irrevocable legal arrangement used to minimize estate taxes, where an account is set up to hold assets that will eventually be transferred to a named beneficiary. The creator (also known as the "grantor") keeps the use of or the income from the account assets for a set number of years.
> See also: Estate tax, Trust

The financial planner suggested a **GRIT** *to address both the needs of the older gentleman and his son's inability to pay estate taxes on the eventual inheritance.*

Guaranteed replacement cost provision
A covenant in an insurance policy that promises to pay out the amount of money needed to buy new assets similar to those that have been lost or damaged as per the policyholder's claim.
> See also: Insurance

Due to the risk of damage in a kitchen, most restaurants make sure their insurance policies include a **guaranteed replacement cost provision.**

Guaranteed-investment contracts (GICs)
Insurance agreements that promise regular principal and interest payments for a fixed time period. The agreement interest rate can be either fixed or floating, but promise the holder a minimum rate of return. Used to mitigate portfolio risk. Primarily purchased by institutional investors, such as banks or mutual funds.

See also: Fixed-income securities, Institutional investors

James made sure his fixed-income funds held plenty of **GICs** *so he knew he could count on his dividends.*

Health insurance
Coverage that provides financial payment and reimbursement for medical expenses.

See also: Insurance

Amber took the job because the **health insurance** *offered by the company was comprehensive and reasonably priced.*

Identity theft
When someone illegally takes and uses the identifying information of another person to make fraudulent purchases. Essentially, the thief pretends to be the other person, then uses that person's existing credit cards to make purchases, and possibly gets even more credit cards in that person's name.

See also: Skimming

Jack realized he had been a victim of **identity theft** *when he got a call from his credit card company inquiring about suspicious charges.*

Idle funds
Money that isn't earning anything, such as money in a change jar or a non-interest-bearing checking account.

See also: Demand deposit, Time deposit

She kept part of her paychecks in short-term CDs in order to avoid **idle funds** *but still have scheduled access to her money.*

Immediate annuity
An annuity purchased with a single, large payment. This annuity starts making regular income payments right away. Also called an "income annuity."

See also: Annuity

Bob used his settlement to open an **immediate annuity** *and ensure a longer-term income.*

Income annuity
An annuity that's purchased with a large lump-sum payment, which starts paying out an income stream right away.

> See also: Annuity

Jackie knew she would spend the large inheritance quickly if she wasn't careful so she bought an **income annuity** *in order to regulate the amount of cash she had on hand.*

Income shifting
A tax-saving strategy where earnings are transferred from a high-bracket taxpayer to a lower-bracket taxpayer, such as holding investments in a child's name.

> See also: Marginal tax rate, Taxable income

When their first child was born, the couple decided to try **income shifting** *with their quarterly investment returns in order to save on their taxes.*

Indemnity insurance
A form of insurance that protects business owners and their workers from financial losses due to on-the-job mistakes and misjudgments. An example is malpractice insurance.

> See also: Insurance

Prior to opening the new water park, the company strengthened its **indemnity insurance**.

Inherit
To receive assets from someone who has died.

> See also: Bequest

She worked every summer at her grandfather's business because she knew she would eventually **inherit** *it.*

Insolvency
The inability to pay debts as they come due.

> See also: Bankruptcy

The primary reason small businesses fail in the first five years is **insolvency**.

Insurance
A purchased policy that transfers risk of loss to the issuing company for a fee. When invoked, the policy pays out benefits to cover a loss, as specified by the contract.

> See also: Loss

Many apartment complexes and condo associations require tenants to carry **insurance** *on their properties.*

Inter vivos trust
A legal arrangement where one party ("trustee") holds assets for the benefit of someone else ("beneficiary"). The arrangement is created by a living person (as opposed to being created in a will). Also called a "living trust."

See also: Testamentary trust, Trust, Trustee

*Mame hoped to set up an **inter vivos trust** for her autistic nephew.*

Intestate
To die without a will.

See also: Probate

*The millionaire's family fought over his estate when it was discovered he died **intestate**.*

Irrevocable trust
A legal trust agreement that cannot be canceled by the creator.

See also: Trust

*After Tom's diagnosis of Alzheimer's disease, he created an **irrevocable trust** to protect his estate for his heirs.*

Joint and survivor annuity
A long-term financial tool that accepts and invests deposits for a set period of time, then makes regular payments to at least two beneficiaries (usually a husband and wife). Also called a "joint-life annuity."

See also: Annuity

*Wendy and Tomas set up a **joint and survivor annuity** when they were married so they could both make deposits and have a dependable income after retirement.*

Life insurance
A purchased policy that transfers to the issuing company the risk of loss of future earnings due to the death of a named individual. Death benefits are paid out when the named individual dies.

See also: Insurance, Term life insurance, Whole life insurance

*John bought a **life insurance** policy to protect his family from financial difficulties in case he died.*

Living trust
A legal arrangement, created by a live person (as opposed to being created in a will), where a trustee holds the title to assets for the benefit of another person or people (called "beneficiaries"). A useful estate planning tool, it is also called an "inter vivos trust."
See also: Testamentary trust, Trust, Trustee

Susan's concern for her autistic grandson caused her to set up a **living trust** *in his name.*

Long-term care insurance
A health-related guarantee agreement where the purchaser pays periodic premiums in exchange for reduced health costs in the case of a major illness or debilitation that requires constant attention for an extended period of time. Typically available to people aged sixty-five and older.
See also: Insurance

Jeremiah bought **long-term care insurance** *for his grandmother to help supplement her health insurance just in case she needed extra benefits.*

Management fee
A set charge paid to an experienced financial advisor to maintain and enhance an investment portfolio. Typically paid to private financial advisors or as a normal charge by mutual fund investors.
See also: Money manager, Mutual fund

A **management fee** *is a necessary budget item for novice investors, as they can benefit greatly from an advisor's expertise.*

Money manager
A professional (or professional firm) that administers the securities portfolio and other holdings of a high net worth individual or an institution, in exchange for a fee. Responsibilities include purchasing and selling securities according to the goals of a fixed financial plan, and tracking and analyzing investment results. Fees are typically based on a percentage of the portfolio value, rather than charged on a per-transaction basis.
See also: CPA, Certified financial planner, Chartered financial consultant

When Helen discovered her portfolio had only been averaging 5% returns, she decided to look for a new **money manager.**

Morningstar
A reliable investment research company that provides its customers with in-depth, detailed data on a variety of securities, though they're best known for their mutual fund rankings.

See also: Reuters

Holly always checks with **Morningstar** *before purchasing a new mutual fund.*

Offshore
Located outside an investor's home nation. For example, investing in Canadian securities counts as offshore for an American. Often done to avoid taxes in the home nation.

See also: Tax shelter

The real estate investor bought most of his properties **offshore** *so he wouldn't have to pay as much in taxes.*

On stream
An investment that's providing returns as expected.

See also: Rate of return, Returns

Lion Joe's stock was **on stream** *with slow but very steady growth as the public embraced its products.*

Opportunity cost
The benefits that could possibly have been received if an investor had made a different investment choice, when only one option can be chosen. Can be quantified by calculating the difference between returns actually earned and the returns that could have been earned if the other choice had been made.

See also: Due diligence

Louis carefully considered the **opportunity cost** *when making his investment choices, and decided to go with a tech stock fund instead of a real estate fund.*

Overweight
When a managed portfolio holds an excessively large position in a single security, in comparison with a benchmark index. Occurs when the portfolio manager thinks that security will quickly increase the overall returns of the portfolio. Usually a short-term situation.

See also: Portfolio

Although Terry's portfolio was temporarily **overweight***, it was succeeding in bringing returns back to her desired levels.*

Paper profit
An increase in the value of an investment that's still being held. No actual profit occurs until the asset is sold.

See also: Capital gains

George's **paper profit** *grew quarterly but he still had trouble making the rent some months.*

Paper millionaire
Someone who has investment holdings in excess of a million dollars. However, until those securities are converted to cash, that person does not really have a million dollars.

See also: Paper profit

Chris tried to live only off her paycheck and ignore the fact that she was a **paper millionaire** *since coming into her inheritance.*

Payable on death (POD)
An account designation that allows a bank depositor to assign beneficiaries to his bank account, so they will automatically receive the account assets in the event of the depositor's death. Allows beneficiaries to receive assets without waiting for probate. No ownership changes hands until the death of the depositor.

See also: Beneficiary, Decedent, Probate, Transfer on death

Charlie was able to pay his grandfather's bills immediately after he died because of the **POD** *notice on the checking accounts.*

Performance
A mathematical measure of the total returns earned on an investment during a specific time period.

See also: Capital gains, Capital loss, Dividend, Interest, Returns

Although it is tempting to use past **performance** *of a stock as an indicator if it is going to be a wise investment or not, it is not fail-safe and must not be depended upon too much.*

Personal property
Any tangible asset that is not land or a building attached to land.

See also: Intangible asset, Real property

Gina included her Yorkshire terrier and her Ravens' season tickets in her **personal property** *list.*

Portfolio
A collection of securities held by one person or company.

See also: Asset allocation, Portfolio manager

Nichelle had a diverse enough **portfolio** *that even if one sector showed a loss, her investments were still making her money.*

Portfolio income
Earnings derived from investments. These earnings include interest, dividends, and capital gains.

See also: Active income, Passive income

The young woman was able to take low-paying jobs for causes that mattered to her because her **portfolio income** *was large enough to pay her bills.*

Portfolio pumping
An illegal price manipulation employed to make a basket of holdings (such as a mutual fund) appear more valuable than they actually are. Accomplished by placing a lot of buy orders on securities already held in the fund to drive their prices up and make year-end returns look better.

See also: Fund manager, Pump and dump

Most investors in the fund didn't realize that the numbers that were so attractive weren't real but a result of **portfolio pumping.**

Premium (insurance)
A periodic fee paid in exchange for loss coverage.

See Also: Insurance, Life insurance

When she moved to Washington, the woman was pleased to discover her monthly **premium** *on her car insurance went down nearly $50 for the same coverage.*

Price risk
The chance that the market value of an investment will decline.

See also: Market risk, Risk

Conservative mutual funds tend to invest in companies whose stock carries a low **price risk.**

Probate
The authentication of a will, followed by the distribution of estate assets to the beneficiaries.

See also: Beneficiary, Estate

The will got stuck in **probate** *for months when the woman's family started arguing over her estate.*

QDOT trust (Qualified Domestic Trust)
A formal legal arrangement used to stave off estate taxes when leaving assets to a spouse who is not a U.S. citizen, therefore not qualifying for the unlimited marital deduction. Used only when the estate exceeds the standard federal estate tax exemption amount. Pronounced "cue-dot" trust.

See also: Estate tax, Marital deduction

Julie set up a **QDOT** trust *for her Canadian husband in case she died before he did.*

QTIP trust (Qualified Terminal Interest Property)
A formal legal arrangement that allows a surviving spouse to enjoy and receive income from estate assets without ever actually owning them. Upon that spouse's death, the assets are distributed to the final beneficiaries, at which time estate taxes are due and payable. A way to leave property to a beneficiary (or beneficiaries) other than a spouse and postpone estate taxes at the same time.

See also: Estate tax, Marital deduction

Ben set up a **QTIP** trust *with his sister, ensuring his wife would also be provided for during her life, and then his family assets would end up back in his family.*

Replacement cost
The amount someone would need to pay to replace a lost asset; the current market price of an asset.

See also: Asset, Insurance

The **replacement cost** *on the truck was more than the cost of keeping it running so the business owners lived with the occasional breakdowns.*

Reserve fund
An account used to save up a minimum amount of money to be used in case of emergency or to fulfill specific future financial needs. For individuals (rather than businesses), this is sometimes called an "emergency fund."

See also: Sinker

The museum kept a **reserve fund** *to pay for the donors' party it hosted every winter.*

Residual income

The monthly income a person has left after paying all of his monthly expenses. A key factor looked at by reputable mortgage lenders to make sure a prospective borrower can afford to make mortgage payments.

See also: Disposable income, Income

After Martin made the last payment on his car loan, his **residual income** *went up by $355 per month.*

Returns

Income earned on an investment while it is held, including interest and dividends.

See also: Dividend, Interest, Total return, Yield

Ralph chose to invest in companies that offered small but steady **returns** *instead of investing in riskier but potentially more profitable stocks.*

Reuters

A company that provides trusted financial news, analysis, and information, 24 hours a day around the world. Pronounced "roy-ters."

See also: Morningstar

Day traders rely on **Reuters** *for the up-to-the-minute scoop on the markets.*

Rider

An attachment to an insurance policy that alters a key provision contained within the original policy.

See also: Insurance

When the couple bought several antique pieces of furniture, the insurance company added a **rider** *to the original policy in order to cover the purchases.*

Risk

The possibility that your investment will not return the yield you expect, including the possibility of total loss.

See also: Returns, Yield

Younger investors can handle greater portfolio **risk** *as they have more time to recover from downturns.*

Risk averse

An investor who does not like risk (especially risk of loss), and therefore will always choose the lower-risk investment given similar expected returns. Often ignores the fact that lower returns, as typically come with lower-risk investments, may not outpace inflation.

See also: Inflation-adjusted return

It took Mac months before he broke through Pauline's **risk-averse** *nature and convinced her to make investments that would have real earnings.*

Risk capital
Money that an investor can afford to lose, and therefore uses to make high-risk investments. Sometimes called "gambling capital."
>See also: Capital loss, Downside risk
>
>*Sarah used her* **risk capital** *to buy stock options.*

Risk lover
An investor willing to take on risk even for relatively low returns.
>See also: Bankruptcy, Default risk, Downside risk
>
>*Jeff had a reputation as a* **risk lover**, *so his friends and family never listened to his "hot tips."*

Risk neutral
An investor who focuses solely on returns when making investment choices, without regard to risk.
>See also: Risk averse, Risk lover
>
>*Although being* **risk neutral** *had indeed lost Jackie money in the past, it had earned her more than it had cost her.*

Risk tolerance
The amount of uncertainty an investor can handle regarding the possible loss of value of his investments; the amount of money an investor is willing to lose.
>See also: Asset allocation, Reward, Risk
>
>*As Rex got older, his* **risk tolerance** *decreased because he had less time to recoup losses prior to retirement.*

Risk-adjusted return
A measurement of the earnings on an investment after the risk level has been accounted for. Helps investors compare investments of different risk levels on an even playing field. Adjustment factors include things such as beta and standard deviation.
>See also: Beta, Standard deviation
>
>*When deciding which corporate bonds to buy, Elisa looked at the* **risk-adjusted return** *for each.*

Risk-return tradeoff
The idea that, in investing, taking bigger risks provides the opportunity to earn higher returns.
>See also: Returns, Risk
>
>*Callie checked into the* **risk-return tradeoff** *before making any investments.*

Rule of 72
A simple, rough method of figuring out how long it will take an investment to double in value. Calculated by dividing the annual rate of return for an investment into 72, where the result gives an approximation in years of the time it would take to double the investment.
> See also: Time value of money
>
> *According to the* **rule of 72***, Che's investments would double in approximately eight years.*

Second-to-die insurance
A form of life insurance that covers the lives of two people (usually husband and wife), and pays out to the named beneficiaries when both named parties have died.
> See also: Life insurance
>
> *Susan received $500,000 after the death of her stepmother, under the dictates of the* **second-to-die insurance** *her father had purchased.*

Seed capital
Money used to start a new business, often obtained from family and friends, or from angel investors.
> See also: Angel investor
>
> *Clay was thrilled when his parents presented him with the* **seed capital** *to open his own salon.*

Sharpe ratio
A calculation created by renowned economist William F. Sharpe to measure portfolio performance adjusted for risk. Helps investors compare the risk levels of different investments with similar returns, so they can choose the lower risk investment without sacrificing returns.
> See also: Returns, Risk tolerance
>
> *Nathan used the* **Sharpe ratio** *to help explain his recommendations to his clients.*

Skimming
An identity theft strategy, where the thief steals his victim's credit card information (but gives back the card itself) electronically to obtain the details contained in the magnetic strip. Done with small handheld machines that are similar to the ones retailers use to swipe credit cards.
> See also: Identity theft
>
> *Clarice suspected* **skimming** *when her credit card bill showed up with charges from hotels and restaurants in San Diego, when she hadn't left Washington.*

Strategic asset allocation
An investment strategy where portfolio holdings are rebalanced as their market values rise and fall in order to maintain preset proportions. For example, if the proportion of a portfolio is set at 50% stocks and 50% bonds, when stock prices drop while bond prices rise, bonds will be sold off and stocks purchased to get back to the 50-50 allocation.

See also: Asset allocation

Santos insisted on **strategic asset allocation** *within the investments he set up for his son in order to maintain a certain level of stability.*

Tactical asset allocation (TAA)
An investment strategy where a portfolio is actively managed and rebalanced to take immediate advantage of strong market sectors and special profitable situations; then returned to a prescribed asset mix after short-term goals are attained.

See also: Asset allocation, Sector

Thanks to **tactical asset allocation***, Manuel was able to take advantage of surges in a wide variety of markets he wouldn't usually be invested in.*

Tax attorney
A lawyer who specializes in the complexities of IRS code, and uses the code to create wealth-preserving plans for clients. Most of these professionals hold two degrees, a J.D. (juris doctor, for law) and an LL.M. (a master of law, with a focus in taxation).

See also: CPA, Tax preparer

Since Clint couldn't decide between a career in law and a career in finance, he chose to become a **tax attorney** *in order to combine his loves.*

Term life insurance
A purchased policy that pays out death benefits only if the named individual dies during the time period specified by contract.

See also: Whole life insurance

Kara got **term life insurance** *coverage as part of her benefits package when she started her new job.*

Testamentary trust
A legal arrangement, created in a will, that calls for assets to be held by one party for the benefit of another.

See also: Living trust, Trust

McConnell Incorporated was in charge of the **testamentary trust** *set up in the woman's will to care for her niece.*

Total return
The income earned on investment while it's held (including interest and dividends) plus the capital gain (or loss) earned upon the sale of the investment.
> See also: Capital gains, Capital loss, Dividend, Interest

Susan was shocked at the **total return** *she earned after only two years when she sold her corporate bonds.*

Trailing commission
A fee paid to a financial advisor every year that an investor holds a particular investment, rather than only at the time of purchase. Seems like a bad idea, but it can help keep the advisor from making excessive trades. Conversely, it also pays the advisor repeatedly for a single piece of advice.
> See also: Commission

Deanna refused to work with any advisor who charged **trailing commissions.**

Transfer on death (TOD)
An investment account designation that allows beneficiaries to receive assets automatically upon the death of the original account holder. Allows assets to change hands without first going through probate.
> See also: Beneficiary, Payable on death, Probate

The old man was concerned some of his children would contest his will so he designated his largest investment accounts as **TOD** *in order to ensure they went directly to his long-time companion.*

Trust
A legal arrangement where one person or other entity, such as a financial institution, has control over property donated by another person for the benefit of a third person.
> See also: QDOT trust, QTIP trust

The day she was born, Helen's grandfather set up a **trust** *to pay for her education so she would have the money when she needed it.*

Trustee
The person or institution that manages the assets of a trust, strictly according to the terms of the trust.
> See also: Fiduciary

The day after his eighteenth birthday, the young man met with his **trustee** *to arrange to take control of the money.*

UGMA (Uniform Gifts to Minors Act)

A state law that lets minors have bank accounts and own securities, as long as an adult is the custodian of the account. The account is set up when an adult makes a gift (of cash or securities) to a child in the child's own name. The account management reverts to the child as soon as he hits the age of majority, as decided by state law (anywhere from eighteen to twenty-five depending on the state). Similar to a trust, but much easier to set up.

See also: Fiduciary, Kiddie tax, UTMA

Marc gave each of his children $100 and some oil stock in order to set them up with accounts under **UGMA**.

Umbrella insurance

A guaranteed liability reimbursement policy meant to supplement the standard group of protection policies, which cover home, health, and automobile. Guarantees protection against losses over and above the norm in exchange for regular premium payments.

See also: Insurance, Premium (insurance)

Many people choose to carry **umbrella insurance** *to help cover costs above and beyond those paid for by their primary insurance policy.*

UTMA (Uniform Transfers to Minors Act)

An add-on to the UGMA that allows minors to own additional types of assets, such as real estate, through the custodial account.

See also: UGMA

To avoid the look of impropriety, Chris asked her attorney to be the custodian of her nephew's account when she used **UTMA** *to put the condo in his name.*

Value Line Investment Survey

An independent newsletter, produced by a highly trusted financial source, that offers detailed information about approximately 1,700 stocks, ranking each based on its probable upcoming performance.

See also: Due diligence

Many brokers will cross-reference any materials sent by a corporation to the **Value Line Investment Survey** *to ensure they get a true and accurate picture of the health of the company.*

Variable annuity

A contract between an individual and an insurance company, where the individual makes current premium payments in exchange for future regular payouts from the company. The premium payments are invested according to the individual's wishes, within the scope of the company's investment options, and the account value varies based on total returns. Advantages of the contract include tax-sheltered investing and death benefits, in addition to the payment stream.

See also: Premium (insurance), Whole life insurance

As a part-time employee, Kim wasn't eligible for her company's retirement plan so she signed up for a **variable annuity** *with her insurance company.*

Viatical settlement

An investment where one party purchases the life insurance policy of a terminal patient in exchange for a portion of the policy's cash value.

See also: Whole life insurance

To help relieve her grandmother's financial burden, Kimberly entered into a **viatical settlement** *with her during the last year of the woman's life.*

Wall Street Journal

The most prominent daily financial newspaper in the United States. Includes daily detailed listings of stock market quotations to help investors keep track of their investments.

See also: Morningstar, Reuters

The broker started every morning with a cup of coffee, a bran muffin, and the **Wall Street Journal.**

Whole life insurance

A contract that combines the death benefits of a term policy with an investment component. A portion of the premium paid by the policy holder goes toward the death benefits guarantee, and the rest goes into an investment reserve; as the policy holder ages, more of the premium is used for benefits, and less for reserve. Often used in retirement and estate planning.

See also: Premium (insurance), Term life insurance

Joe believed **whole life insurance** *to be a useful tool for both retirement money and protecting his family from financial difficulties after his death.*

FUND INVESTING

12B-1 fees
An annual distribution expense charged by mutual funds to their investors to cover promotional costs.
See also: Load, Mutual fund, No-load
Investors need to be aware of the fact that many mutual funds charge **12B-1 fees** *as part of their total expenses, which further diminish investor profits.*

Active risk
The chance that an actively managed mutual fund will not perform as well as a passively managed fund (such as an index fund).
See also: Index fund
Some investors prefer the hands-on approach and are willing to accept the **active risk** *inherent in an actively managed mutual fund.*

Adjustable-rate mortgage fund
An investment pool that holds mortgages with variable interest rates. Offers investors increasing returns during periods of rising interest rates.
See also: Adjustable-rate mortgage, Mutual fund
Although people purchasing property aren't thrilled with rising interest rates, investors in **adjustable-rate mortgage funds** *look forward to them.*

Aggressive growth
An investment whose primary purpose is to produce substantial capital gains. Usually used in reference to mutual funds.
See also: Capital gains, Mutual fund
Katja was looking to pay for her next overseas vacation so she talked to her broker about **aggressive growth** *options.*

Aggressive growth fund
An investment pool that holds stocks in companies expected to bring in substantial capital gains. Looks for maximum gain potential without regard to risk level.
See also: Capital gains, Mutual fund
Since Erin had plenty of time to make money for her retirement, she chose an **aggressive growth fund** *with the hopes of spectacular gains.*

All-cap fund
An investment pool that holds stocks of companies of different sizes.

See also: Market capitalization

It was important to George to support new, smaller companies as well as large conglomerates, so he invested heavily in an **all-cap fund.**

Average cost basis
The simplest way to track the purchase price of mutual fund shares, necessary to calculate gains or losses when shares of the fund are sold. Calculated by taking the original price paid for the shares plus any fees paid, adding in all reinvested taxable distributions (such as gains or dividends), and dividing that sum by the total number of shares held. That "new" per share price is then multiplied by the number of shares currently being sold to determine their worth for tax purposes. Often provided by the mutual fund company on annual statements, as a service to shareholders.

See also: Capital gains, Mutual fund

Al kept track of the **average cost basis** *of his clients' stocks in order to give them sound tax advice at the end of the year.*

Back-end load
A brokerage commission paid when an investors sells shares in a mutual fund.

See also: Mutual fund, No-load, Redemption charges

Rita's **back-end load** *kept her returns from being quite as large as they might have been but she still ended up with overall gains.*

Balanced fund
An investment pool that contains both income and growth investment to manage portfolio risk. Investments would normally include common and preferred stock, and bonds of varying maturities.

See also: Mutual fund

Samantha invested in a **balanced fund** *so she wouldn't have to worry about asset allocation.*

Blend fund
An investment pool consisting of different types of securities, such as stocks and bonds. Sometimes called a "hybrid fund."

See also: Bond fund, Mutual fund, Stock fund

New investors often use a **blend fund** *to establish how much risk they can handle.*

Bond fund

An investment pool which holds only long-term debt securities, usually all of the same quality (as evidenced by their ratings).

See also: Bond rating, Moody's ratings

Since he was looking for a steady income stream rather than capital gains, Phillipe invested in a **bond fund** *with a high rating.*

Breakpoint sale

The sale of a specific dollar value of mutual fund shares necessary for an investor to get fee breaks on her account. Can be reached with a slightly lesser purchase and a letter of intent from the investor to purchase the balance within a specified time frame. For example, if the breakpoint is $50,000 and you go to buy $47,000 worth, they have to tell you you're almost at the breakpoint sale level, and let you do a letter of intent.

See also: Load fund, Mutual fund

When her broker realized the amount of her request, he offered her a **breakpoint sale.**

Broke the buck

When the net asset value (NAV) of a money market fund sinks below $1. Occurs rarely, as the funds strive to maintain the $1 NAV.

See also: Money market fund, Net asset value

The fund managers scrambled to rebalance the investments after the money market fund **broke the buck** *due to problems in the mortgage market.*

B-share

A class of mutual fund ownership units that have different fee schedules and come with different investor services than the standard class (usually called "A-shares" or "Class A"), even though all classes of a single fund are invested in the same securities pool. Due to the different fee schedule, total net investment returns may not be the same as they are for other classes. Also called "Class B shares."

See also: 12B-1 fees, Fee schedule, Fund management fees, Mutual fund

Tim's portfolio included a mix of A-shares and **B-shares** *because he wanted to own some funds for which the A-shares were sold out.*

Capital appreciation fund
An investment pool that holds growth stocks, focusing on companies expected to garner substantial capital gains regardless of potential loss risk. Sometimes called an "aggressive growth fund."

See also: Capital gains, Mutual fund

Denny had time to recoup any losses so he invested in a **capital appreciation fund** *in the hopes that it would create large earnings.*

Capital gains distribution
Payment of profits earned by an investment pool (usually a mutual fund) to its shareholders on a proportional basis. Investors may receive cash payments or directly reinvest these earnings in additional shares. Either way, though, the amount allocated to the investor is taxable.

See also: Capital gains, Mutual fund

She chose to reinvest her quarterly **capital gains distribution** *since she was living well within her budget.*

Closed-end mutual fund
An investment pool whose shares are issued once in an initial public offering, then traded publicly in a manner similar to stocks. The pool offers investors shares in a specific, actively managed securities portfolio.

See also: IPO, Mutual fund

The **closed-end mutual fund** *had a strong enough history that Meghan decided to buy into it once she was able.*

Core plus
A twist on a fixed-income investment style, where a fund manager may add more risky securities to a portfolio primarily consisting of investment-grade debt securities in order to boost returns.

See also: Fixed-income assets, Investment grade, Investing style

Marshall was mainly conservative, but willing to take on a little calculated risk, so he invested in a **core plus** *fund.*

Corporate bond fund
An investment pool that holds only debt securities issued by publicly held companies.

See also: Bond rating, Corporate bonds, Mutual fund

Steve's portfolio held only stocks, so his financial advisor suggested he add in shares in a **corporate bond fund** *for balance.*

Country fund
An investment pool that invests solely in the securities of a single nation.

See also: Global fund, International fund

Gina felt strongly enough that the small nation was about to burst onto the international scene that she had her broker invest in a **country fund**.

Crossover fund
An investment pool that holds both private and publicly traded securities.

See also: Private placement

The **crossover fund** *gave Toby access to investments he could never participate in on his own.*

Cubes (QQQQs)
An exchange-traded fund that copies the NASDAQ 100 Index (holds the same securities that are included in that index). Trades under the ticker symbol QQQQ on the NASDAQ.

See also: Exchange-traded funds, NASDAQ, NASDAQ 100 Index

Shelly couldn't afford to buy all the stocks she wanted, so she put her money into **Cubes**.

Debt fund
An investment pool that holds only fixed-income securities such as bonds and notes. Typically come with lower portfolio turnover and, therefore, lower fees.

See also: Debt instruments, Fixed-income assets, Turnover rate

Clarice used her **debt fund** *investments as her safety net while she took greater risks by investing in aggressive growth stock funds as well.*

Declaration date
The day on which the directors of a public corporation or a mutual fund announce the details of an upcoming dividend distribution. Lets the shareholders know that they can expect a dividend, and how much they'll receive for each share they hold.

See also: Dividend, Ex-dividend date, Record date

On the **declaration date**, *Wayne found out he'd be getting a fat dividend check for his Lion Joe shares.*

Diamonds (Diamonds Trust Series 1)
A unit investment trust based on the Dow Jones Industrial Average index, where shareholders actually own fractional shares of the thirty stocks included in the index. Trades under the ticker symbol DIA. Mistakenly referred to as an exchange-traded fund quite frequently in the media.

See also: Dow Jones Industrial Average, Exchange-traded funds, Unit investment trust

After much consideration, Joan decided to buy **Diamonds** *because she wanted to participate directly in the DJIA's growth.*

Dollar cost averaging
A low-risk investment strategy that employs periodic small purchases of specific securities (usually mutual funds) rather than a single large purchase. Allows investors to automatically take advantage of price dips. These fixed-dollar purchases are made on a regular schedule, regardless of market price.

See also: Mutual fund, Trade

Rita found it easier to use **dollar cost averaging** *to invest in mutual funds so she never had to put down a big chunk of money all at once but would still end up with a sizable investment by the end of the year.*

Emerging growth fund
An investment pool that attempts to meet its primary goal of higher-than-average capital appreciation by investing in small, promising companies with the potential to become corporate giants.

See also: Income fund, Mutual fund, Small-cap stock

Justin invested in **emerging growth funds,** *hoping to catch the next Microsoft while it was still in its infancy.*

Enhanced index fund
A managed investment pool that basically mimics a prominent index (such as the S&P 500 or the Russell 2500 Index) but can tweak some of the positions to grab higher returns.

See also: Index fund

The **enhanced index fund** *was the most productive part of Helen's portfolio.*

Exchange privilege
A special benefit offered by some fund families that allows investors to move their money from one fund to another without paying sales fees. This transaction counts as a sale and purchase for tax purposes.

See also: Fund family

When looking for a new fund, Jack was hoping to find one that shared **exchange privileges** *with one he was already invested in.*

Exchange-traded funds (ETFs)
Investment pools whose shares are bought and sold like stocks. Different from mutual funds because of the way they are bought and sold, their lack of active management, and their transparency (ETFs disclose all of their holdings, while mutual funds do not).
See also: Exchange, Mutual fund, Trade

Poppy invested in **ETFs** *instead of mutual funds because they don't require a big initial investment, and she only had $200 to spare.*

Exit fee
A charge incurred when an investor sells an investment, usually mutual fund shares. Intended to discourage redemptions. Also called a "redemption fee."
See also: Commission, Mutual fund

Morgan was shocked at the **exit fee** *his broker quoted him prior to the sale.*

Expense limit
A formal cap on the amount of fees that can be charged by a specific mutual fund.
See also: Total expense ratio

Charles only bought mutual funds with an express **expense limit** *because he knew exactly how much of the earnings would be eaten by expenses.*

Fair weather fund
An investment pool that performs well when the overall market is doing well.
See also: Bull market, Mutual fund

She wanted a more diverse portfolio than just a **fair weather fund.**

Family of funds
All of the mutual funds administered by a single company. Also called a "fund family."
See also: Mutual fund

The benefits of investing in a single **family of funds** *outweighed the management risks because she wanted to be able to track her investments and needed exchange privileges.*

Fee schedule
A list of charges an investor or depositor may incur on his account.
See also: Load fund

All investors should carefully examine the **fee schedule** *before they purchase shares in a mutual fund.*

Foul weather fund

An investment pool that performs well when the overall market is doing poorly.

See also: Bear market, Mutual fund

Suzanna didn't worry when the market started to drop because she had a **foul weather fund** *as part of her portfolio.*

Front-end load

A sales fee charged when a security (usually a mutual fund) is purchased. The fee is deducted from the invested amount, which results in fewer shares being purchased with that initial investment. Frequently waived for retirement plan investments.

See also: Mutual fund, No-load fund

When considering a budget for purchasing mutual fund shares, it is important to remember the **front-end load** *to ensure you know how many shares can actually be bought.*

Fund family

A group of mutual funds managed by the same company. Also called "family of funds."

See also: Mutual fund

Sticking with a single **fund family** *offers investors a lot of benefits, such as exchange privileges and easier investment tracking, but it also increases some risk (such as management risk).*

Fund management fees

Charges paid to investment pool advisors in exchange for their portfolio selection and management services. Can decrease the total return for shares in the pool.

See also: Fund manager, Mutual fund

The firm charged surprisingly low **fund management fees** *considering the quality of its holdings.*

Fund manager

The financial professional responsible for determining the investment strategy for an investment pool, as well as selecting and managing the investment portfolio for it. A critical factor to consider when choosing an investment.

See also: Mutual fund

The **fund manager's** *track record was so profitable that investors were willing to pay higher than average fees to benefit from his judgment.*

Fund of funds
An investment pool that invests in other investment pools.
> See also: Mutual fund
>
> *Alec couldn't choose among mutual funds so opted to invest in a* **fund of funds.**

Fund overlap
A phenomenon that occurs when a single investor owns multiple investment pools, some of which hold the same securities. This increases portfolio risk and reduces diversification. Many investors are unaware that their portfolios have this problem, which can be corrected by taking a closer look at their holdings.
> See also: Diversification, Due diligence, Exchange-traded funds, Mutual fund
>
> *Chuck's new accountant pointed out several places of* **fund overlap** *his previous financial advisor had never mentioned.*

Global fund
An investment pool that holds foreign and U.S. securities. Also called a "world fund."
> See also: International fund, Mutual fund
>
> *To boost his portfolio's diversification and offset some inflation risk, Ethan bought shares in a* **global fund.**

Gold fund
An investment pool that holds only securities associated with the mining or production of the precious metal.
> See also: Exchange-traded funds, Mutual fund
>
> *Ruben was pleased to learn that his* **gold fund** *was steadily increasing in value while many of his other funds were going down.*

Green fund
An investment pool that holds only securities of companies that have made a commitment to improving, maintaining, or supporting the environment.
> See also: Green investing, Mutual fund
>
> *As more people have come to understand the human impact on the environment,* **green funds** *have been easier to find.*

Growth and income fund
An investment pool that strives to maximize investor returns by holding shares in companies that both pay out dividends and have strong growth potential.
> See also: Dividend, Mutual fund
>
> *Ethan advised his mid-life clients to invest in* **growth and income funds.**

Growth fund
An investment pool that holds a diversified selection of stocks chosen with the aim of returning extensive capital appreciation (i.e., increase in market value).

See also: Growth stock, Value fund

When there's plenty of time on the investment horizon, a **growth fund** *is a must for the portfolio.*

Hidden load
A mutual fund fee that an investor may not realize he's paying.

See also: 12B-1 fees, Load fund, Mutual fund, No-load fund

It is always wise to read all the paperwork that comes with investing in a new mutual fund to avoid a **hidden load.**

HOLDR (Holding Company Depository Receipt)
A single security that holds a basket of securities from a single sector, allowing an investor to diversify within a sector. A HOLDR holder actually owns shares in the underlying securities. Developed by Merrill Lynch, and traded on the AMEX.

See also: American Stock Exchange, Exchange-traded funds, Sector

Natalie chose to invest in **HOLDRs** *so that she could invest widely, yet easily, in the aerospace industry.*

Hybrid fund
An investment pool that holds a variety of securities classes, including stocks and bonds. Security category proportions can remain fixed or vary over time.

See also: Bond fund, Mutual fund, Stock fund

A **hybrid fund** *can be a good starting point for new investors looking to learn how much risk they can stand and what exactly their financial goals are.*

Income fund
An investment pool that focuses on steady earnings (from income and dividends, for example) rather than on capital growth.

See also: Growth fund, Mutual fund

As an addition to his annual budget, Luis invested part of his savings in an **income fund.**

Index fund
An investment pool whose holdings mirror those of a benchmark group of securities. These pools see little investment turnover, which enables them to keep both expenses and taxable events to a minimum.

See also: Index, Mutual fund, No-load fund

A lot of investors prefer **index funds** *because they usually charge very low fees.*

Index hugger
An actively managed mutual fund that closely mimics a related major financial benchmark.
> See also: Index, Index fund, Mutual fund

Cole bypassed the **index hugger** *and chose the straight-out index fund instead.*

Intelligent ETF (Exchange-traded fund)
An actively managed investment pool that loosely follows a named index, but may alter the proportion of the securities included in that index. Also called a "smart ETF."
> See also: Exchange-traded funds, Index

One of Sam's investment goals was to beat the S&P 500, so he opted for an **intelligent ETF**.

International fund
An investment pool that holds only securities not issued in the United States.
> See also: Global fund, Mutual fund

As the U.S. dollar began to weaken, interest in **international funds** *became more widespread.*

Inverse ETF
An exchange-traded fund (ETF) that looks to perform opposite to its underlying index by taking short positions and holding derivatives on the securities that make up the index.
> See also: Derivatives, Index, Short position

Eric expected the S&P 500 Index to drop in value, so he bought the **inverse ETF** *to cash in on the decline.*

Investing style
Also known as "investment style," it is a securities selection philosophy that highlights specific securities' characteristics. Usually used in reference to institutional investors, such as mutual funds.
> See also: Institutional investors, Securities

Since Jenna only wanted to invest in corporations that used fair trade practices, she found a fund that had a similar **investing style**.

iShares
Units of exchange-traded funds (ETFs) issued by Barclays Global Investors, reported to be the largest family of ETFs in the world.
> See also: Exchange-traded funds

Daniel invested in **iShares** *because he liked knowing exactly what securities his fund was holding.*

Large-cap fund
An investment pool that holds only shares in sizable corporations whose total market value exceeds $5 billion.

See also: Large-cap stock, Mutual fund

Margo didn't have enough money to buy individual blue-chip stocks, so she bought **large-cap fund** *shares instead.*

Life-cycle fund
A mutual fund designed to rebalance its asset allocation over time, based on a targeted shareholder age range. For example, in a fund aimed at forty-year-olds, the initial investment pool might hold 60% stocks and 40% fixed-income securities. Periodically, the portfolio is adjusted to reflect the advancing age of the shareholders, so when those forty-year-olds turn fifty, the portfolio would decrease the stock holdings and increase the fixed-income holdings. Saves the investor the trouble of periodically re-examining and rebalancing his portfolio on his own.

See also: Asset allocation, Mutual fund

Dina bought a **life-cycle fund** *so she could stop worrying about her asset allocation.*

Lifestyle fund
An investment pool that bases security selection on a combination of shareholders' age range, and risk level (such as aggressive investors in their fifties or conservative investors in their forties). Designed to be a primary holding for an investor, as it employs asset allocation strategies that will be rendered irrelevant if the investor buys other securities as well.

See also: Life-cycle fund, Risk tolerance

Rissa bought a **lifestyle fund** *instead of a life-cycle fund because she has a an aggressive investing style and a higher risk tolerance than most people her age.*

Load
Transaction fee. Usually used in reference to mutual funds.

See also: Fee schedule, No-load

The **load** *on Spencer's mutual fund was reasonable enough that he still managed very high earnings.*

Load fund

An investment pool whose shareholders are charged commissions or sales fees.

> See also: Mutual fund, No-load fund

The most popular **load funds** *tend to be those with the highest historical returns.*

Long/short fund

A mutual fund that uses some of the same high-risk strategies as hedge funds, such as trading derivatives and short selling securities. Typically require higher minimum investments ($1,000 and up) than standard mutual funds.

> See also: Derivatives, Hedge fund, Short selling

After Melinda inherited $3 million she put a little money into a **long/short fund** *for a gamble.*

Management risk

The chance that the advisors at the helm of a mutual fund make poor investment choices on behalf of the fund.

> See also: Mutual fund, Risk

Major mutual funds hire well-known, well-established professionals in order to mitigate **management risk***.*

Momentum fund

An investment pool that chooses securities based on prevailing growth trends (such as earnings or price increases).

> See also: Mutual fund, Uptrend

Even though she wasn't overly interested in the latest gadgets, Judy's **momentum fund** *made her a lot of money during the technology boom.*

Money market fund

An investment pool that holds highly liquid short-term debt securities (which are also called "cash equivalents") with maturities of thirteen months or less, and an overall average maturity of ninety days. Net asset value aims to stay steady at $1 per share. Profitability comes from interest rate changes rather than changes in net asset value.

> See also: Mutual fund, Money market account, Net asset value

Eric and Laura moved some money from a bond fund into a **money market fund** *because they were concerned about interest rates and risk.*

Municipal bond fund
A typically tax-advantaged investment pool that holds only debt instruments issued by local and state governments.

See also: Bond fund, Municipal bond, Mutual fund

She invested in **municipal bond funds** *as a way to take advantage of the tax breaks and, at the same time, invest in communities throughout the country.*

Mutual fund
A professionally managed investment pool structured to meet specific investing goals. Shares must be bought and sold directly from the issuing fund, as opposed to being traded on an exchange.

See also: Fund manager, Investing style

Most people's portfolios include several **mutual funds.**

Net asset value (NAV)
The per-share price for a mutual fund or exchange-traded fund. Calculated by adding the current value of all fund holdings, then subtracting any fund liabilities, and dividing that difference by the number of shares outstanding.

See also: Exchange-traded funds, Mutual fund

Financial advisors keep an eye on the **NAV** *of funds to ensure their clients are still making money.*

No-load
Free of transaction fees.

See also: Commission

Index funds are almost always **no-load** *because they don't require active management.*

No-load fund
A mutual fund that does not charge transaction fees to shareholders.

See also: Load fund, Mutual fund

In order to avoid extra fees, Tera invested in **no-load funds.**

Open-end mutual fund
An investment pool with no fixed limit on the number of shares it may issue. Shares are sold and redeemed directly with shareholders, instead of on the open market. Shares can only be bought from the fund (either by the investor directly or through a broker) and can only be sold back (redeemed) to the fund. They are not traded on an exchange like stocks or closed-end fund shares.

See also: Closed-end mutual fund, Mutual fund

Individuals looking to buy large numbers of stock may be drawn to **open-ended mutual funds.**

Pooled funds
Money from a lot of different investors, all combined to invest in common securities. This strategy helps small investors buy securities in bulk, and to limit fees, which can result in higher net returns than they would have earned individually.
See also: Mutual fund, Unit investment trust

The members of the union used **pooled funds** *in order to invest above and beyond their retirement plans.*

Portfolio manager
The person or group in charge of investment decisions for a mutual fund's or exchange-traded fund's portfolio. Determines portfolio strategy and makes all day-to-day choices, such as buy and sell decisions.
See also: Mutual fund, Portfolio

The fund was stable enough that there was no noticeable fluctuation between the retirement of the old **portfolio manager** *and the hiring of the new one.*

Quant fund
An investment pool that chooses its holdings based strictly on computer quantitative analysis. Counts on the computer to "beat" the market.
See also: Mutual fund, Quantitative analysis

The senior partner and the junior associate often debated if it was better to choose investments through instinct and research or by entrusting them to a **quant fund.**

Redemption charges
A fee charged by a mutual fund company when an investor sells back his shares.
See also: Back-end load, Mutual fund

Robin was willing to pay the **redemption charges** *when he cashed out his shares in order to pay for his daughter's wedding.*

Regional fund
An investment pool that only holds securities issued by companies and government entities in a specified geographic area.
See also: Global fund, Mutual fund

Her love of Rio de Janeiro caused her to invest heavily in a South American–based **regional fund.**

Sector fund
An investment pool that holds only securities from a single market niche, such as precious metals or real estate.

See also: Mutual fund

As limited in scope as **sector funds** *are, they can be a valid and valuable part of a well-rounded portfolio.*

Short-term investment fund (STIF)
An investment pool that holds high-quality, low-risk securities that mature within a year. Holdings typically include bank notes, cash, and short-term Treasury instruments.

See also: Government securities, Mutual fund

Since Carol needed to stay relatively liquid with her money but still wanted to invest, she was grateful to learn about a **short-term investment fund.**

Socially responsible fund
An investment pool that selects securities based on moral, ethical, and environmental criteria, while still attempting to maximize investor returns.

See also: Green investing, Mutual fund

As an environmentalist, it was important to Steve that his broker only invest him in **socially responsible funds** *that followed his beliefs.*

SPDR (Standard & Poor's Depository Receipt)
An exchange-traded fund designed to correspond with the S&P 500 Index. Pronounced "spider." Listed on the AMEX under the symbol SPY.

See also: American Stock Exchange, Exchange-traded funds, S&P 500 Index

Ethan invested in **SPDR***s because he wanted to capture big returns (and because he liked the name).*

Stock fund
An investment pool that holds only publicly traded corporate equity shares.

See also: Mutual fund, Stock

When most people think about investing, they think about buying into **stock funds***, even if they don't know what they're called.*

Style drift
A deviation from the stated investment objective for a mutual fund, usually caused by a deliberate change in investment approach or a change in fund management.

See also: Fund manager, Investing style, Mutual fund

The managers of the mid-cap fund started to **style drift** *as large-cap stocks became more profitable.*

Target-date fund
An investment pool that reallocates assets over a specific time horizon based on an expected future date, such as retirement. Similar to a life-cycle fund (which is based on shareholder's current age, rather than an upcoming event).

See also: Life-cycle fund

Chen opened a **target-date fund** *when he was twenty years away from retirement.*

Targeted distribution fund
An investment pool with a primary aim of paying out earnings to shareholders. Often used by retirees to supplement pension and social security income.

See also: Earnings, Mutual fund

After trying to live on her pension, Marta invested in a **targeted distribution fund** *in order to have some extra play money.*

Tax efficient fund
An investment pool that seeks to keep tax burdens to a bare minimum while still bringing in returns. Uses a combination of tax-advantaged investments (such as municipal bonds), low turnover rates (to keep taxable capital gains to a minimum), and minimal or no income-producing investments (such as stocks that pay regular dividends).

See also: Capital gains, Dividend, Municipal bond

Kay paid enough taxes that she was more than willing to invest in a **tax efficient fund** *in order to help alleviate any further tax burden.*

Total expense ratio
A calculation that divides all of the expenses of a mutual fund by its total assets, reported as a percentage. Helps investors gauge mutual funds by comparing expected return percentages to this calculated percentage. For example, a fund with 5% returns and a total expense ratio of 2.5% won't be as lucrative for a shareholder as a fund with 5% returns and a ratio of 1.25%. (5 − 2.5 < 5 − 1.25).

See also: 12B-1 fee, Management fee, Mutual fund

Boris liked to preserve his earnings, so he always looked for funds with low **total expense ratios.**

Tracker fund
An investment pool in which the securities held correspond to those of a benchmark pool of securities. Commonly called an "index fund."
See also: Index, Mutual fund, No-load fund

Mekho appreciated the lower fees charged by her **tracker fund**.

Trailer fee
A commission paid to a mutual fund salesperson by the mutual fund while an investor who bought through the salesperson (who may be his investment advisor) holds on to that fund. Investors should ask whether their salesperson receives this fee, as it can color investment advice.
See also: Commission

Phil refused to take **trailer fees** *because he didn't want to feel obligated to the fund managers, but chose instead to be an objective advisor for his clients.*

Turnover rate
A measure of trading activity for a portfolio over a specific time period, typically one year. For a mutual fund, this is calculated by taking the lesser of total securities sold or total securities bought and dividing that by the fund's NAV. High turnover rates cause more transaction fees and more taxable transactions, which can eat away at the portfolio. Also called "portfolio turnover."
See also: Mutual fund, Net asset value

The young woman was shocked at the number of transaction fees her broker was charging her until she realized how high her portfolio's **turnover rate** *was.*

Ultra ETF
A special type of exchange-traded fund (ETF) that uses leverage to increase the returns on an investment pool that mimics a specific market index. The goal is to earn returns double that of the performance of the index.
See also: Exchange-traded funds, Index, Leverage

Freddie was pleased when the index did so well because he knew his **ultra ETF** *was doing even better.*

Ultra-short bond fund
An investment pool that holds only debt securities that mature within one year.
See also: Bond, Maturity, Mutual fund

Since Eve wanted to make as much money as she could but had very little time to do so, she invested in several **ultra-short bond funds**.

Unit investment trust (UIT)
A company that holds an unmanaged, set pool of income-producing securities. People can purchase shares in that company, and then receive periodic income payouts from the company for a set time period. The investments in the pool never change (unless something such as a bankruptcy or merger takes place for one of the securities).

See also: Mutual fund

The couple invested in a **UIT** *rather than a managed mutual fund because they didn't want their returns eaten up by transaction fees.*

Value Added Monthly Index (VAMI)
A measure of the progress of a hypothetical $1,000 investment, calculated every month based on the previous month's result plus the current month's returns. Often used to analyze mutual fund performance.

See also: Rate of return

The **VAMI** *indicated Ricardo would be better served putting more money into the fund he already had rather than investing in the second one he was considering.*

Value fund
An investment pool that buys securities that are underpriced compared to their innate worth.

See also: Value stock

Investing in a **value fund** *gave Jonah a chance to invest in companies he couldn't usually have afforded.*

Vanguard Exchange-Traded Funds
Offered by Vanguard, it is a group of more than thirty-five index-based investment pools for which shares trade like stocks on the AMEX. Formerly known as "VIPERS."

See also: American Stock Exchange, Exchange-traded funds, Index

Some investors appreciate the combination of easy trading and broad coverage offered by investing in **Vanguard Exchange-Traded Funds.**

Vice fund
An investment pool that holds securities from tobacco, alcohol, gambling, and defense industries.

See also: Mutual fund, Socially responsible fund

Although she lived cleanly, Lilith had no compunction making money through **vice funds.**

VIPERS

The original name for a group of index-based investment pools that trade on the AMEX. Now known as the "Vanguard Exchange-Traded Funds."

See also: American Stock Exchange, Exchange-traded funds, Index

Rex had a quaint habit of referring to **VIPERS** *rather than Vanguard Exchange-Traded Funds.*

Vulture fund

An investment pool that buys up the securities of struggling companies.

See also: Hedge fund

The weakening airline industry made for excellent pickings for **vulture fund** *managers.*

Window dressing

Improving the appearance of a mutual fund portfolio's performance at the end of the year by dumping losing securities and buying the current market favorites to make the portfolio look stronger in the annual report.

See also: Mutual fund

The **window dressing** *didn't accurately portray the true performance of the fund but made it look good for potential investors.*

World fund

An investment pool consisting of both U.S. and foreign securities. Also called a "global fund."

See also: International fund, Mutual fund

Rachel invested in a **world fund** *because she wanted to diversify beyond the U.S. markets.*

INVESTING

2% stop
A preset limit on the dollar amount an investor is willing to lose on an investment. Usually refers to a percentage of his entire portfolio, converted into dollars. For example, a 2% stop on a $200,000 portfolio means the investor would sell any security whose price declined by $4,000. Sometimes called a "money stop."
> See also: Stop order, Trailing stop
>
> *In order to help control losses, Zach made sure his broker always knew where his* **2% stop** *was set.*

52-week high
The top price for which a security has traded over the past year.
> See also: Record high
>
> *Eric was lucky to have sold his stocks at their* **52-week high**.

52-week low
The lowest price for which a security has traded over the past year.
> See also: Record low
>
> *Sandra assured her clients that the* **52-week low** *was still more than they had paid for the securities. In spite of the drop, they were still making money.*

Above the market
An order to buy or sell a security at a price that's higher than the prevailing trade price. Often used when a trader expects a stock to break through resistance and go on an uptrend, in order to get in at the start of that uptrend.
> See also: Resistance, Uptrend
>
> *The speculator told his broker to buy* **above the market** *because he expected prices to rise in the next few months.*

Absolute Breadth Index (ABI)
A measure of the movement and volatility of the New York Stock Exchange (though it can be used to measure any exchange), regardless of which direction the market is moving. It is the difference between the number of advancing and declining issues. The larger the difference, the higher the market volatility, which may indicate a rollercoaster ride in the upcoming weeks.
> See also: Advance/decline line, Breadth indicator
>
> *Investors held their breath as the* **ABI** *started increasing because they knew the market was going to start fluctuating rapidly.*

Absolute return
The actual earnings on an investment.

See also: Relative return

Even after fees and taxes, Todd was pleased with the **absolute return** *on his mutual fund.*

Accredited Investor
A person or entity (such as a bank or corporation) that is allowed, under securities laws, to invest in extremely high-risk investments. Defined under the Securities Act of 1933; to qualify as an accredited investor a person must either have a net worth (either on her own or combined with her spouse) of more than $1 million at the time she invests or have more than $200,000 income ($300,000 if it's joint income with a spouse) in each of the past two years and reasonably expect to continue earning at the same income level.

See also: Institutional investor

Since Gina earned $225,000 per year for the past two years, she qualified as an **accredited investor.**

"Across the board"
A phenomenon where most market activity moves in the same direction, a market-wide movement.

See also: Big board, Stock market

Since the crash of 1929, there have been safeguards to avoid an **"across the board"** *drop from causing another depression.*

Actuals
Physical goods that are interchangeable with other goods of the same type, such as sugar, corn, precious metals, and oil. Also called "commodities."

See also: Chicago Mercantile Exchange, Futures

Investors keep an eye on hurricanes because they can affect the **actuals** *markets for the rest of the year and beyond.*

Advance/decline index
A technical analysis measurement used to judge the overall strength of the stock market based on its movement as a whole. Takes the current number of securities whose prices have gone up (advanced) less those whose prices have gone down (declined) and adds that total (whether negative or positive) to the previous cumulative value. This benchmark can go down even when others increase as it's not based on dollar values.

See also: Index, Technical analysis

The **advance/decline index** *indicated a steady weakening of the market over the past three years.*

Advance/decline line (A/D)
A graphical representation of the movement of the advance/decline index over a period of time. Used in trend analysis to determine the overall health of the stock market.

See also: Advance/decline index

The administration's senior economists couldn't ignore or rationalize the drop in the market any longer once they were faced with the reality of the **advance/decline line** *during the presentation.*

ADX (Average Directional Index)
Used in technical analysis to evaluate the strength of a prevailing security price trend (with no regard to its direction, despite the name) on a scale of 0 to 100. Ratings below 20 indicate a weak trend and over 40 suggest a strong trend. Usually found at the bottom of price charts in a separate box. Used by investors to help them decide when to invest.

See also: Downtrend, Uptrend

Elizabeth looked to the **ADX** *to confirm that her portfolio positions still made sense.*

After-hours trading
Buying and selling securities when the major markets are closed.

See also: Online trading

Online investors have increased the frequency of **after-hours trading**.

Against the box
Short-selling securities that the investor also owns and holds, creating a situation where gains and losses on the two security positions will balance each other out. Was used as a way to defer capital gains taxes before a loophole was closed in 1997. Still used by investors who prefer risk-neutral positions. Also called "short selling against the box" or "shorting against the box."

See also: Long position, Short position, Short selling

Back in the early 90s, Sam used to short **against the box** *to put off paying taxes, and he continues to do that even without the inherent tax break.*

Angel investor
A person who gives money (and other forms of capital, but usually money) to startup companies to help them get on their feet, in exchange for a piece of the business. Makes high-risk investments to reap very high returns. May become involved in management activities.

See also: Silent partner, Venture capital

Without an **angel investor**, *the small communications company would never have gotten off the ground because mainstream donors were too uncertain about the technology.*

APY (annual percentage yield)
The true interest rate earned in one year when the effects of compounding are considered. Used to help investors compare different fixed-income investments on an even scale.

See also: Interest, Rate of return

Marge knew she had to look at the **APY**, *not just the coupon rates, to figure out which investment fund was right for her.*

Arbitrage
The act of simultaneously buying and selling an investment to take advantage of a price difference. Arbitrage typically involves two different markets.

See also: Exchange, Market

Jenny used **arbitrage** *to take advantage of a minor price difference between the New York Stock Exchange and the London Stock Exchange in order to make a $5,000 profit.*

Ascending tops
A descriptive term for a security price chart pattern where the periodic (daily, weekly, or monthly) high price for that security keeps increasing.

See also: Descending tops, Technical analysis

The analyst was able to assure the board that they would see **ascending tops** *during the presentation.*

Ask
The amount a seller is willing to accept for a security or other asset.

See also: Bid, Bid-Ask spread

Joan's **ask** *for the stock she owned in the company was $21 per share.*

Asset allocation
An investment strategy where the total portfolio is divided into specific investment categories.

See also: Portfolio

Nicole's **asset allocation** *included 30% bonds, 60% stocks, and 10% cash.*

At-the-money
A phenomenon where the strike price of the option is the same as the current market price of the security underlying the option.

See also: Options, Strike price

Meg didn't bother exercising her option because the stock was **at-the-money**, *but she hoped the market price would change soon.*

Back up the truck
Industry lingo for a very large securities purchase.
> See also: Securities
>
> *The mutual fund manager placed a* **back-up-the-truck** *order for 50,000 shares of Lion Joe to capitalize on the corporation's projected growth.*

Bagel land
Industry lingo for a security whose market price is dropping to $0.
> See also: Bankruptcy
>
> *The word spread quickly that, with the failure of the last product, Lion Joe's stock was heading toward* **bagel land***.*

Below the market
An order to trade a security at a price that's less than the current trading price. Often used to help investors limit their losses when a stock price starts declining.
> See also: Stop loss
>
> *Harvey was worried about an upcoming market drop so gave his broker the order to sell* **below the market** *if necessary.*

Benchmark
A standard against which similar things are measured. Used to gauge the relative success of investments.
> See also: Index
>
> *The Lipper indexes make great* **benchmarks** *for judging mutual funds' performance.*

Beta
A calculation used to determine the relative risk of an investment or an investment portfolio in comparison to the whole market.
> See also: Portfolio, Risk
>
> *Based on the* **beta***, Al advised his clients to invest in the small company, even though it wasn't on most brokers' radars yet.*

Bid
The amount an investor is willing to pay for an investment.
> See also: Ask, Bid-Ask spread
>
> *David's* **bid** *was higher for the Lion Joe stocks than he was typically willing to pay because he expected the company to do so much better than average.*

Bid-Ask spread
The difference between the highest price a buyer is willing to pay and the lowest price a seller is willing to accept for a security or other asset.

See also: Ask, Bid

Barbara's trading profits varied based on the current **bid-ask spread**.

Block trade
An order to buy or sell a large quantity of securities. Typically refers to at least $200,000 worth of bonds or 10,000 shares of stock.

See also: Round lot

The broker was always pleased when the older woman called him because he knew she would place a **block trade** *order and he would make an enormous commission.*

Bloomberg
One of the biggest providers of up-to-the-minute financial information in the world.

See also: Ticker tape

Most financial news networks rely on **Bloomberg** *for their information.*

Blue sky laws
State (rather than federal) laws of the United States that govern local securities trades, which are designed to protect their citizens from securities fraud.

See also: SEC

Although the **blue sky laws** *vary from state to state, every state takes securities fraud seriously and the laws reflect that.*

Bogey
The benchmark index used to evaluate a specific mutual fund's performance.

See also: Index

Marc was sure to explain to his new clients which **bogey** *to watch in order to have a feel for their own fund's activity.*

Boiler room
An unscrupulous, high-pressure sales scheme where brokers cold-call prospective clients and induce them to make inadvisable securities transactions.

See also: Churning and burning

Seniors are particularly susceptible to **boiler room** *tactics because the deals can sound so appealing and promise quick money.*

Bollinger band

A commonly used technique in technical analysis that tracks volatility on a price chart using standard deviation. Made up of three lines: a centerline and two channels, one above and one below. The centerline tracks a tewnty-day moving average of the stock price, and the channels follow that centerline but two standard deviations away. When the security is more volatile, the channels will be further apart; when there's less volatility, the channels will be closer to the center line. When the current price skates close to the bottom channel, that means the price is going down due to excess selling (such as panic selling), making it a good time to buy.

See also: Standard deviation, Technical analysis

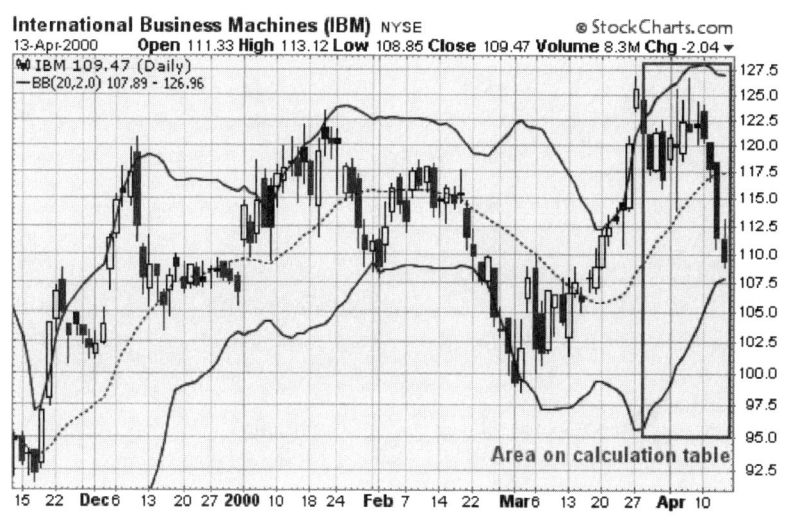

Bollinger band

Samir encouraged his clients to buy the stock because the center line on the **Bollinger band** *was closer to the bottom channel than it had been in years.*

Book-entry securities

Stocks, bonds, or derivatives whose ownership is recorded electronically, rather than with physical paper certificates.

See also: Bearer bonds, Record date

The old-school broker never really felt completely comfortable with **book-entry securities**, *preferring to have a paper trail.*

Bottom-up investing
An analysis strategy, used in security selection, that focuses on a single company, regardless of any other factors (such as the overall economy or industry comparisons). Relies on the theory that a solid company can succeed even if its industry or the overall economy are doing poorly.

See also: Due diligence, Top-down investing

Since the alternative energy company had such promising products in their pipeline, it fit into Carly and Luke's **bottom-up investing** *plan, despite the fact that most energy sector stocks were doing poorly.*

Breakout
When a security price rises above a resistance level. Usually signifies an impending increase in trading volume and price volatility. Also used (but not as frequently) when a security price sinks beneath a support level.

See also: Resistance, Support level, Volatility

Lion Joe Metals seemed stuck at $17 until a **breakout** *sent it soaring above $20.*

Broker
The person (or firm) that executes trade orders for an investor in exchange for commissions or fees.

See also: Discount broker, Full-service broker

The firm of Lion Joe Financial had a reputation for hiring **brokers** *who could handle major clients and increase portfolios even when the market was shaky.*

Bullion coins
Pure, precious metals formed into minted negotiable currency. Value fluctuates based on market forces, as these pieces are traded as investments rather than spent like money.

See also: Commodity, Gold bug

Burt was proud of his collection of **bullion coins,** *especially when they tripled in value as precious metal prices rose to their highest levels ever.*

Bullpen
The seating arrangement for newer professionals in a brokerage firm, who all sit together in a big room rather than in individual offices with doors.

See also: Broker

Sarah was proud to be the first female employee to make it out of the **bullpen.**

Buy-and-hold
A long-term investing strategy that focuses on purchasing securities and retaining them despite ups and downs in their market value.

See also: Day trading, Market timer

Maddie wanted a **buy-and-hold** *strategy because she was building a nest egg.*

Buy on margin
Borrowing money from your broker to purchase securities, with those securities as the collateral.
> See also: Margin account, Margin call

Stephen only allowed his most creditworthy long-term clients **buy on margin.**

Call option
A derivative security that gives its owner the right, not the obligation, to purchase the named underlying security at a stated price within a time frame.
> See also: Derivatives, Put option

Chris exercised his **call option** *and bought stock at far below the going market price, netting him a tidy profit.*

Called away
The investing-world phrase used to describe an investing contract that's terminated before its defined maturity date. Examples include an exercised option and a bond issue redeemed before stated maturity.
> See also: Call risk, Callable bond, Options

Jamie asked his financial professional to explain the impact on his portfolio of the bonds being **called away.**

Candlestick
A picture of a stock's trading activity for the day. Includes the open and closing prices, as well as the daily high and low. The color of the candlestick body and the positioning of the open and close data points depends on whether the price has gone up or down since the open.
> See also: Chartists, Technical analysis

Some traders make all of their buy and sell decisions based on **candlesticks.**

Chartists
Investors and analysts who use graphical representations of key factors (such as stock prices and trading volume) in their technical analysis of a security.
> See also: Ratio analysis, Technical analysis

Dan made sure he had **chartists** *in the firm because many investors responded better to the visual explanation over the verbal one.*

Chicago Board of Trade (CBOT)
A commodities exchange where agricultural products (such as corn and wheat) and financial products (such as options and futures contracts) are bought and sold.
> See also: Commodity, Futures, Options

The farmers paid close attention to prices on the **CBOT** *to have an idea of what their crops would be selling for.*

Chicago Board Options Exchange (CBOE)
A marketplace for the trade of particular derivative investments, specifically those that offer the holder the opportunity but not the obligation to trade on the underlying securities at preset prices.

See also: Derivatives, Equity LEAPS, Index options, Interest-rate options, Stock options

The **CBOE** *first opened for trading on April 26, 1973.*

Chicago Mercantile Exchange (CME)
The largest U.S. marketplace for trading futures and futures options.

See also: Futures

The **CME** *is as busy as the New York Stock Exchange on any given day of trading.*

Chooser option
A security that gives the holder the right to trade a certain stock for a certain price and to choose at a specific time whether it will be a sell trade (a put) or a buy trade (a call). For example, the chooser option is for 100 shares of stock for $10 each, and the holder can decide whether he wants to sell those shares for $10 or buy those shares for $10. The decision is made at a certain time before the expiration date, but the option does not have to be used at that time.

See also: Call option, Put option

Addison bought **chooser options** *because he wasn't sure whether Lion Joe's stock price would go up or down.*

Close a position
Finish off an investment strategy by either buying or selling a security. Long investment arrangements are terminated by selling a security, while short investment arrangements (i.e., short sales) are terminated by buying a security.

See also: Long position, Short position

When Corey **closed a position** *in Lion Joe Corporation, he made a lot of money.*

Closing price
The amount paid for the last trade of a security on any day.

See also: At-the-close order, Closing bell

Investors pay attention to the **closing price** *on stocks to see how their portfolios performed over the course of the day.*

Coattail investing
A financial strategy where the security-buying and -selling choices of a well-known successful trader or fund manager are mimicked. Works best with the buy-and-hold style.

See also: Buy-and-hold

The senior partner was consistently so successful that brokers from other firms, not just his own, managed their clients' portfolios through **coattail investing**.

Coffee, Sugar & Cocoa Exchange (CS&CE)
The New York sales forum used for trading these three commodities futures and options. Shares room with four other sales forums in the Commodity Exchange Center.

See also: Commodity, Futures, Options

The **Coffee, Sugar & Cocoa Exchange** *is far busier than the average person may originally expect.*

COMEX
The primary sales forum for trading futures and options on metals (the underlying commodity). Short for COMmodities EXchange.

See also: Commodity, Futures, Options

Her mentor insisted Angie spend time at the **COMEX** *before specializing in the trading of precious metals.*

Commodity
A physical good that is interchangeable with other goods of the same type, such as coffee, soybeans, gold, and oil.

See also: Chicago Mercantile Exchange, Futures

The floods in the Midwest affected many of the **commodity** *markets around the world.*

Conservative growth
An investment style that looks for low-risk investments expected to increase in value over the long-term.

See also: Aggressive growth

Since Wendy had fifteen years left before retirement, she was happy with **conservative growth** *from her investments.*

Contrarian
An investor who acts against prevailing market trends, buying when a security is performing poorly and selling when a security does well. Tend to seek out unpopular investments that have low P/E ratios.

See also: Price-to-earnings ratio, Value investing

Although unconventional, Jamal's **contrarian** *ways had made him a very successful investor.*

Country risk
The chance that a security will lose value because of the country of the issuing company. Includes things such as political risk (the chance of an unfavorable regime change) and currency risk (such as a negative change in exchange rates).

See also: Country fund, Risk

Until recently the **country risk** *inherent in investing in non-Western countries scared most investors away.*

Covered call
An investment strategy where an investor buys shares of a particular stock, then sells call options against those shares (which gives the option holder the right to buy his stock at a specific price); done when the stock price is expected to stay steady or drop. Called "covered" because if any of these options are exercised (used) by their purchaser, the underlying stock is already in possession of the option writer, so he doesn't have to buy it at the higher price to fulfill his obligation.

See also: Call option, Derivatives

William wanted to make money on his Lion Joe shares even though the price was down, so he created and sold **covered calls**, *expecting that the price would stay low.*

Cumulative return
The total amount an investment has gained over time, no matter how much time has passed.

See also: Capital gains, Returns

Jack was surprised that Nelson's three month, aggressive investing had netted him the same **cumulative return** *as Jack's six years with a mutual fund.*

Currency basket
A specific collection of monies whose weighted average value acts as a benchmark for the movement of monetary values based on international fluctuations. Typically used to settle contracts while minimizing the impact of value fluctuations, which happen frequently in the global marketplace.

See also: Currency risk, Exchange rate

The international coalition agreed to base all contracts on the **currency basket**, *rather than dealing with varying exchange rates.*

Currency risk
The chance that investment returns will be decreased due to changes in relative currency values.

See also: Exchange rate

Since Lion Joe Exports' sales were made overseas, investors could expect higher than normal **currency risk**.

Dawn raid
A surprise attack to takeover a target company, executed by buying up shares as soon as the market opens, before the word gets out and the price goes up.

See also: Hostile takeover

The **dawn raid** *shocked everyone because there hadn't even been rumors that a takeover was being considered.*

Day trader
A person who buys and sells securities extremely frequently, based on up-to-the-minute information, trying to capitalize on price changes throughout the day.

See also: Day trading, Market timer

Russell was the envy of his friends because he had such an instinct for the markets that he was able to make a living as a **day trader**.

Day trading
A risky strategy of buying and selling securities within the same market session, so that all investment positions are closed by the end of that session.

See also: Day trader, Market timer, Market timing

Most people who made money **day trading** *in the 1990s eventually lost it again because of the high risk involved.*

Derivatives
Investment contracts (such as stock options) with value that is based on other securities, and which have no value on their own. It takes its value (*derives* it) from price changes of the underlying security, sort of like a bet on how the price of the underlying security will move.

See also: Stock options, Futures

Derivatives *are very risky investments, but can offer the possibility of higher than average returns.*

Descending tops
A pattern on a security price chart that shows decreasing periodic high prices for that security. This can indicate that the security value is in decline.

See also: Ascending tops, Technical analysis

The **descending tops** *for Lion Joe's stock concerned the mutual fund manager because they were occurring sooner than expected.*

Disclosure
Providing all the information an investor would need to make an informed investment decision.

See also: Due diligence

The marketing department made sure every packet had all the documentation necessary to meet the requirements of **disclosure**.

Discount broker
A licensed professional through whom you can buy and sell investments at lower cost. These professionals typically receive no commissions on client trades, and do not offer investment advice.

See also: Full-service broker

Informed investors can save money by using **discount brokers** *to facilitate their trades.*

Don't fight the tape
Conventional wisdom that says an investor should not make trades contrary to market activity, such as buying aggressively during a downtrend.

See also: Downtrend

Since her father's financial advisor held with the **don't fight the tape** *mindset, Gail bought stocks online herself, hoping to beat the odds.*

Double bottom

A graphical pattern where a stock price drops down, then rises up, then drops back to the same level as the first drop, then heads up again. Looks like a "W." May indicate a long-term reversal for a downtrend.

See also: Downtrend, Technical analysis

*The CFO was cautiously optimistic when a **double bottom** appeared at the end of the company's long losing streak.*

Double top

A chart pattern where a stock price hits a peak, drops down, rises back to the level of the original peak, and then drops down again. Looks like an "M." Can indicate a reversal for an uptrend.

See also: Technical analysis, Uptrend

*Since the new technology was due to be introduced within the month, no one in the company was concerned when the current stock prices showed a **double top**.*

Downside risk

An estimate of how much an investor can lose on a security.

See also: Risk, Stop loss

*Nate always knew his clients' **downside risk** before making any investment suggestions.*

Downtick

A securities transaction that happens at a lower price than the previous transaction for the same security.

See also: Closing tick, Tick, Uptick

*Market timers often obsess about **downticks**.*

Downtrend

A steady downward movement in a securities price. Can be profitable for investors with short positions, and dangerous for long positions. Paying attention to this pattern can help investors avoid large losses.

See also: Long position, Short position, Sideways trend, Uptrend

*Andrew sold his stock immediately before the current **downtrend**, which earned him a large profit and avoided major losses.*

Due diligence

A complete investigation and analysis of a potential investment.

See also: Fundamental analysis, Ratio analysis, Technical analysis

*A wise trustee will engage in **due diligence** before allowing any of the trust monies to be invested in an unknown or unproven corporation.*

Equity LEAPS (Long-term Equity AnticiPation Securities)
Stock or index options with terms extending as long as three years (unlike regular options which normally expire within three months).

See also: Index options, Stock options

Stuart preferred **equity LEAPS** *to standard options because he took a long-term view of the market.*

Evergreen option
An employee stock option plan where more shares are given every year, usually without expiration dates.

See also: ESOP, Options

The company's **evergreen options** *made them more appealing to prospective employees than other corporations with more restrictive benefits.*

Exit strategy
A plan for closing an investment position.

See also: Close a position, Stop loss, Trailing stop

Virginia's **exit strategy** *was to sell the stocks as soon as they would provide enough to buy her next property in cash.*

Fee-based investment
A portfolio account where the account manager charges a flat fee (either in dollars or in percentage of total assets invested) rather than commissions. Helps protect investors against excessive and unnecessary trading practices.

See also: Churning and burning, Commission

As more people start investing, many firms are moving towards **fee-based investment** *to attract clients.*

Fill or kill
An order to a broker to execute a stock transaction exactly as specified immediately or not at all. Also called an "all or none" order.

See also: Market order

David recognized the small window for a good trade so issued a **fill or kill** *order on the stock.*

Financial Industry Regulatory Authority (FINRA)
A nongovernment organization that regulates and monitors all U.S. securities firms, with a goal of protecting investors. Created when the National Association of Securities Dealers combined with the regulators of the NYSE.

See also: SEC

FINRA examines securities firms in order to ensure fair and ethical business practices.

Floor
A preset minimum. Examples include rate floors in adjustable-rate mortgage contracts and minimum acceptable share prices when a new stock is issued.

See also: Offering price, Rate floor

The underwriter tried to buy the newly issued stocks for $15 per share, but the company's CFO set the **floor** *at $18.*

Forex
A marketplace where global currencies can be traded, i.e., a "foreign exchange." Rather than a big central exchange, this marketplace is more like a big network of interconnected dealers, such as banks and brokers.

See also: Currency basket

Investors can find a **forex** *in most major cities throughout the world.*

Full-service broker
An investment agent (or agency) that offers a wide range of services to clients, rather than merely executing trades for them. Services may include investment advice, portfolio design, and basic tax planning to optimize returns. Usually charge relatively high commissions for their services.

See also: Broker, CPA, Certified financial planner, Chartered financial consultant, Commission, Discount broker

Since Maddie knew very little about finances, she decided to pay a higher commission for a **full-service broker** *than try to figure out her investments by herself.*

Fundamental analysis
An investment evaluation technique that focuses on information about the issuing company itself. Based primarily on the company's financial statements and other information about the company (such as that contained in the annual report), determines the true value of the company, and its profit-generating potential. Regarded as the opposite of technical analysis.

See also: Annual report, Financial statements, Technical analysis

The company was strong enough that brokers felt comfortable advising clients based solely on its **fundamental analysis.**

Futures
Often called a "futures contract," it is an agreement to buy or sell a named asset for a specific price at a later date. This agreement constitutes a binding obligation to fulfill the terms of the agreement as specified.

See also: Derivative

Many analysts believe the oil **futures** *trade is having a huge impact on prices at the pump today.*

Going long
An investing strategy in which a security is bought with the belief that it will be worth more in the future. Also called a "long position."

See also: Buy-and-hold, Short position

Mac assured his clients that **going long** *was an appropriate response to the current market fluctuations.*

Going short
An investing strategy where a security is purchased with the belief that its price will decrease. Also known as a "short position."

See also: Long position, Short selling

In light of the potential set backs with the new drugs, Al advised his clients that **going short** *was important if they insisted on investing in the pharmaceutical company.*

Gold bar
Bricks made up of at least 99.5% pure bullion, as measured in karats. Typically weigh 400 troy ounces (the standard measure for this precious metal), but can weigh as little as one gram.

See also: Commodity, Fungibles

Fort Knox is the largest holding facility for **gold bars** *in the United States.*

Gold bullion
The pure, investment-grade form of the precious metal, which is the raw material used to create bars and coins.

See also: Bullion coins, Gold bar

The myth of a pirate's treasure is usually represented by a trunk full of coins, not actual **gold bullion.**

Gold certificate
A piece of paper held by an investor that shows proof of ownership of bullion. The actual gold is kept in a special storage facility because most people don't have the room or proper facilities to store a lot of gold.

See also: Gold bullion

His granddaughter was shocked to discover **gold certificates** *in the safety deposit box after the man's death.*

Gold bug
Investors who choose to hold gold and gold-based investments in their portfolios, believing that the price of gold will always rise over the long run.

See also: Gold bar, Gold bond, Gold fund

In spite of being encouraged to diversify, Brad was a staunch **gold bug** *and preferred to invest what little he had in gold.*

Good through order
An instruction to a broker to buy or sell a security for a named price, usually within a specified time period. This instruction remains open until it's altered or canceled by the investor, or the time expires.

See also: Day order, GTM order, GTW order

Sofia wanted her broker to keep an eye on the new electronics stock, and so she placed a **good through order** *for the next several months.*

Green investing
A portfolio style where securities are selected based on the issuing company's dedication to preserving and conserving natural resources and developing or implementing environmental safeguarding strategies. A subset of socially responsible investing.

See also: Socially responsible fund

Green investing *is a result of society's priorities shifting away from wanting to make money at any cost.*

Growth at a reasonable price (GARP)
An investment style that seeks companies poised for strong earnings increases that are still trading below their inherent value.

See also: Growth stock, Value investing

Margo had always profited by finding **GARP** *investments at bargain prices and riding the wave to success.*

GTC order (Good till canceled order)
An instruction to a broker (to buy or sell a security at a specific—or limit—price) which remains open until it's executed by the broker or terminated by the investor. Typically used to purchase securities at a price that they aren't expected to hit for quite some time.

See also: Broker, Limit order

Evelyn had enough faith in the stock that she gave her broker a **GTC order** *to sell when the price reached $50 per share even though the current market price hovered in the teens.*

GTM order (Good this month order)
An instruction to a broker to buy or sell a security for a specified price. The instruction expires upon execution or at the end of the current month.

See also: Limit order, Market order

Scott was hoping to use specific stocks for a graduation present so he gave his broker a **GTM order** *in the hopes that the price would make the purchase a good deal before the date of the party next month.*

GTW order (Good this week order)
An instruction to a broker to buy or sell a security for a specified price within the business week. The instruction is valid only during the week in which it was placed.

See also: Limit order, Market order

Lee suspected that Lion Joe Inc. would announce strong earnings next Monday, so he placed a **GTW order** *to get in before the announcement would be made.*

Gunslinger
A portfolio manager with a jittery investment style, who favors high risk–high return investments. Only people with extremely high risk tolerance (and money to lose) should invest with such managers.

See also: Portfolio manager, Returns, Risk

Amanda's reputation as a **gunslinger** *drew clients who thrived on high-stake risks.*

Hedge
An investment that helps offset the downside risk in another investment.

See also: Downside risk

Christie bought gold as a **hedge** *against inflation when prices started going through the roof.*

Hedge fund
A private investment pool that is actively and aggressively managed using complex investment strategies with the goal of producing remarkably high returns. Typically open to a limited number of high net-worth investors.

See also: Accredited investor, Derivatives

Miguel's brokers were pleased with their work when he qualified to invest in a **hedge fund.**

Horizontal analysis
A method for evaluating financial statements over time, by looking at changes in key line items (such as revenues, cash, or net income) between different periods.

See also: Financial statements, Vertical analysis

Joanna used **horizontal analysis** *to see how much the company's earnings had grown since last year.*

Horizontal trend
Signifies a security price that is not fluctuating much over a specific time period. Also called a "sideways trend."

See also: Downtrend, Uptrend

The development team worked overtime to complete the new product, hoping the new line would break the **horizontal trend** *the company had been in for so long.*

Iceberg order
An instruction to a broker to trade a very large block of securities but in several smaller trades. Typically used by institutional investors who don't want the public to know such large amounts are being traded because that could cause extreme price movement. Named such because the public only sees the tip of the "iceberg."

See also: Block trade, Institutional investor

When rumors of the founder's retirement started circulating, the primary investor issued an **iceberg order.**

Immediate or cancel order
An instruction to a broker to trade all or some of a preset number of securities right away or not at all. Typically used for extremely large orders that may not be able to be filled in their entirety.

See also: Fill or kill, Market order

When Evan won the lottery, he wanted to put the money into 50,000 shares of his favorite coffee retailer right away, so he put in an **immediate or cancel order** *with his broker.*

In and out
Buying and selling a security in the same day.

See also: Day trader

Melissa preferred to hold onto stock but was willing to go **in and out** *if the price was right.*

In the money
When a stock option becomes profitable. For calls, when the market price is higher than the strike price; for puts, when the market price dips below the strike price.

See also: Call option, Put option, Strike price

Ethan was thrilled when his Lion Joe stock options were **in the money** *and he sold them for a hefty profit.*

In the penalty box
When a company's stock price drops down and stays down, without prospects for a rebound soon.

See also: Contrarian, Value investing

The scandal caused the stock to end up **in the penalty box** *in spite of the board's best efforts to regain the public's trust.*

In the pink
Industry lingo for an investor with a healthy financial position.

See also: Accredited investor, Paper millionaire

When the older man retired from the brokerage firm, he made sure his protégé ended up with the clients who were **in the pink.**

Incentive stock option (ISO)
A special employee bonus where an employer gives tax-advantaged (as long as specific conditions are met) stock options to an employee. Unlike other bonuses, these are taxed only when the underlying stock (bought when the option was exercised) is sold. Also called "qualified stock options."

See also: Capital gains tax, Stock options

Chester hadn't realized how long he'd held his **incentive stock options**; *he was pleasantly surprised at the lower tax rate he received on them.*

Index futures
A futures contract based on a financial index, such as the DJIA or the S&P 500.

See also: Dow Jones Industrial Average, Futures, S&P 500 index

Tammy preferred to invest in **index futures** *because they let her make bets on whole markets instead of individual companies.*

Index options
A derivative investment contract where the holder has the right but not the obligation to capitalize on changes in the underlying financial benchmark, such as the S&P 500. Essentially a bet on the direction of the overall market or a market segment.

See also: Index, Stock options

As a risk lover, Doug always bought **index options** *instead of index funds to cash in on market movement.*

Indexing
An investment strategy where securities portfolios are created to mimic a specific financial benchmark, such as the DJIA or the S&P 500. Primarily used by mutual funds or other institutional investors, since most individual investors don't have the means to buy that many stocks. Trades are far less frequent—which is beneficial for tax purposes.

See also: Index, Portfolio

As a novice investor, Tal used **indexing** *to create his own stock portfolio.*

Inflation-indexed securities
A special class of securities (usually bonds) that comes with a provision that promises a return higher than the inflation rate, if the security is held to maturity.

See also: Bond, Inflation

Since Lori was looking for a long-term investment, **inflation-indexed securities** *were a good option for her.*

Institutional investors
Organizations (such as pensions, mutual funds, and insurance companies) that have ready access to large sums of cash with which to purchase and hold large blocks of securities, entitling them to preferential service and lower fee schedules.

See also: Mutual fund, Securities

Institutional investors *tend to wield more power than individuals simply due to their size and sheer number of investments.*

Interest-rate options
A derivative security whose inherent worth depends on the direction of prevailing borrowing rates. Holders have the right but not the obligation to cash in on these securities. Buying a put option indicates an expectation of declining rates, where buying a call option indicates an expectation of rising rates.

See also: Call option, Interest rate, Put option

Kat bought **interest-rate call options** *when she heard that the Fed might raise interest rates.*

Investment banker
A financial professional who deals with corporations and municipalities, primarily orchestrating IPOs and bond issues.

See also: Bond, IPO

As an international **investment banker,** *Marion had worked with some of the biggest corporations on the globe.*

Key reversal
The point where a prevailing trend changes direction. Trades made very close to that point typically provide the biggest profit opportunities.

See also: Downtrend, Uptrend

Madge was lucky enough to sell her stock just at the **key reversal** *point and made more money than investors who waited another few days.*

Lead underwriter
An investment bank that manages public offerings (both initial and secondary) for corporations. They bring other investment banks into the deal to increase the size of the sales force and generate interest in the offering. They help determine the offering price and size of the offering. The underwriters receive a hefty commission and a big payoff if the issue does well.

See also: IPO, Investment banker, Offering price

Even though all the banks stood to make money on the deal, as the **lead underwriter,** *Lion Joe Bank had the most riding on the project.*

Limit order
An instruction to a broker to buy or sell a security for a preset price. The broker cannot buy the security for more than that price, or sell it for less than that price.

See also: Broker, Order

When the new company's stock took off, many investors set very high sell **limit orders** *because of the belief the stock would reach those prices.*

Liquidity risk
The chance that an investor will not be able to sell a security when he needs to in order to prevent a loss.

See also: Market risk, Risk

When Adrianna wanted to buy 5,000 shares of penny stocks, her financial advisor warned her about the **liquidity risk.**

Long position
An investment strategy where a security is purchased with the expectation that its value will increase.

See also: Buy-and-hold, Short position

Angela decided to take a **long position** *in biotech stocks, because she believed in their future success despite current market setbacks.*

Long-term growth
An investment approach that looks for the value of a security to increase, but over an extended time period.

See also: Buy-and-hold

As a more conservative investor, he was looking for **long-term growth** *rather than glamour stocks.*

Maintenance margin
The minimum equity balance that must be sustained in a margin account, in most cases at least 25% of the value of securities bought on margin. Many brokers have a higher minimum percentage. If the account value falls below this minimum, the broker will make a margin call.

See also: Margin account, Margin call

Lance breathed easier when his margin stocks went up in value, exceeding his **maintenance margin,** *because he had been dreading a phone call from his broker.*

Margin
Using money borrowed from a broker to purchase securities, with those securities pledged as collateral (also known as "buying on margin").

See also: Collateral, Margin call

Most brokers will need an established relationship with a client before they will agree to give the client the privilege of buying on **margin**.

Margin account
A special brokerage account where the investor borrows money from the broker in order to buy securities, and holds those securities in the account as collateral for the loan.

See also: Margin buying, Margin call

Clark knew he had built a strong relationship with his broker when she offered him a **margin account**.

Margin buying
Purchasing securities using funds borrowed from the broker, with those securities as the loan collateral.

See also: Margin account, Collateral, Leverage

Hannah employed **margin buying** *to invest in Lion Joe Inc. because she did not have enough cash to buy the stock outright.*

Margin call
A demand for immediate cash when the balance in a margin account falls below a specific level. Occurs when the securities used for collateral in the account lose market value (i.e., their market price goes down), making the account balance lower.

See also: Margin account, Margin buying

When the stock price of the corporation went down by 50%, Brian knew he'd hear from his broker with a **margin call**.

Margin debt
The total dollar amount of securities bought with borrowed funds, which may change based on the current market value of those securities.

See also: Margin buying, Margin call

Jean-Paul only bought stocks on margin that he believed would see huge price gains, in order to keep his **margin debt** *under control.*

Market maker
A brokerage company that ensures people can buy or sell stock shares at any time by completing the other side of the transaction, making certain shares are always liquid. For example, if an investor wants to sell 500 shares of Microsoft, the brokerage firm will buy them (unless there's an investor at the exact same time who wants to buy 500 shares of Microsoft). They literally make a market for investors.

See also: Liquid

The firm had a reputation for being such a good **market maker** *that they had never had to turn down a transaction.*

Market order
An instruction to a broker to buy or sell a security right away at the best available price.

See also: Limit order

When Jeff needed to liquidate as quickly as possible, he sent a **market order** *to his broker and hoped for the best.*

Market risk premium
The expected return on a portfolio over and above the risk-free rate. Calculated by deducting the risk-free rate from the anticipated market return. An add-on return to compensate for the additional risk of loss an investor faces.

See also: Returns, Risk-free rate

If it weren't for the **market risk premium**, *no one would invest in anything except risk-free securities, such as T-bills.*

Market timer
A person who makes trades based on the belief that he can predict market movements based on technical analysis.

See also: Technical analysis

Jeff lost all his savings trying to be a **market timer** *when his analysis turned out to be irrelevant, and the market tanked.*

Market timing
A risky investment strategy where securities are bought and sold based on anticipated price movements.

See also: Day trading

A substantial part of the dot-com boom, and its crash, was caused by **market timing** *investing.*

Mixed lot
A purchase of an unusual number of securities where the quantity falls between normal trading units; a combination of a round lot and an odd lot, such as 125 shares of stock or seventeen bonds. Commission percentages are higher than with round lots. It is common among people giving gifts—such as eighteen bonds on the eighteenth birthday, for example.

See also: Odd lot, Round lot

Gracie's mother bought her a **mixed lot** *of 170 IBM shares when she scored 170 on her LSATs.*

Money stop
A limit on the amount of money an investor is willing to lose on a single security. Usually determined as a percentage of his whole portfolio, translated into dollars. For example, a 2% stop (the most commonly used percentage) on a $100,000 portfolio means the investor would sell any investment that declined by $2,000.

See also: Stop order, Trailing stop

When Sarah changed brokers, she made very clear what her **money stop** *was so that she wouldn't lose more than she expected.*

Morgan Stanley
One of the world's most prestigious financial services firms, known for their underwriting, brokerage, and investor services.

See also: Broker, Money manager, Underwriter

Oscar worked with his **Morgan Stanley** *advisor to set up college funds for his children.*

Morgan Stanley Capital International (MSCI)
A company that developed some of the most widely used investment indexes, particularly global benchmarks.

See also: Index

Most financial professionals rely heavily on information developed by **Morgan Stanley Capital International.**

Naked call
An investment strategy where a person creates and sells call options on a security he does not already own. If the option is exercised, he would have to purchase that security at the current market price. Riskier than writing covered calls.

See also: Call option, Covered call

Although Lou had made a lot of money writing **naked calls,** *he never grew complacent about their risk.*

Noise trader
An investor who makes impulsive buy and sell decisions without doing any due diligence. Trade decisions are based on reactions to news items and popular opinion.
> See also: Due diligence
>
> *Mac was constantly trying to dissuade his* **noise trader** *clients from making poor investment decisions.*

Odd lot
A purchase of less than the normal trading unit for a security: fewer than 100 shares of stock or fewer than five bonds.
> See also: Mixed lot, Round lot
>
> *Many parents purchase* **odd lots** *for their children in order to teach them investment practices without spending too much money.*

Online trading
Self-directed buying and selling of securities over the Internet using an online brokerage account. Can help investors minimize trading fees.
> See also: Discount broker
>
> *Many people who would never have considered investing are doing so thanks to the ease and relatively low cost of* **online trading**.

Open order
A buy or sell order to a broker that stays open until either executed by the broker or canceled by the investor. May be used to buy (or sell) securities for a price that they may not reach in the near future. Also known as a "good till canceled" or "GTC" order.
> See also: Broker, Limit order
>
> *Joseph expected the stocks to do well enough that he gave his broker an* **open order** *for $118 while the price was still below $70.*

Open position
An ongoing investment.
> See also: Close position
>
> *Luna held an* **open position** *in Chevron, shares which she'd gotten from her grandfather almost forty years ago.*

Opening price
The amount for which a security's first trade of the day is made.
> See also: Closing price
>
> *Lion Joe Inc. shares had an* **opening price** *of $38 on Thursday, thanks to a great news story about the company on Wednesday night.*

Option writer
The person who creates and sells a derivative security (called an "option") which gives the purchaser the right but not the obligation to buy or sell an underlying security at a predetermined price.

See also: Call option, Options, Put option

Bradley became an **option writer** *because he was sure he could predict stock price movements accurately.*

Options
Derivative securities that give the holder the right to buy or sell another named security (usually a stock) at a set price, usually within a set time period. For example, an option (a call option in this example) could give its holder the right to buy 500 shares of a stock at $60 per share within six months.

See also: Call option, Derivative, Put option

Some investors like trading **options** *because they might get big returns on a relatively small investment.*

Out of the money
A description of the current status of an option. For a call option (one that gives the holder the right to buy), it's when the market price of the underlying security is trading for less than the price specified on the option (also known as the "strike price"). For a put option (one that gives the holder the right to sell), it's when the underlying security is trading for more than the strike price. In either case, the option is currently worthless because no one would buy a stock for more than the market price, or sell a stock for less than the market price.

See also: In the money, Options, Strike price

Marguerite was frustrated because all of her options were **out of the money.**

Painting the tape
When a group of market players illegally (and unethically) manipulate trading activity by trading a security among themselves to make it appear that the security is drawing interest, and luring in unsuspecting investors.

See also: Due diligence, Noise trader, Pump and dump

The young brokers set up an arrangement for **painting the tape** *in order to build up their reputations for being hotshots.*

Ponzi scheme
An investing swindle, created by Charles Ponzi, that tantalizes new (often unsuspecting) investors with the promise of low-risk huge returns. Each new investor pays into the scheme, and his funds go directly to the scheme's creator (also known as the "mastermind") who then distributes a portion of the funds to other existing investors down the chain. As long as enough new investors keep joining, the plan holds up—but at some point, the source of fresh funds dries up and the whole thing falls apart. The newer investors typically lose money on the deal. Differs from a pyramid scheme in that all new investments go directly to the top, then trickle down.

See also: Pyramid scheme

Sonia was wary of the investment her neighbor was talking about, because it sounded like a **Ponzi scheme.**

Poop and scoop
An illegal Internet investing scheme where a group of people conspires to knock down a security price by spreading false, negative information about the security (the poop). When the price drops, they buy it. When the price rebounds based on true information, they sell for a quick profit (the scoop).

See also: Pump and dump

Jolene didn't know that the web report about Lion Joe Corporation being investigated by the FBI was just part of a **poop and scoop** *scheme, so she sold her shares at a loss.*

Pork bellies
The actual pigs that are the underlying commodity for a futures contract (i.e., pork belly futures).

See also: Commodity, Futures

The sausage company depended on a steady supply of **pork bellies.**

Principal
1. The initial amount invested in any security.
2. The original loan amount borrowed, less any noninterest payments made to pay down the loan balance.
3. The stated value of a bond.

See also: Bond, Interest

1. Even though Akira's **principal** *was small, his investments grew rapidly under the control of a smart financial advisor.*

2. The couple made an extra payment on the **principal** *of their mortgage every month, so they were able to pay off their house sooner than expected.*

3. She found bonds in her grandfather's safety deposit box with **principals** *of $50, $100, and $500.*

Private placement
A security issue that is not offered to the public, but rather to a handful of investors who are usually institutional investors. Due to the strictly limited offering, the issue is not required to be registered with the SEC.

See also: IPO, Institutional investor

The national bank was one of the corporations most often offered **private placements**.

Pump and dump
An illegal scam where a group of people who own a specific stock spread positive (but false) rumors about the company to run up the stock price (the pump). When the price has gone high enough for them to score substantial gains, they sell their shares (the dump). Usually happens with very small and microcap stocks.

See also: Due diligence, Poop and scoop

The original investors of the jewelry company tried to run a **pump and dump** *when they realized the artist had lost interest and wanted to do something else.*

Pure play
The security of a company that has only one business line or product, and its value is completely dependent on that single item. Very common among R&D companies. An example would be a small biotechnology firm that's developing one or more cancer therapies.

See also: Conglomerate, Diversification, Research and Development

Lion Joe Gear earned its reputation for making the best cold-weather clothing because, as a **pure play** *corporation, it could focus all of its development monies on improving upon its line.*

Put option
The right to sell a specific number of shares of a security for a specific price by a named date. Option holders are not obligated to make that sale, but they are entitled to if they so desire. Put options are typically exercised when the current market price of the named security is less than the specified sell price (see strike price). Also called "put."

See also: Call option

Maria exercised her $40 **put option** *when shares of the tech company fell to $38 per share.*

Pyramid scheme
An illegal investing scheme where participants make money by recruiting new "investors" by promising very high returns with very little risk. Works by convincing new members to contribute money, which then gets distributed to existing members. There is no other money-making mechanism in place, and the scam relies solely on getting money from new members, each of whom "invests" a lump sum with his recruiter. Each recruiter keeps a portion of the new investment, and sends the balance to his recruiter, and so on until the balance reaches the top of the "pyramid." Differs from a Ponzi scheme in that investments go from the bottom up.

See also: Ponzi scheme

Maxine suspected her boyfriend's "can't lose" investment deal was really a **pyramid scheme.**

Quantitative analysis
A securities evaluation method that reduces all variables to mathematical values as a way to measure them. Relies extensively on statistical modeling.

See also: Fundamental analysis, Technical analysis

As a scientist, Stephanie appreciated her broker sharing her portfolio's **quantitative analysis** *with her because she was used to dealing with numbers and statistics.*

Quotation
Either the highest bid price or the lowest ask price for a security.

See also: Ask, Bid

Amanda refused to buy any stock where she thought the **quotation** *was unreasonably optimistic.*

Quoted price
The dollar amount at which the last trade for a security was made.

See also: Closing price, Opening price

In the hour that Helen considered the purchase, the **quoted price** *of the stock rose $10.*

Relative return
The difference between actual earnings (also known as the "rate of return") on an investment compared to an appropriate financial benchmark.

See also: Absolute return, Index, Rate of return

The fund was particularly attractive to investors because its **relative return** *was higher than average.*

Resistance

The price at which a security trades for a long time, without going higher (though it may go lower, and then rise back up to the prevailing price level). Also called the "resistance level."

See also: Break

*Aisha was convinced the stock would go up to $55, even though it had met **resistance** at $52.*

Risk-free rate

A hypothetical return percentage for an investment with absolutely no risk attached. In practice, since there's no such thing as a wholly risk-free investment, the stated return on the three-month U.S. Treasury bill is used.

See also: Interest rate, Returns, Risk

*Alice finally convinced Peter that holding only **risk-free** securities was still risky, because they couldn't possibly keep pace with inflation.*

Risk premium

Compensation for investors willing to take the chance that an investment won't perform as expected (including a complete loss), where the security issuer pays more than the risk-free rate. For example, the interest rate on corporate bonds (which may default) is always higher than the rate on Treasury bonds (which are considered to have no default risk).

See also: Risk-free rate

*Larry invested in junk bonds, because the **risk premium** made it worthwhile.*

Roll back

When an investor sells (but does not exercise) his options, then replaces them with virtually identical options (same underlying security, same strike price) but with an earlier expiration date.

See also: Options

*Angela expected Lion Joe shares to take off—and soon—so she **rolled back** her call options.*

Roll forward

When an investor sells (but does not exercise) his options, then replaces them with virtually identical options (meaning with the same strike price for the same underlying security) but with a later expiration date.

See also: Options

*John didn't see the kind of price movement he'd been counting on, but he still expected a big jump so he did a **roll forward** with his options.*

Roll up
When an investor buys options similar to ones he already had, but the new ones have a higher strike price.

See also: Options, Strike price

Since Daisy was relatively pleased with Lion Joe Feed and Grain, she **rolled up** *her options to take advantage of more price increases.*

R-squared
A statistical measure that shows what portion of an investment's performance can be tied to the performance of a relevant index or to the market as a whole. A result of zero means there's absolutely no performance correlation, and a result of 100 indicates an exact correlation.

See also: Index, Performance

Joanna questioned her index fund's performance because it had a low **R-squared** *result.*

Scalping
An investing strategy where large numbers of trades (sometimes more than 100 in a single day) are made with very small gains expected on each.

See also: Day trader

Jeff tried to make a living **scalping** *but was unable to follow the daily market trends closely enough.*

Secondary market
A forum for investors to trade securities with each other, rather than only buying from and redeeming with the securities' issuers.

See also: NASDAQ, New York Stock Exchange

Susanna preferred buying ETF shares on the **secondary market** *to buying mutual fund shares from the fund company.*

Sector rotation
The act of moving investment dollars out of one industry-type or economic segment into another.

See also: Sector

Some mutual funds use a **sector rotation** *strategy to maximize shareholder earnings.*

Securities
Negotiable instruments that hold financial value. Come in two main categories: debt and equity. A catch-all phrase for almost everything someone could invest in, with the exception of physical goods (such as actual commodities, precious metals, and art).

See also: Debt instrument, Equities

Her financial planner discussed the possibility of investing in real estate as well as **securities**, *during their quarterly meeting.*

Securities law
The legal code associated with the buying and selling of securities.

See also: Blue sky laws, SEC

Ethical professionals will go out of their way to ensure compliance with **securities law**.

Short position
An investment strategy based on the premise that a security price is expected to go down.

See also: Long position, Short selling

Martin took a **short position** *in the mortgage company stock, because he figured their share price would go down when the housing market bottomed out.*

Short selling (shorting)
A risky investment strategy where an investor sells a borrowed security to another individual at the current market price. The investor hopes to purchase the security at a lower price than he'll receive from his buyer, use those as replacement shares, and profit from the differential. Used when a security price is expected to decline.

See also: Derivatives, Market value, Risk lover

The businessman lost a fortune when he went on a **short selling** *spree but the market rebounded.*

Speculation
A high-risk, short-term financial strategy where investment selection is based on expected price movement.

See also: Day trading, Market timing, Risk

While **speculation** *has the potential for bringing in a large return, it is not a wise investment strategy for people unwilling or unable to absorb a loss.*

Spot market
An exchange where commodities (and sometimes securities) are sold for cash and delivered immediately. So-called because transactions occur "on the spot." Also called the "cash market."

See also: Commodity

Tobacco was traditionally sold at **spot markets** *because the buyers wanted to see the quality of each lot first hand.*

Spread
The difference between the bid and ask prices for a security. One way brokers and dealers make money.

See also: Ask, Bid

The **spread** *was large enough that Mac made a lot of money on his client's trade.*

Sterile investment
An investment that doesn't pay out steady income streams like interest and dividends. Rather, its value comes solely through capital appreciation. Examples include precious metals, such as gold coins, and art.

See also: Capital gains

The young woman was shocked to learn that her great-grandmother's furniture would count as a **sterile investment** *and increase her overall worth.*

Stop limit order
An instruction to a broker to trade a security at a specific price only after a particular preset price has been surpassed. A combination of a stop order and a limit order.

See also: Limit order, Stop order

Tammy wanted to buy the stock low but not before it started to rise a little bit, so she set a **stop limit order** *with her broker for a dollar above its current price.*

Stop loss
A standing order to sell a security when its market price declines by a fixed percentage. Investors use this order to limit their losses on any given security.

See also: Capital loss

Paul ordered a **stop loss** *should any of his stocks decline in value by 10%.*

Stop order

An instruction to a broker to buy or sell a security when its market price gets better than a preset price point. Once the preset price has been passed, the instruction turns in to a market order. Typically used to limit losses or lock-in profits.

See also: Market order

Jane placed a **stop order** *with her broker just in case the price on her stock continued to drop.*

Strike price

The preset dollar amount for which a derivative security (such as an option) can be exercised (used). Set by whomever creates the derivative. For example, if a call option states that a stock can be bought for $40 per share, $40 is the strike price. Also called the "exercise price."

See also: Derivatives, Options

Dominic was hoping that Lion Joe shares would exceed the **strike price** *on his options so he could make a quick profit.*

Support Level

The lowest price for which a stock tends to sell historically. Also called "support."

See also: Resistance

Jack bought into the company at the **support level** *because of his expectation that the price would rise from there.*

Swing trading

A short-term investment strategy where securities are held for predefined periods, usually between one and four days, for (hopefully) quick gains.

See also: Buy-and-hold, Capital gains

Brandon decided to see if he could use **swing trading** *to finance his spring break trip.*

Tailgating

When a broker makes the exact same trades in his account right after he's made them for a client. Not illegal, but may be unethical if the broker is capitalizing on insider information known by his client.

See also: Insider trading

Jack had a difficult time proving he had been considering the trade prior to speaking to his client and wasn't just **tailgating**.

Take a bath
To lose a substantial amount of money—even everything—on an investment.
> See also: Capital loss
>
> *The investor knew he might* **take a bath** *on the new computer firm but was intrigued enough by the new design to risk it.*

Take a flier
To invest in extremely high-risk securities looking for a big payoff... though the investor may end up taking a bath instead.
> See also: Speculation, Take a bath
>
> *William's decision to* **take a flier** *by investing heavily in penny stocks went directly against the advice of his financial advisor.*

Technical analysis
A security evaluation method that looks at historical market data trends, such as price movement and trading volume, to predict future performance.
> See also: Fundamental analysis
>
> *Chuck decided not to invest in the company in spite of the representative's claims because the* **technical analysis** *didn't back up any of the sales pitch.*

Tick
The smallest amount by which the price of a security can move up or down.
> See also: Exchange, Securities
>
> *Few investors worry when a stock price goes down a* **tick** *because such movement is to be expected.*

Trade
The act of buying or selling a security.
> See also: Broker, Exchange
>
> *In another ten years, teenagers won't understand what a big deal it is to be able to* **trade** *online or globally because it will be a matter of course for them.*

Trailing stop
A special instruction to a broker to sell a security if it declines in value by a specific percentage, rather than falling to a preset dollar amount. The dollar value of the order changes as the stock price increases, which has the effect of locking in gains and limiting losses. For example, a 10% trailing stop tells the broker to sell the stock if its price declines by 10%. This order does not kick in while the price is going up, but the watch starts right away if the price starts dropping.
> See also: Limit order, Stop loss
>
> *The price when the* **trailing stop** *kicked in was higher than the original purchase price of his stock so James enjoyed big gains when it sold.*

Transaction fee
A charge applied to a security sale or purchase.

See also: Commission

Some online trading companies are popular because they charge **lower transaction fees** *than traditional brokerage firms.*

Trend following
An investment strategy where trends are assumed to continue indefinitely, and trades are made based on the prevailing trend, i.e., long positions are taken during uptrends, and short positions during downtrends. Also called "trend trading."

See also: Long position, Short position

Trend following *has cost short-sighted investors once the public's interest in an industry or new gadget has waned.*

Trend reversal pattern
A repeated series, as plotted on a graph, characterized by sudden changes in direction of a securities price (looking sort of like repeated Ms or Ws). This pattern can help technical analysts make decisions about the type of position they want to take with the security. Also called a "reversal pattern."

See also: Long position, Short position, Technical analysis

The **trend reversal pattern** *indicated the security would be dropping in price soon so the brokers decided to take a short position.*

Triple top
A graphical pattern characterized by the up and down movement of a security top. The price moves up to a peak then drops down, and repeats this action two more times to the same levels. Typically used to predict the reversal of a long uptrend, as it indicates the peak price can no longer be sustained.

See also: Technical analysis, Trend reversal pattern, Uptrend

As soon as Brady saw the **triple top,** *he knew it was time to sell his Lion Joe shares.*

Troy ounce
An historical measure still used for weighing precious metals, particularly gold. When an investor buys an ounce of gold, he's buying a troy ounce, not a standard ounce. One troy ounce is slightly heavier than a standard ounce.

See also: Gold bullion

The groom had a necklace made out of a full **troy ounce** *of gold for Helen, his bride-to-be.*

Underwriter

A company that manages the issuance of securities (such as stocks or bonds) for another company. Services include helping the client company set an offering price for their securities, buying the full issue from the client company, and selling the security to the public.

See also: IPO, Securities

According to the **underwriter**, *the company could offer the stocks a few cents cheaper and all parties involved would still make money.*

Uptick

A security transaction that closes at a higher price than the previous transaction for the same security did.

See also: Downtick, Tick

The **uptick** *in Lion Joe Coffee Inc. shares caused several investors to show an interest where they hadn't cared previously.*

Uptrend

A consistent, sustained upward movement in a security price. On the technical analysis charts, this may be marked by ups and downs as long as the overall direction is up, and no downward movement sinks below a previous drop. Tracking this can help investors avoid big losses.

See also: Downtrend, Sideways trend, Technical analysis

The cosmetics company noticed an **uptrend** *as soon as they changed their marketing strategy.*

Value investing

A style where stocks are purchased when they are believed to be undervalued. The investor looks for securities whose prices are down because of reactions to new items or other factors that don't take into account what the company is really worth.

See also: Investment style, Value fund

With **value investing**, *Hal was able to uncover some very good companies that soon took off and gave him great returns.*

Venture capital

Private funds invested in small and startup businesses with huge expected growth potential. Sometimes includes managerial advice in addition to financial support.

See also: IPO

The philanthropist was always ready to provide **venture capital** *to new businesses that she found interesting or worthy.*

Wallpaper
Industry lingo for securities that have become worthless.

See also: Bankruptcy

After the dot-com bubble burst back in the 1990s, investors were stuck with **wallpaper.**

Warrant
A derivative security attached to another security (usually a bond) that gives the holder the right to buy an underlying security (virtually always stock) for a specific price within a specific timeframe. Similar to a call option, but issued by the company that issued the underlying stock (rather than by a third party). Often used when a corporation is issuing bonds; they attach stock warrants to their bonds to make their bonds more attractive to investors.

See also: Call option, Derivatives

Even though Lion Joe stocks had risen to $65, David was able to exercise his **warrant** *and buy the stock for $50 since he was within the allotted timeframe.*

Yield
The return on an investment, expressed as a percentage, calculated by dividing the purchase price of one share into the related earnings (i.e., interest and dividends).

See also: Dividend, Interest, Returns

Investors were impressed with the fund's 12% **yield** *because it was so much greater than most projections.*

REAL ESTATE

2-1 buydown
A mortgage loan that comes with initial temporary interest rates that start out lower than normal, then increase twice before hitting the loan's ultimate fixed rate. Borrowers have to pay more points up front for this benefit (i.e., buying down the interest rate).
> See also: Mortgage, Points
>
> *Due to the current high interest rates, the couple went with a* **2-1 buydown** *for a better initial rate.*

2/28 ARM (Adjustable-rate mortgage)
A home loan that comes with a two-year initial fixed-rate period, after which interest rates begin changing according to an agreed-upon formula for the remaining twenty-eight years of the thirty-year loan. Usually used by people with poor credit ratings who expect to repair their credit in a couple of years and then qualify for a better fixed rate when they refinance.
> See also: Adjustable-rate mortgage, Credit rating
>
> *After defaulting on his credit cards, Bob went with a* **2/28 ARM** *with an eye toward refinancing in a few years.*

3-2-1 buydown
A kind of mortgage where interest rates start out low, and then step up with three timed increases before settling at the permanent rate. Borrowers normally pay extra points for these loans, so they're used by people with a lot of cash up front but not a lot of income (such as someone who inherits a good down payment, but still has to make the mortgage payments with low regular income). Sometimes offered by builders as an added incentive to buy.
> See also: Mortgage, Points
>
> *Janet's parents gave her enough money for a down payment, so she was a perfect candidate for a* **3-2-1 buydown** *mortgage.*

3/27 ARM (Adjustable-rate mortgage)
A variable-rate home loan that comes with an initial fixed rate for the first three years of the loan. Pushed on people with poor credit, who are typically only eligible for higher-rate subprime mortgage loans. Borrowers may sign up for these loans with an eye on refinancing before the variable rate kicks in.
> See also: Adjustable-rate mortgage, Subprime mortgage
>
> *Many people are shocked at how drastically a* **3/27 ARM** *payment can rise after the first three years.*

5-1 hybrid ARM (Adjustable-rate mortgage)
A home loan that comes with a five-year initial fixed-rate period, followed by a twenty-five-year period where the interest rate changes annually. Usually used by people who plan to move or refinance within five years.

See also: Adjustable-rate mortgage

The young family suspected the move to Austin was temporary so chose a **5-1 hybrid ARM.**

5-6 hybrid ARM (Adjustable-rate mortgage)
A home loan that comes with a five-year initial fixed-rate period, followed by a twenty-five-year period where the interest rate changes every six months. Typically used by borrowers who plan to move or refinance within five years.

See also: Adjustable-rate mortgage

As a contractor who moved every three years, Marisa looked for a **5-6 hybrid ARM** *when she bought her condo.*

80-10-10 mortgage
A special home loan transaction where two mortgages (a first and a second) are generated on the same property at the same time. The borrower makes a 10% down payment, takes out an 80% first mortgage, and a 10% second mortgage. Often used by borrowers so they can avoid the primary mortgage insurance required when the primary mortgage is more than 80% of the home value.

See also: Mortgage

Carol didn't have a lot of money to put down, but she really wanted to avoid mortgage insurance, so she opted for an **80-10-10 mortgage** *to help save a little money.*

100% loan
A mortgage that is equal to the full amount of a property, where the buyer makes no down payment. Usually comes with higher-than-normal interest rates.

See also: Mortgage

Since Craig qualified for a **100% loan,** *he decided to use his savings to remodel the house instead of putting it toward a down payment.*

125% loan
A mortgage where the borrower gets 25% more than the value of the property. Considered a high-risk loan, and usually comes with an interest rate much higher than average prevailing rates. People get these loans when they have no down payment and no money to pay closing costs or other prebuying activities (such as the home inspection.)
> See also: Default, Mortgage

The bank agreed to a **125% loan** *for the couple since their incomes would easily meet the proposed mortgage payments, even though they hadn't been able to save a down payment.*

Acceleration clause
A section commonly found in reverse mortgage agreements where a loan can be called in (a demand for payment in full) if certain covenants (such as proper property maintenance or payment of property taxes) are not maintained by the homeowner.
> See also: Reverse mortgage

Paul was careful to maintain the requirements of his **acceleration clause** *so that he wouldn't lose his house for an avoidable reason.*

Acquisition debt
Money borrowed to buy, build, or fix up a first or second home. The most common form is a mortgage.
> See also: Debt, Mortgage

The couple used **acquisition debt** *to rehab their beach house by borrowing against their primary home.*

Adjustable interest formula
The equation used to determine the current interest rate on an adjustable-rate mortgage. Usually equal to a named benchmark (such as LIBOR) plus a fixed percentage, possibly subject to minimum and maximum values.
> See also: Adjustable-rate mortgage, LIBOR, Rate cap, Rate floor

The lenders ran the **adjustable interest formula** *every quarter to set new payments for homeowners.*

Adjustable-rate mortgage (ARM)
A home loan with a variable interest rate.
> See also: Variable interest rate

Bettina got an **adjustable-rate mortgage** *to take advantage of the very low introductory rate, but began to have financial problems when the loan's interest percentage increased.*

Assumable mortgage
A home loan that can be transferred intact to a new borrower with no change in terms. It follows as if the original borrower still held the loan.

See also: Mortgage

Instead of signing a new lease, Bobbie offered her tenant the option of taking over an **assumable mortgage** *on the condo.*

Bimonthly mortgage
A home loan where payments are made twice per month, for a total of twenty-four payments per year. Allows the borrower to pay less interest over the life of the loan.

See also: Mortgage

Due to the timing of her paychecks, Jane was able to handle a **bimonthly mortgage***.*

Biweekly mortgage
A home loan where payments are made every other week, for a total of twenty-six payments per year. Comes in two possible styles, either where the first payment in a month is held until the second one is received and then they're processed as a single payment or where each payment is immediately applied to principal and interest, thus lowering the loan balance with each payment (called a "simple interest biweekly mortgage"). Either way allows the borrower to save significant interest over the life of the loan, with the second method allowing for even more savings.

See also: Mortgage

Andrew's income was such that he could make a **biweekly mortgage** *easily so he chose to do so in order to save money in the long run.*

Cash-out refinance
A new mortgage transaction that pays off an existing mortgage plus leaves the borrower with additional cash.

See also: Mortgage

The **cash-out refinance** *gave the couple a better interest rate and money for the redecorating they wanted.*

Closing
The end of a home sale process, where the mortgage loan is recorded, the loan contract goes into effect, and the property ownership is transferred to the purchaser.

See also: Mortgage

Jessica and Jeremy took the afternoon off from work in order to celebrate the **closing** *on their first house.*

Closing costs
The expenses associated with a property transfer (other than the price of the property itself). Also called "settlement costs."

See also: Closing, Mortgage

The Realtor had his clients bring a money order covering the **closing costs** *to his office.*

Comparables
A real estate term used to aid in determining a fair price for a home by looking at recent selling prices for similar homes in the area.

See also: Appraisal

Prior to setting a price for their condo, Chris and Terry checked the **comparables** *to ensure they asked an appropriate amount.*

Conforming loan
A mortgage that fits into the size limits and meets the lending standards set by Fannie Mae and Freddie Mac. The limit on the loan amount is set each year by the Office of Federal Housing Enterprise Oversight.

See also: Freddie Mac, Fannie Mae, Jumbo loan, Subprime mortgage

The couple was buying a very expensive home, so they did not qualify for a **conforming loan.**

Conventional loan
A mortgage that meets specific criteria (such as loan amount) and standards set by Fannie Mae and Freddie Mac. Also called a "conforming loan."

See also: Freddie Mac, Fannie Mae, Jumbo loan, Subprime mortgage

The young man was thrilled that, due to the price of the small house he was buying, he qualified for a **conventional loan.**

Counteroffer
A response to an unacceptable proposal, usually involving property sales. Technically, a rejection of the original offer and the submission of a new one.

See also: Godfather offer

The woman's bid on the condo had been intentionally low so she wasn't surprised when the owners came back with a **counteroffer.**

Deed
A legal document declaring real property ownership, and by which title of the named property can be transferred from one party to another.

See also: Real property, Title

Max and Kayla put the **deed** *to their house in a safe deposit box.*

Deferred payment loans (DPL)

A low-cost reverse mortgage offered by state and local governments to help homeowners make repairs and improvements. Use of funds is limited to the contracted purpose.

See also: Home equity loan, Reverse mortgage

David and Maddie were able to refurbish their old Victorian house due to a **deferred payment loan.**

Down payment

A lump sum used to partially purchase a costly asset, such as a house or car.

See also: Mortgage

Marguerite put away part of every paycheck in order to save for a **down payment** *on a new condo.*

Escrow

A safekeeping arrangement, where assets owed by one party to a second party are held by a third party until such time as they are due to be disbursed.

See also: Settlement, Closing costs

The rental agency held all deposits in **escrow** *until the tenants moved out again.*

FHA (Federal Housing Administration)

A government agency that insures home loans for individuals to help first-time home buyers with very small down payments qualify for mortgages. The agency makes no actual loans.

See also: Mortgage

Although the elderly couple had never owned a home before, Wilbur and Ruth were able to qualify for an **FHA**-*insured loan.*

Foreclosure

A legal proceeding that terminates the right to hold property, usually due to nonpayment of collateralized loans such as mortgages.

See also: Collateral, Mortgage

Whenever the housing market bottoms out, **foreclosure** *rates increase.*

Freddie Mac (FHLMC)

Formally known as the Federal Home Loan Mortgage Corporation (FHLMC), it is a government-sponsored corporation set up to make a secondary market for specific mortgage loans. The corporation purchases home loans from lenders; then repackages them into pass-through securities that can be sold to investors.

See also: Mortgage-backed securities, Pass-through security

Freddie Mac *has helped families for generations to get home loans by keeping money in the mortgage markets.*

Growing equity mortgage (GEM)
A unique home loan whose monthly payments get bigger over time, even though the interest rate is fixed, to allow the borrower to pay down the balance more quickly.

See also: Adjustable-rate mortgage, Mortgage

Janet knew her income was going to rise steadily every year so she arranged for a **GEM** *in order to own her home faster while not exceeding her immediate payment abilities.*

Home equity line
A form of revolving credit (sort of like a credit card) with a primary residence as collateral. The original balance is set, then the homeowner takes out funds as needed. In most cases, the borrower is required to make minimum annual withdrawals. Interest is charged on the withdrawal amounts until they're fully repaid. The interest paid by the homeowner is tax-deductible.

See also: Home equity loan, Itemized deductions

Whenever the couple needed to make large purchases, they preferred to use their **home equity line** *rather than a credit card so they could take the interest payment off their taxes.*

Home Equity Loan (HEL)
Money borrowed using residential real estate for collateral, usually in addition to a primary mortgage.

See also: Collateral, Mortgage

Josh took out a **home equity loan** *to refinish his basement.*

HUD-1
A detailed report that itemizes all the particulars of a single home-buying deal. Includes all the amounts (such as property purchase price and title transfer fees) paid by both parties to the transaction. Commonly known as a "settlement statement."

See also: Mortgage, Settlement

Charlie was proud to show the **HUD-1** *to her grandfather after the sale of her first home was complete.*

Interest-only mortgage
A home loan where the homebuyer pays no principal on the loan, therefore not paying down the loan or building equity. Instead, he makes only interest payments on the original principal balance until the loan term expires. At that time, the loan may be renewed as is or refinanced as a regular mortgage. Often offered to first-time home buyers who don't earn enough to make full monthly mortgage payments. A VERY bad idea!

See also: Mortgage

Although the unethical lender tried to convince the couple to get an **interest-only mortgage**, *they were savvy enough to wait until they could afford a standard mortgage.*

Joint tenancy with rights of survivorship (JTWROS)
A legal property ownership arrangement where all parties own equal portions of the property, and upon the death of one owner, his interests are automatically transferred to and split equally by the remaining owners. Property owned in this manner cannot be transferred in any other way (i.e., cannot be passed down via a will) until there is only one owner left.

See also: Community property, Tenancy in common

Blanche didn't worry about where she would live when her boyfriend died because they owned their home under **joint tenancy with rights of survivorship**.

Jumbo loan
A mortgage that's bigger than the size limits set by the Office of Federal Housing Enterprise Oversight, and therefore not eligible for FNMA or FHLMC programs.

See also: Conforming loan, Freddie Mac, Fannie Mae

Since Mick and Mary's dream house cost $760,000, they needed a **jumbo loan** *even though they had saved up a substantial down payment.*

LTV ratio (loan to value)
A calculation based on the relationship between a mortgage and the appraised value of the related property. Used to evaluate default risk, and may impact interest rate charged. Higher values may lead to higher interest rates and required mortgage insurance.

See also: Default, Mortgage

Rhonda and Scott had trouble refinancing their mortgage for a lower rate because of the high **LTV ratio** *on the property.*

Landlord
A property owner who rents his property to another individual or company. Also called a "lessor."

See also: Rental property

Rob was a fair-enough **landlord** *that, while he paid the property mortgage with his rents, he didn't make much money off his tenants.*

Lease
A rental agreement, where a property owner allows another party to use that property in exchange for regular periodic payments.

See also: Rental property

Rob frequently introduced current tenants to prospective ones before offering the applicants a **lease.**

Like-kind exchange
The act of simultaneously buying and selling the same type of asset (such as trading in one car when buying another car), which can result in deferred tax treatment for any taxable gains on the transfer. Also called a "Section 1031 Exchange."

See also: Capital gains, Section 1031 exchange

The real estate investor always had a property ready to sell before he bought another one in order to receive all the benefits of the **like-kind exchange.**

Mortgage
A loan taken out to purchase real estate, secured by that real estate. The borrower pays this loan following an amortization schedule and gains equity in the property as the loan principle is paid down.

See also: Amortization schedule, Down payment, Real property

Joan bought her home with a 20% down payment and a thirty-year **mortgage** *from her local bank.*

Mortgage rate lock
A binding agreement between a lender and a borrower that sets a firm interest rate for a mortgage that's executed within a specific time period. A deposit is usually necessary to ensure the agreement is legally binding.

See also: Mortgage

Clint was worried about drastic changes in interest rates so he made sure to get a **mortgage rate lock** *from his lender.*

Negative amortization
An increase in the principal balance of a mortgage. A phenomenon that occurs when a mortgage payment is not enough to cover the current interest due, causing the unpaid interest portion to be added to the loan's principal balance. Sometimes occurs with adjustable-rate mortgages, when loan interest rates increase more quickly than loan payments.

See also: Adjustable-rate mortgage, Amortization, Payment cap

Many homeowners will find themselves in foreclosure if they face too many months of **negative amortization.**

Negative equity
A situation where the value of an asset is less than the remaining balance of the loan taken out to buy the asset. Can occur, for example, because of a combination of a high loan-to-value ratio and declining home price.

See also: LTV ratio, Negative amortization

Walt and Liz realized that buying at the height of the housing boom had been a mistake when, just five years later, they were faced with **negative equity.**

Payment shock
The surprise felt by people when loan payments suddenly increase, often by more than they've planned for. Often occurs with adjustable-rate mortgages.

See also: Adjustable-rate mortgage

As teaser rates started to expire, homeowners were suddenly dealing with **payment shock.**

Points
Interest fees paid when a loan is obtained, rather than over the life of the loan. Usually paid in regard to mortgage loans. Measured as a percentage of the total loan; for example, one point on a $125,000 would be $1,250 (one percent).

See also: Interest, Mortgage

To save money on his mortgage payment, Ed bought three **points** *and lowered his interest rate to 5.5%.*

Property tax
A state or local levy based on the value of real estate.

See also: Itemized deductions

As renters, Lionel and Daisy were exempt from having to pay any **property tax** *on their home.*

Quitclaim deed
A legal document that transfers all ownership rights to a specific property. Often used in divorces.

See also: Deed, Title

She wrote a **quitclaim deed** *on the timeshare so her ex-husband could own it outright.*

Rate and term refinance
Getting new features—either interest rate or maturity—on a mortgage loan by swapping the old loan for a new one with the same principal balance. Often done when rates have dropped substantially, and often through the same lender.

See also: Cash-out refinance

When interest rates dropped by almost 5%, the couple looked into a **rate and term refinance** *on their house.*

Real property
Land and assets attached to land, such as buildings and fences (also known as "real estate").

See also: Assets, Personal property

Conservative investors often hold **real property** *in their portfolios because it tends to be less risky and hold value better than stock market investments.*

Recording fee
An expense charged by the government for documenting a real estate transaction in the public records.

See also: Mortgage

The Realtor paid the **recording fee** *at the same time he filed the deed transfer.*

Refinance wave
When droves of homeowners refinance their mortgages, almost always following a decline in prevailing interest rates.

See also: Mortgage, Rate and term refinance

The real estate market experienced a wide-spread **refinance wave** *when the Fed dropped interest rates another point.*

REIT (Real Estate Investment Trust)
A specially formed company that buys and manages real estate (equity REITS) or mortgages using funds invested by shareholders. Equity REITs (pronounced "reets") typically own and operate income-producing properties such as shopping malls, apartment buildings, hotels, and office complexes.

See also: Real property, Rental property

Joe was able to own pieces of two Las Vegas casinos, a New York luxury hotel, and three shopping malls through his **REIT** *shares.*

REMIC (Real Estate Mortgage Investment Conduit)
A bond issue, backed by mortgages, that is divided up into several tranches, each with different payment and maturity characteristics. Similar to a CMO, except for federal tax treatment. Practically speaking, the terms REMIC and CMO are used interchangeably, as the tax impact is only to the bond issuer. Pronounced "rem-ick" (rhymes with hem stick).

See also: Mortgage-backed securities, Tranche

When Chet learned his client was interested in real estate, he suggested she invest in a **REMIC** *so she wouldn't have to deal with property upkeep.*

Rental property
An asset owned by one party and leased to another for a periodic fee.

See also: Asset, Landlord

Rental property *can be a good investment, especially when home prices are dropping.*

Reverse mortgage
A financial arrangement where a homeowner borrows money against the equity in his home and receives the money in monthly installments rather than in a lump sum. The homeowner continues living in his home during this arrangement, which ends when the home is no longer his primary residence. Often used by older people who need extra money but don't want to leave their homes.

See also: Equity, Mortgage

Betty used the money from her **reverse mortgage** *for monthly visits to her grandchildren.*

Right of first refusal
A contractual obligation to offer an item for sale to specific people (or companies) before offering it to anyone else. Common in real estate deals.

See also: Real property

The author's contract for her first book included granting the publisher **right of first refusal** *on her second novel.*

Roll in
Adding all or most of the costs associated with a loan into the loan balance. Common with mortgages, though certain costs are not allowed to be added in.

See also: 125% loan, Mortgage

The Realtor assured the couple they could **roll in** *everything but the prepaid interest into their mortgage so they didn't need to worry about having extra cash on hand.*

Section 1031 exchange
The portion of U.S. tax code that allows investors to defer the taxes due on capital gains associated with a like-kind property swap, as long as they follow some very strict rules. Often used in reference to real estate "swaps," where an investor sells one property and immediately buys another with the same characteristics. Under the tax code, that original investment is considered to remain intact, just housed in another asset.

See also: IRS, Like-kind exchange

Real estate investors need to pay close attention to the rules, or they'll lose the tax benefits they'd get with a perfect **Section 1031 exchange**.

Servicing fee
A small percentage (usually from 0.25 to 0.50% of the mortgage balance) of every mortgage payment that's kept by the company that processes the payments, then sends the balance to the lender.

See also: Mortgage

The mortgage processor took a hit during the housing crash because they lost many **servicing fees** *out of their budget.*

Settlement
When all terms of a contract have been fulfilled. For house purchases, this is the same as the closing. For securities trades, this occurs when the buyer has paid in full and the seller has delivered the securities.

See also: Settlement statement, Trade

The Realtor always breathed easier when the **settlement** *for a home purchase he had facilitated was completed.*

Settlement risk
The chance that one party to a contract will fail to meet the terms of the contract.

See also: Settlement

Lion Joe Inc. was a strong enough company that few of its partners ever considered the **settlement risk** *of doing business with them.*

Settlement statement
A report that includes all the details of a single home-buying transaction, including all amounts paid by both the buyer and the seller (such as the property purchase price and Realtor fees). Also called the "HUD-1" (because the form comes from the Department of Housing and Urban Development).
See also: Mortgage, Settlement

After she bought her first home, Michele framed the **settlement statement.**

Skip-payment mortgage
A special home loan that lets the borrower not make (skip) a scheduled payment. The interest portion of that skipped payment is added to the principal balance of the loan, causing negative amortization (the loan balance increases).
See also: Mortgage

When the National Guardsman realized he was going to be deployed, he arranged for a **skip-payment mortgage** *in case money got tight while he was overseas.*

Subprime mortgage
A home loan typically offered to people with bad credit and higher default risk. Comes with higher (often substantially higher) interest rates than regular mortgages.
See also: Credit rating, Default, Mortgage

Jason knew he would only be able to qualify for a **subprime mortgage** *so decided to wait until he had rebuilt his credit before buying a house.*

Tax lien
A legal claim placed on property to secure payment for previously unpaid government assessments.
See also: Property tax

The IRS put a **tax lien** *on the man's boat because he hadn't paid taxes in the last two years.*

Tenancy by the entirety
A type of community property ownership where each spouse retains the right of survivorship. Similar to joint tenancy, but for a married couple.
See also: Joint Tenancy with Rights of Survivorship

Because Lisa and Mike were married, they owned their house under **tenancy by the entirety.**

Tenancy in common

A legal arrangement where two or more people own portions of a single piece of property. Each owner can dispose of his property upon his death as he sees fit.

See also: Joint Tenancy with Rights of Survivorship

Since they had owned the store through **tenancy in common,** *Greg had no choice but to work with a new partner after his first partner left his half to a nephew.*

Title

A legal document conveying ownership of an asset.

See also: Asset

The woman was so proud when she paid off her car loan and received the **title** *in the mail.*

RETIREMENT

401(k) plan
A special tax-advantaged investment account designed to help employees save for retirement. Pretax contributions are deducted directly from employees' paychecks and deposited into their individual accounts.

See also: Pretax contribution

A **401(k) plan** *is often used as an enticement for potential employees.*

403(b) plan
A retirement savings account available only to public school employees, employees of certain tax-exempt institutions, and some ministers. Investments in these accounts get the same tax-advantaged treatment of other retirement accounts, such as tax-deferred contributions and earnings.

See also: 401(k) plan

As a guidance counselor at Rydell High, Laura had a **403(b) plan** *as part of her benefits package.*

457 plan
A tax-advantaged deferred compensation program for government employees, wholly funded by payroll deductions from those employees. Similar to a retirement plan, but not considered as such by legal definition.

See also: Retirement plan

Once she started working for the senator, she was eligible for the **457 plan** *offered.*

Catch-up provisions
A special rule added into the U.S. tax code that lets people age fifty and older contribute more to retirement plans than younger people can.

See also: Retirement plan

Minnie hadn't saved much during her younger years so began to take advantage of the **catch-up provisions** *immediately after her fiftieth birthday.*

Cliff vesting
A special benefit of some employee retirement plans where employer contributions become the property of the employee all at once, rather than gradually over an extended time period.

See also: Vested

The company's **cliff vesting** *policy allowed the employees to own 100% of their retirement accounts after they'd worked there for three years.*

Defined benefit plan
A retirement arrangement based on specific, guaranteed payouts to be made to the account holder upon retirement. Payments into the fund may vary, and are recalculated periodically to ensure the account will attain sufficient value to make the promised payments in the future.
>See also: Defined contribution plan, Retirement plan
>
>*Daisy knew she could easily afford to live in the first-rate retirement community because, thanks to her* **defined benefit plan**, *she knew exactly what her monthly budget would be.*

Defined contribution plan
A retirement arrangement where payments into the account are fixed, and the eventual payment benefit depends on the account balance at the time of retirement.
>See also: Defined benefit plan, Retirement plan
>
>*The 401(k) plan offered by Lionel's employer was a* **defined contribution plan**, *and his payroll deductions were always the same.*

Direct rollover
A distribution from a qualified retirement plan that gets deposited straight into another qualified retirement plan.
>See also: Rollover IRA
>
>*When Heather changed jobs, she used a* **direct rollover** *to keep from taking a tax hit on her retirement monies.*

ERISA (Employee Retirement Income Security Act)
A federal law designed to protect workers who participate in retirement and other benefit plans by requiring strict adherence to rules by employers in exchange for tax benefits.
>See also: Retirement plan
>
>*The CFO worked with the human resource department to ensure strict compliance with* **ERISA** *so as to not lose the government tax advantages.*

ESOP (Employee Stock Ownership Plan)
A form of defined contribution retirement plan that allows workers to become investors in the corporation they work for by giving them shares of the corporate stock.
>See also: Defined contribution plan, Retirement plan
>
>*The airline's employee satisfaction ratings turned completely around once it started an* **ESOP**.

Extended IRA (Individual retirement account)
A special retirement arrangement that lets the original owner of an IRA pass on the tax-advantaged distributions to his heirs. Annual payments are made from the IRA as if the original owner were collecting them. Also called a "stretch IRA."

See also: Beneficiary, IRA

Maddie made her nephew the beneficiary of her **extended IRA**.

Five-year rule
A regulation that states retirement account holdings must be distributed by December 31 of the fifth year after the original owner dies if he died before required distributions began and the beneficiary did not opt to take distributions over his own life expectancy.

See also: Required minimum distribution, Retirement account

George's daughter made arrangements to extend her father's retirement benefits so she wasn't constrained by the **five-year rule**.

Hardship withdrawal
An emergency early distribution taken from a retirement account before distributions are allowed (currently when the account holder is at least fifty-nine and a half years old), subject to special tax rules, potentially including a 10% penalty. This withdrawal cannot be repaid into the retirement account, so it permanently decreases the value of the account.

See also: Retirement account

After the flood, Jacob was qualified for a **hardship withdrawal** *but didn't want to use it because he wouldn't have time to replace the funds.*

IRA (Individual retirement account)
A tax-advantaged personal savings and investment fund from which monies cannot be withdrawn without penalty until the owner has attained an age specified by law (currently fifty-nine and a half).

See also: 401(k), Retirement plan, Roth IRA

Having an **IRA** *is a convenient and practical way to save for retirement.*

Inherited IRA (Individual retirement account)
A special IRA setup that allows a testamentary beneficiary to continue the tax-advantaged distributions as if he had been the original owner. Basically "stretches" the time period over which the retirement account earnings can grow tax-deferred. Also called a "stretch IRA."

See also: Beneficiary, IRA

In order to extend the time on tax-deferred growth, Marc set up an **inherited IRA** *for his kids.*

Keogh plan
A tax-advantaged retirement account available only to self-employed individuals. May be designed in the money purchase or profit-sharing format. (Pronounced KEE-oh.)
>See also: Money purchase plan, Profit-sharing plan, Retirement plan, SEP plan, SIMPLE plan
>
>*When Shay became a self-employed artist, she was thrilled to learn about the* **Keogh plan** *because she had been concerned about retirement savings.*

Longevity risk
The chance that a pension or life insurance company may run out of funds due to increased life expectancies, which call for bigger payouts (and longer payment streams) than planned for.
>See also: Life insurance, Pension
>
>*As the average person lives longer, the* **longevity risk** *increases for everyone.*

Lump-sum distribution
A one-time payout instead of a steady payment stream. Often talked about in regard to things such as retirement accounts and lottery winnings.
>See also: Required minimum distribution, Rollover IRA
>
>*Jane took the* **lump-sum distribution** *from her lottery winnings and invested it wisely enough that she made more than if she had taken it in increments.*

Money purchase plan
A retirement arrangement where an employer makes legally mandatory contributions to individual employee accounts in proportion with their (the employee's) earnings, regardless of the company's profitability.
>See also: Keogh plan, Profit-sharing plan
>
>*Many small business owners avoid* **money purchase plans** *because they don't want to be forced to make contributions when they're not making profits.*

PBGC (Pension Benefit Guaranty Corporation)
A not-for-profit entity (operating under the Department of Labor) that insures retirement payments for specific retirement plans should the plans themselves be unable to make those payments to retirees.
>See also: Defined benefit plan
>
>*The* **PBGC** *took steps to help protect Enron employees' pensions after the company's financial fiascos came to light.*

Pension
A retirement plan where an employer contributes money into an account on behalf of an employee for that employee's future use.

See also: Defined benefit plan, Defined contribution plan

The steel workers' **pension** *plan was known as one of the best in the state.*

Pretax contribution
Paycheck deductions that are made before federal and state obligations are calculated.

See also: After-tax contribution, Retirement account

Linda's paycheck included **pretax contributions** *toward her health insurance and 401(k) plan.*

Profit-sharing plan
A retirement arrangement where an employer makes contributions to individual employee accounts based on a percentage of profits earned by the company.

See also: Keogh plan, Money purchase plan

Many small companies offer a **profit-sharing plan** *as part of their benefits package.*

Qualified retirement plan
A deferred savings vehicle that meets both IRS and ERISA requirements, allowing participant accounts to retain special tax benefits.

See also: 401(k) plan, ERISA, IRS

In order to reap all the available tax benefits of financial planning, it is important be invested in a **qualified retirement plan.**

Required minimum distribution (RMD)
The amount that people have to take out of their retirement accounts when they hit the official retirement age (currently seventy and a half). Calculated based on factors including the account balance and owner's life expectancy. Often called "minimum required distribution."

See also: Retirement account

As soon as Susan turned seventy, she began taking the **required minimum distributions** *from her IRA in order to avoid IRS penalties.*

Retirement account
A tax-advantaged vehicle into which employees and self-employed individuals contribute money that will not be withdrawn until they retire. There are many types of retirement accounts, including IRAs and 401(k)s.

See also: 401(k), IRA

Pauline had no clue which **retirement account** *was right for her until she spoke with a trusted financial advisor.*

Retirement plan
An arrangement where funds are held for participants until they reach retirement age and stop earning money from employment. Typically holds tax-advantaged funds. May be offered by an employer as an employee benefit.

See also: Defined benefit plan, Defined contribution plan, Pension

As an independent contractor, Jessica couldn't depend on an employer to provide a **retirement plan** *so she found herself a financial advisor.*

Rollover
To transfer the holdings in a retirement account to a different retirement account with no alteration in tax status. Also used to describe the transfer of funds from a matured investment into another investment of the same type, such as with a certificate of deposit.

See also: Certificate of deposit, Retirement account

When Nichelle changed jobs, she was able to **rollover** *her 401(k) monies into the new company's investment plan.*

Rollover IRA (Individual retirement account)
A tax-advantaged savings plan that is moved from one financial institution to another. Must be done correctly to ensure there is no loss in tax benefits.

See also: IRA, Retirement plan

When Randi left her corporate job and started her own company, she opened a **rollover IRA**.

Roth IRA (Individual retirement account)
A special form of tax-advantaged savings where current contributions are taxed but distributions—including earnings—are completely tax-free when the owner meets certain requirements.

See also: IRA, Retirement plan

Many people have a **Roth IRA** *in order to complement the retirement plans offered by employers.*

Roth IRA conversion

When a person transfers their traditional IRA into a Roth IRA. Income tax is usually assessed on the IRA at that time, as traditional IRAs are based on pretax dollars and Roth IRAs are based on after-tax dollars.

See also: IRA, Rollover IRA

When Akira's IRA started earning more money and he could afford the current tax bill, he did a **Roth IRA conversion** *to help save more in taxes down the line.*

SEP plan (Simplified Employee Pension)

A retirement savings arrangement specifically designed for small businesses (with twenty-five or fewer employees) to allow them to offer a retirement benefit to their workers without dealing with the tax and paperwork complexities or prohibitive administrative costs of standard arrangements. Can be set up either like an IRA or like a 401(k). Employers can contribute up to 25% of earnings (employee salaries or business earnings for the owner) each year, subject to annual dollar limits set by the IRS. Pronounced "sep."

See also: IRA, Keogh plan, Retirement plan, SIMPLE plan

The small factory won its employees' loyalty by offering plenty of benefits, including a **SEP plan.**

SEP-IRA (Simplified employee pension-individual retirement account)

A tax-advantaged savings arrangement used by small business owners so they can make deductible contributions on behalf of their workers (which include the owners themselves). Each worker receives a separate, personal IRA into which those contributions are made.

See also: Retirement plan, SEP plan, SIMPLE plan

Danni is self-employed, so her accountant advised her to set up a **SEP-IRA** *to shelter more of her current income.*

SIMPLE plan (Savings incentive match plan for employees)

A retirement arrangement geared toward small-business owners and self-employed individuals with no more than 100 employees. Allows for tax-advantaged investing with minimal administrative burdens for the business owner, where the tradeoff for simplicity is smaller annual contributions than are available with other retirement arrangements. Employees contribute pretax dollars into the plan, and the employer *must* make contributions as well. Employer may not offer any other types of retirement benefits with this plan.

See also: Keogh plan, Retirement plan, SEP plan

The designer was excited when her shop became successful enough that she could offer her staff a **SIMPLE plan.**

Saver's tax credit
A direct deduction from income taxes due given to people who put money into a qualified retirement plan (such as a 401(k) or an IRA). Prorated based on the person's income and his retirement contribution (up to maximum of $2,000 under current law).

See also: Retirement plan, Tax credit

Learning about the **saver's tax credit** *was what finally got Mandy to open an IRA.*

Social Security
A federal insurance program that offers small monthly stipends to citizens who are either unable to work or have attained the legal retirement age.

See also: Retirement plan

Workers pay into **social security** *throughout their careers in order to receive benefits after retirement.*

Stretch IRA (Individual retirement account)
A special IRA setup that allows the original owner, upon his death, to pass on the tax-advantaged distributions to a beneficiary. Annual payments continue to be made from the account as if the original owner were collecting them, rather than as a lump sum that would be subject to immediate taxation. Essentially "stretches" the amount of time over which account earnings can grow tax-deferred.

See also: Beneficiary, IRA

Jan's retirement account was a **stretch IRA** *because he had every intention of being able to leave money to his children.*

Target benefit plan
A retirement arrangement where contributions are variable, and calculated based on desired future payouts, though the amount of those payouts is not guaranteed.

See also: Defined benefit plan, Defined contribution plan

Since Rachel had other investments as well, she opted for a **target benefit plan** *hoping the payouts would meet her goals.*

Tax-deferred
Describing current earnings which will be taxed in the future.

See also: Retirement account

The contributions made to a 401(k) plan, as well as any plan earnings, are **tax-deferred.**

Vested

Having full ownership rights. Usually used in regard to employer contributions to employees' retirement accounts, where the employee doesn't own those contributions right away. Instead, he accrues portions of ownership over time (for example 20% vested after one year of service, 40% vested after two years of service, 100% vested after five years of service). Once the employee is fully vested, he is the sole owner of the funds, and they cannot be taken back by the employer.

See also: Retirement account

On her five-year anniversary at Lion Joe, Shula was finally fully **vested** *in her 401(k).*

STOCKS

10-K (Form 10-K)
A formal annual report required by the SEC of publicly traded companies, which must include specific information about the prior year's financial performance, such as audited financial statements.

See also: Annual report, Financial statements, SEC

Martin always examines a company's **10-K** *in addition to its glossy annual report before deciding whether to invest.*

Accumulated dividend
An earnings distribution that is due but not yet distributed to a preferred stockholder.

See also: Cumulative preferred stock, Dividend, Preferred stock

The shareholders were glad when their **accumulated dividends** *were finally paid.*

Acquisition
When one company buys another company (called the "target company"), usually by purchasing the target company's stock.

See also: Hostile takeover, Takeover bid

The **acquisition** *of Lion Joe Aviation raised the aviation company's stock almost immediately because of LJA's excellent reputation.*

After-market performance
The price activity of a security right after its initial public offering.

See also: IPO

Although the stock price skyrocketed initially, its **after-market performance** *was weak.*

After the bell
Following the close of the stock market. Based on the NYSE, which ends the daily trading session by ringing a bell.

See also: Closing tick, New York Stock Exchange

In the last few minutes of trading, there tends to be a frantic push so brokers aren't holding orders **after the bell.**

Air pocket stock

Corporate shares whose price suddenly plunges (as sometimes happens in airplanes), usually due to bad news.

See also: Selloff

After the scandal broke, shares in the energy corporation became **air pocket stocks** *as investors scrambled.*

All or none order

An instruction to a broker to complete a stock transaction exactly as specified right away or not at all. If the instruction cannot be carried out during the trading day, it's canceled at the market close.

See also: Market order

Since Rob was heading out of the country, he placed an **all or none order** *so if the stock was to be purchased, it would be done before he left.*

American Stock Exchange (AMEX)

The second-largest U.S. marketplace for buying and selling corporate equity securities.

See also: Exchange-traded funds, New York Stock Exchange, Stock

Josie's broker had a seat on the **AMEX** *rather than the NYSE.*

Ankle biter

Stock in a corporation whose market capitalization (calculated by multiplying all outstanding shares by current market price) is less than $1 billion. The slang name for a small-cap stock.

See also: Large-cap stock, Market capitalization

Investing in the right **ankle biter** *can earn investors high returns if the corporation becomes a major player.*

At-the-close order

An instruction to a broker to buy or sell a security as the market stops trading for the day, or as close to the end-of-day price as possible. A last-minute market order.

See also: Closing bell, Market order

Anticipating that the price of the stock would peak near the end of trading, Marc put in an **at-the-close order** *to sell with his broker.*

At-the-opening order
An instruction to a broker to buy or sell a security the moment the market begins trading that day. If not executed at that time, the instruction is canceled.

See also: Market order, Opening bell

Maria expected the price of the new stock to climb steadily throughout the day so she put in an **at-the-opening order** *to buy with her broker.*

Authorized shares
The total number of stock shares that are allowed to be issued by a corporation, as expressed explicitly in its articles of incorporation; if a corporation authorizes 10,000 shares in its articles, only 10,000 shares may be issued unless those articles of incorporation are legally amended.

See also: IPO, Subsequent offering

The corporation could not raise any more capital by issuing stock, as they had already issued all of the **authorized shares.**

Average daily volume
A market measurement calculated by dividing the total number of shares traded during a specified time period by the number of days in the period. Changes in this measurement can indicate future price movements.

See also: Performance, Stock market

The **average daily volume** *in March seemed to indicate that April and May would continue to bring large gains to investors.*

Barometer stock
A stock whose price changes parallel to overall market changes. Almost always stock in a blue-chip corporation whose success (or failure) impacts the economy. Also called a "bellwether."

See also: Leading indicator

Mac suggested his clients track **barometer stocks** *before making certain investment decisions.*

Bellwether
A stock whose movement indicates overall market movement. Usually stock in a major corporation whose success or failure impacts the entire economy.

See also: Leading indicator

James tracked certain **bellwether** *stocks for a few weeks before making any major investments.*

Big Board
A nickname for the New York Stock Exchange, the oldest and largest exchange in the United States.

See also: New York Stock Exchange, Stock exchange

Many global economies are affected by the movements of the **Big Board**.

Blue chip
A phrase used to describe the stock of very large, financially stable, steadily profitable corporations.

See also: Corporation, Stock

After retirement, Ben invested only in **blue chip** *stocks in order to ensure a steady, reliable income.*

Bucket shop
An unethical brokerage firm that tries to unload unprofitable stocks on unsuspecting investors with aggressive sales tactics.

See also: Boiler room, Broker

The young broker quit as soon as he realized the firm that had hired him was nothing more than a **bucket shop**.

Click and mortar
A company that does business both in physical stores and on the Internet (such as Barnes & Noble).

See also: Dot-com

Christine preferred doing business with the **click and mortar** *video store because she could keep a steady stream of movies coming but could also rent one on a whim.*

Close corporation
A small privately held company whose equity is based on stock shares for which there are very few owners, usually all family members. In certain states, these companies operate under modified, easier-to-follow laws than publicly held companies.

See also: Common stock, Corporation

The **close corporation** *had been in the family for generations and no one had any thoughts of going public.*

Closing bell
A ringing signal that indicates the end of a trading session.

See also: Closing tick, Stock market

Anna hoped her broker received her sell order prior to the **closing bell** *of the day.*

Closing tick
A daily stock market measurement used to determine the overall direction of that day's trading. Calculated by subtracting the number of stocks that ended the day lower than their previous trade from the number of stocks that ended the day higher than their previous trade. Can be either positive or negative.

See also: Closing price, Tick

According to the **closing tick,** *the stock market had one of the strongest days of the decade.*

Common stock
The main class of stock of every corporation. Shares signify units of ownership, and come with voting rights and the right to receive a proportional share of declared dividends.

See also: Dividend

Investors can buy shares of **common stock** *in any publicly held corporation.*

Controlling interest
A shareholder (or group of shareholders acting as one) who have enough shares (usually more than 50%, but not necessarily) to win all shareholder votes and directly impact corporate policy.

See also: Voting stock

The family agreed to let the company go public so long as they would retain **controlling interest** *in it.*

Countercyclical stock
Corporate shares whose price moves in the opposite direction of the general economy, thriving even during economic decline.

See also: Cyclical stock

Ron encouraged all of his clients to have at least some shares in a **countercyclical stock** *such as Lion Joe Discount Stores, because more people shop there during tough economic times.*

Cumulative dividend
A per-share earnings distribution from a corporation that accumulates until actually paid to the shareholders. Usually associated with preferred stock.

See also: Dividend, Preferred stock

When Rachel finally got the check for her **cumulative dividends,** *she was able to pay for a long spa weekend for her and her best friend.*

Cumulative preferred stock

Form of equity security where unpaid guaranteed dividends accrue, and have to be paid before dividend payments can be made to common shareholders.

See also: Dividend, Preferred stock

The corporation was having cash flow problems even though it was profitable, so the dividends on the **cumulative preferred stock** *were really stacking up.*

Cup and handle

A visual description of a stock price chart pattern. Usually caused by a pause in an uptrend, where the price dips slowly and steadily, stays flat for a while, then goes back up (this is the cup part). That's followed by a small, quick, sharp decline (the handle), after which the price goes back to a steady uptrend.

See also: Technical analysis

In spite of the minor dips in earnings, Leroy relied on the **cup and handle** *pattern and bought more shares of Lion Joe for his portfolio.*

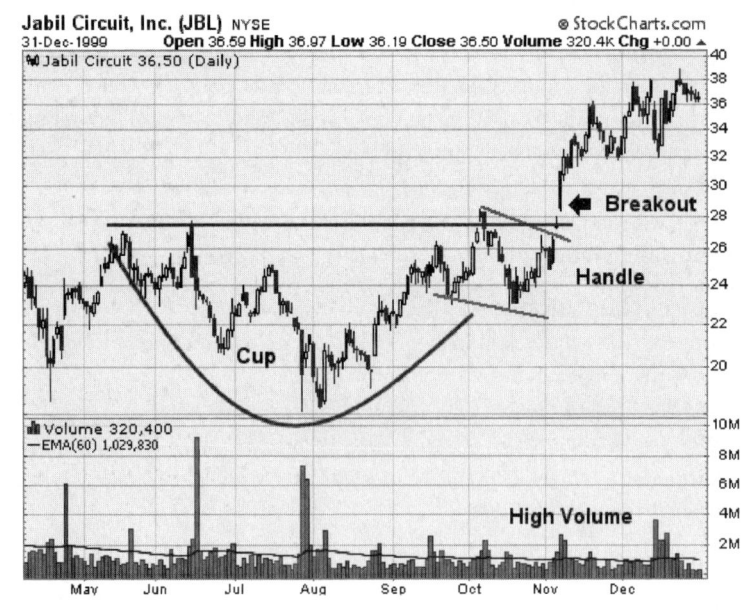

Cup and handle pattern

Cyclical stock

A share in a company that experiences highs and lows on a recurring basis, and whose financial performance is closely tied to prevailing economic factors. Examples include automobile corporations and real estate investments.

See also: Defensive stock

Investors who can stand risk often buy **cyclical stocks** *during their downturns.*

Date of record
The day on which a corporation figures out who is holding the stock entitled to dividend payments. Investors must be recorded as the security-holder on that day in order to receive the dividend. Also called "record date."

See also: Declaration date, Dividend, Ex-dividend date

When buying stock as a gift for someone else, it is important to ensure their name is recorded as the owner by the **date of record** *rather than your own.*

Day order
Instructions to a broker that expire at the end of the current trading period. Most broker instructions fall into this category unless otherwise specified.

See also: Good till Canceled order, Market order, Stop order

Nate gave his broker a **day order** *to sell if the stock reached $110 per share.*

Defensive stock
An equity security whose value and dividend payouts remain stable despite fluctuating economic conditions. Typically shares of corporations that deal in necessities, such as food and energy.

See also: Cyclical stock

As the economy started to weaken, interest in **defensive stocks** *began to rise.*

Delisted
When a security is no longer allowed to continue trading on an exchange. Usually occurs because the issuing company no longer meets the requirements for being listed on the exchange.

See also: Exchange, Listing requirements

The regional bank had been **delisted** *long before it finally failed.*

Dilution
A decrease in earnings per share caused by the issuance of additional shares of stock or by converted securities. The EPS is reduced because the same amount of earnings is now being divided by a greater number of shares.

See also: Convertible bonds, Earnings per share

The corporation decided against issuing new stock because they didn't want **dilution** *to knock down the share price and upset investors.*

Dividend
A distribution of earnings to shareholders by corporations or mutual funds. Corporate distributions can be paid in money or with additional shares.

See also: Earnings, Mutual fund, Stock

Missy received quarterly **dividend** *checks from her blue-chip investments.*

Dividend in arrears
Corporate earnings that were supposed to be paid out to shareholders but were not, and are therefore still owed to the shareholders. Considered a liability of the corporation.

See also: Cumulative dividend, Dividend

As the company began to falter, its **dividends in arrears** *became a concern.*

Dividend payout ratio
A statistical measure of the corporate earnings distributed to shareholders. Calculated by dividing total annual earnings distributions by annual net income. Shows what proportion of corporate earnings are distributed to shareholders.

See also: Dividend, Ratio analysis

Erika loved her Lion Joe stocks, because the high **dividend payout ratio** *provided her with ample cash and still left the company with enough funds to promote growth.*

Dividend rate
Expected corporate earnings distributions made annually. Expressed on a per share basis. Includes any special or extra distributions that may be made, which can occur when earnings are higher than predicted. Expressed as an annualized dollar amount. For example, a quarterly dividend of $1 per share plus a special dividend of $0.30 per share would equal a dividend rate of $4.30 per share.

See also: Dividend

Danica bought shares of Lion Joe when her broker told her the **dividend rate** *was more than $4 per share.*

Dividend reinvestment plan (DRIP)
A program offered by some corporations where investors' earnings are automatically used to purchase additional shares instead of being paid out in cash.

See also: Dividend

Lee opted to participate in a **DRIP** *to help her invest more regularly.*

Dog and pony show
When upper-level executives (such as company CEOs) travel around in an attempt to create interest in their company's upcoming IPO. Also called a "road show."

    See also: IPO, CEO

    The executives enjoyed the **dog and pony show** *as a way to network with other industry professionals.*

Equities
Securities that represent ownership interest, such as stocks.

    See also: Debt securities

    Although the Edith didn't appear to have many assets, the **equities** *in her portfolio showed her to be a wealthy woman.*

Ex-dividend date
Two business days before the date of record. Investors who purchase a security on this day will not be entitled to its dividend. Sometimes called "ex-date."

    See also: Declaration date, Dividend, Record date

    Jared ended up buying stocks on the **ex-dividend date** *so had to wait a full quarter before receiving any payments from it.*

Face value
The token dollar value assigned to each share of stock issued by a corporation. Appears on the stock certificate. Also called "par value" or "stated value."

    See also: Stock, Stock certificate

    Lion Joe Industries intentionally set its shares' **face value** *at zero so it could never trade lower than par.*

Fitch sheet
A report that contains detailed historical securities trading data. Stored in massive financial data banks (the most commonly known is called "Quotron").

    See also: SEC

    The **fitch sheet** *confirmed that the Lion Joe shares really had sold for $108 per share.*

Fortune 500
An annual listing of the 500 highest revenue-generating companies in America.

See also: Bellwether, Blue-chip

*Many new investors start their research with the **Fortune 500**.*

Fully diluted shares
The number of shares in a company that could be outstanding if all employee stock options were exercised and all convertible bonds were converted to shares. Important because it would impact the earnings per share and the per-share dividend payouts, and (probably) the current share price.

See also: Dilution, Dividends, Earnings per share

*Investors should not ignore the information about **fully diluted shares**, because there's a possibility it could impact the value of the shares they hold.*

Glamour stock
An extremely popular security, made so by a strong earnings growth rate and a price that increases faster than normal for the current market.

See also: Coattail investing, Stock

*Sara wanted to buy 100 shares of the **glamour stock**, but her broker advised against it, as the price was already so high there was little chance of profits.*

Going public
When a private company issues and sells shares of common stock to the masses for the first time. Also known as an "IPO" (initial public offering).

See also: Common stock, Prospectus

*Investors were very excited when Lion Joe Communications announced they were **going public**.*

Greensheet
The summary of a prospectus for an upcoming security issue, typically prepared by the underwriting firm for its employees only.

See also: Prospectus, Underwriter

*The brokers were given copies of the **greensheet** to look over in order to build excitement around the new release.*

Growth stock
Shares in a corporation that are expected to show revenue or earnings increases greater than their industry average or than the market as a whole, and therefore provide greater than average increase in market price.

See also: Growth fund, Value stock

*Many investors bought into the new technology stock because it was predicted to be a strong **growth stock**.*

Head-and-shoulders pattern

A descriptive term for a technical analysis graph of a stock's price. This graphical shape occurs when the price first goes up to a high point then drops back down, then goes up to a higher point before falling back down, then returns to a level close to the first high point before falling back down. Considered to be a very reliable trend reversal pattern.

See also: Technical analysis, Trend reversal pattern

Based on the **head-and-shoulders pattern** *of the stock analysis, it appeared to be a good time to sell the investment.*

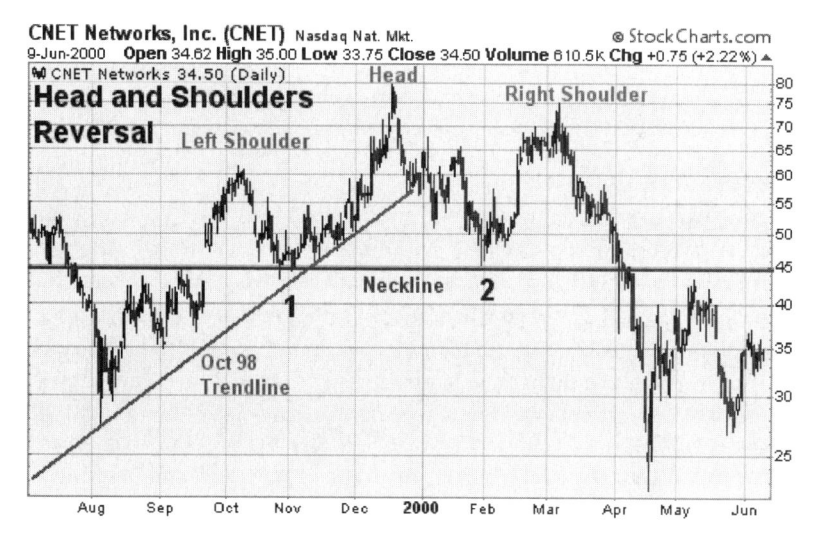

Head-and-shoulders pattern

Hot issue

An IPO that trades for more than the offering price on its first trading day, usually due to overwhelming demand.

See also: IPO, Offering price

Everyone knew the design maven's new company would be a **hot issue** *due to her overwhelming popularity.*

IPO (Initial public offering)

When a private corporation sells shares of its common stock to the general population for the first time.

See also: Common stock, Prospectus

The upcoming **IPO** *of the new communications firm had created quite a bit of excitement among investors.*

Income stock
A corporate security known for consistently paying out regular, high dividends.

See also: Dividend, Growth stock, Stock

June's grandmother always had a healthy stream of cash thanks to the **income stocks** *in her portfolio.*

Information circular
A letter sent out to corporate shareholders to let them know about agenda items in an upcoming shareholders meeting. Usually also includes a proxy form, for shareholders who will not be present at the meeting.

See also: Proxy

The man always read through the **information circular** *before deciding if it was worth it to attend the shareholders meeting or just vote by proxy.*

Interest-sensitive stock
A stock whose price changes when prevailing interest rates change. Some stocks' values are correlated closely with interest rates, and when rates go up their prices go up. Other stocks' values are inversely correlated with interest rates, meaning they go down when interest rates go up. For example, a corporation that has a lot of adjustable-rate debt on its books would see a stock price drop as rates go up because it would have to pay out more interest; but the holders of that debt would see their share prices go up because they'd be receiving more interest.

See also: Interest rate, Stock

Jerry sold all of his **interest-sensitive stock** *as rates began to go up.*

January effect
A phenomenon where stock prices—especially for small caps—tend to rise as the New Year kicks off.

See also: Calendar effect, Small-cap stock

Pam's CPA advised her to buy in December in order to take advantage of the **January effect.**

Large-cap stock
Shares in a corporation whose total market value exceeds $5 billion (calculated by multiplying the total outstanding shares by their current market price).

See also: Market capitalization, Mid-cap stock, Small-cap stock

Since he wanted to minimize the risk in his investments, Adam held a lot of **large-cap stocks** *in his portfolio.*

Listed
Meeting the requirements to be included and traded on an exchange.
> See also: Exchange

After a decade of hard work and high earnings, Lion Joe Technology was finally able to be **listed** *on the stock exchange.*

Listing requirements
Minimum standards that corporations must meet in order to be eligible for trading on a stock exchange. Should a corporation slip below the minimum, it will be delisted. Each exchange (such as NYSE, AMEX) has its own standards, but each exchange generally includes minimum market capitalization and number of shares issued.
> See also: Exchange, Market capitalization

During its 100-year history, the corporation had always well exceeded **listing requirements.**

Majority shareholder
An individual (or group acting in concert) who holds more than half of the outstanding voting stock of a corporation.
> See also: Minority interest, Shareholder, Voting stock

The woman made sure she stayed the **majority shareholder.**

Market capitalization
The value of a corporation, based on the current trading price of its shares. Calculated by multiplying the total shares outstanding by the current trading price.
> See also: Large-cap stock, Mid-cap stock, Small-cap stock

After a huge rally, Lion Joe's **market capitalization** *grew enough for the corporation to finally join the ranks of the large-caps.*

Metrics
Key performance measures for a company, such as earnings per share.
> See also: Earnings per share, Multiple

Investors were pleased when the **metrics** *on the corporation started to rise again after the change of management.*

Mid-cap stock
Shares in a company whose total market value (calculated by multiplying all outstanding shares by current market price) falls between $1 billion and $5 billion (though some analysts use slightly different values to define the tier).
> See also: Large-cap stock, Market capitalization, Small-cap stock

Jeanne invested in **mid-cap stocks,** *because they were established companies that still had room for substantial growth.*

Minority interest

An individual or company that holds less than 50% but still a substantial portion of a corporation's voting stock.

See also: Controlling interest, Majority shareholder

Even though the Surino family held a **minority interest**, *they were still able to significantly influence the board's decisions.*

Multiple

A measure of a company's financial state that is calculated by dividing one metric (a key financial statistic) into another. For example, a price-to-earnings ratio shows how much people are willing to pay for $1 of earnings, and a result of 10 would mean they were willing to pay 10 times earnings (i.e., the earnings multiplied by 10).

See also: Metrics, Price-to-earnings ratio

Nausheen always looked at price **multiples** *before advising her clients about which stocks to buy.*

NASDAQ (National Association of Securities Dealers Automated Quotation System)

An American stock exchange facilitating the trading of more than 3,200 corporations' shares.

See also: American Stock Exchange, New York Stock Exchange

Changes in the **NASDAQ** *are often precursors to shifts in the American economy.*

Neckline

On a head-and-shoulders graph, the horizontal line that marks the low price points; sort of a floor for the pattern. A price move that sinks far below the neckline indicates the end of any upward movement.

See also: Head-and-shoulders pattern, Technical analysis

The CFO was relieved to see the stocks start moving upward again before they hit the **neckline** *on the chart.*

New York Stock Exchange (NYSE)

The world's largest forum (by dollar volume) for trading stocks. "Big Board."

See also: American Stock Exchange, NASDAQ

The **NYSE** *is located on Wall Street in New York City.*

No-par value stock

Corporate shares that are issued with no defined par value.

See also: Par value, Stock

Lion Joe Inc. issued one million shares of **no-par value stock** *because they didn't want to owe money to their shareholders if the stock tanked on the open market.*

Offering circular
A condensed version of a full prospectus for a new security to develop interest in that security. Available to potential individual investors and brokerage firms.

See also: Greensheet, Prospectus

The aviation company sent out an **offering circular** *announcing its intention to issue additional shares.*

Offering date
The first day on which a securities issue will be available to the public.

See also: IPO, Offering circular

The industry was buzzing with the news of the **offering date** *for the new aerospace corporation.*

Offering price
The initial price assigned to shares being sold as part of an IPO, as set by the underwriters.

See also: IPO

The **offering price** *was intentionally lower than could have been asked in the hopes it would attract even more investors despite the bear market.*

Opening bell
A signal to begin trade on a securities exchange.

See also: Stock exchange

Trading begins hard and fast as soon as the **opening bell** *rings.*

Outside day
When the high and low on a trading day exceed those of the previous day (higher high and lower low). For example, if a stock's high and low were $50 and $40 (respectively) on Wednesday, then $55 and $35 on Thursday. An outside day can suggest increasing volatility.

See also: Volatility

Risk-averse investors were wary when the stock kept experiencing **outside days**.

Over-the-counter (OTC)
When a security is bought or sold outside a formal exchange (such as the NYSE), usually traded directly with a dealer network (a group of brokers who buy and sell shares to each other). Typically involves securities ineligible to be listed (and therefore traded) on a formal exchange.

See also: Exchange, Listing requirements, Penny stock

Rose began her investment career buying **OTC** *stocks with money she made from her lemonade stand.*

Overhang
A percentage measure of the amount of dilution shareholders would face if employee stock options were exercised. If all the employees exercised their stock options, there would be more shares outstanding, and that could lead to lower dividend payouts per share, and lower market price per share.

See also: Dilution, Options

Francesca was concerned that her dividends would be smaller than usual because of the **overhang**.

Par value
The nominal dollar amount assigned to a share of stock by the issuing corporation and printed on each stock certificate. Also called "face value" or "stated value."

See also: Stock, Stock certificate

Many corporations set their shares' **par value** *at zero so the stock can never trade below par.*

Participating preferred stock
Preferred stock shares that allow holders to get their guaranteed dividend, then an additional dividend after common shareholders have been paid a specified dividend. Allows preferred shareholders to participate in profits above and beyond those used to pay the standard dividend.

See also: Preferred stock

Clare had enough capital that she was able to buy **participating preferred stock** *almost every time she bought into a new company.*

Penny stock
An equity security, usually issued by a very small company, which sells for less than $1 per share. In some cases, the definition is expanded to include such securities with market value less than $5 per share. Tend to be considered highly risky investments.

See also: Stock

Many new investors are attracted to **penny stocks** *because they don't cost a lot, not realizing that they are much riskier than other stocks.*

Preferred stock
Shares of a corporation that enjoy dividend priority over common shares, and typically receive regularly scheduled dividends regardless of corporate profitability. These shares do not enjoy voting privileges.

See also: Common stock, Dividend

Sam's **preferred stock** *gave him a steady stream of dividend income.*

Price-to-earnings ratio (P/E ratio)
The market value of a single share of stock divided by the corporate net profit attributable to that individual share; shows the relationship between an investment and its historical earnings, and is typically used to compare stocks with each other. A lower P/E ratio means you're paying less for more earnings.
> See also: Earnings Per Share, Market value, Net income

Patrick always looked for stocks with **P/E ratios** *under 10.*

Price multiple
Any ratio that includes share price as one of the numbers, including price-to-earnings ratio and price/book ratio. Helps investors see how the market price relates to the company's financial information (on a per share basis).
> See also: Price/book ratio, Price-to-earnings ratio

Celia was disappointed by Lion Joe's **price multiples**, *so she sold her shares.*

Prospectus
A formal document, filed with the SEC, that contains detailed information about an investment that will be offered to the public. Legally required before a security can be offered, so potential investors can make informed choices about whether or not to purchase the security.
> See also: IPO, Offering circular, SEC

The marketing department made sure that the **prospectus** *was ready to submit to the SEC a week ahead of schedule.*

Proxy
A person authorized to act on behalf of another person, such as a shareholder who cannot attend a meeting but still wants to vote his shares.
> See also: Voting rights

Since most investors cannot travel to meetings, many votes are cast by **proxy**.

Publicly held
Securities available to be bought and sold by anyone on the open market.
> See also: Private placement

The SEC has strict rules about **publicly held** *securities.*

Quarterly report
An accounting of corporate earnings produced every three months, as required of publicly held companies by the SEC. Also called "quarterly earnings report."
> See also: Annual report, SEC

The **quarterly report** *showed the company had made 2% more than originally predicted.*

Quorum

The minimum number of key people who must be present in order for a corporate meeting—and the resulting decisions—to be considered valid. The minimum number is determined by the corporate charter. Basically used to make sure that plenty of shareholders are present when the board of directors wants to make changes.

See also: Board of directors, Corporation

The vote could not be taken when the secretary realized there wasn't a **quorum** *at the meeting.*

Record date

The day on which a dividend-paying entity determines who is holding the associated securities. Investors must be in the books as the security-holder on that day to be entitled to receive the dividend.

See also: Declaration date, Dividend, Ex-dividend date

Since Josephine bought her grandchildren stocks, she always made sure their names, rather than her name, were listed by the **record date.**

Record high

The top price ever reached by a security or an index.

See also: Index

Investors were thrilled when the new product launch took stock prices to a **record high.**

Record low

The lowest price ever hit by a security or an index. Usually seen as very bad news for a publicly traded security.

See also: Index

Economists and pundits started talking about a recession when the NASDAQ 100 Index headed toward a **record low.**

Reverse stock split

When a company reduces the number of shares it has on the open market, usually to increase individual share price or earnings per share, though its total market capitalization remains unchanged. For example, a 1-for-2 reverse stock split means that for every two shares held by a shareholder, he now has only 1 share; a holding of 100 shares would now be 50 shares.

See also: Market capitalization, Stock split

When the CFO realized the market had been saturated, he recommended a **reverse stock split.**

Road show
When high-level executives travel around trying to generate interest in their company's upcoming IPO.

See also: IPO

The CEO and CFO dreaded the prelaunch **road show** *but knew it would help opening day sales so went along with it for the good of the company.*

Round lot
The standard quantity for a securities trade: 100 shares of stock, or five bonds. Also called a "normal lot."

See also: Odd lot, Trade

Bonnie always bought **round lots** *because the commissions were slightly lower.*

Shooting star
A unique candlestick pattern, with a very short black body (which indicates an overall losing day) and a very long top wick (at least twice as long as the body). Happens when the price of a stock goes much higher than the opening price during the day, but closes at a price lower than the open.

See also: Candlestick, Technical analysis

The stock's heavy trading was confirmed by the appearance of several **shooting stars** *on the graph.*

Small-cap stock
Shares in a company whose total market value (calculated by multiplying all outstanding shares by current market price) is less than $1 billion (though some analysts consider $2 billion as the tier cutoff).

See also: Large-cap stock, Market capitalization

Many people wish they had invested in the blue-chip corporations back when they were just **small-cap stocks.**

Stock
A share of ownership in a corporation. May be bought and sold on the secondary market, or directly from the corporation in a public offering.

See also: Corporation, Secondary market

The old woman made sure all of her **stock** *went to her only grandchild rather than have her children argue over it.*

Stock certificate
A legal document that signifies shares of ownership in a corporation.

See also: Corporation

Rita kept her **stock certificates** *in a safety deposit box at her bank.*

Stock dividend
Earnings distributed by a corporation in the form of additional shares rather than in cash.

See also: Dividend

Maddie didn't mind getting **stock dividends** *because she believed the company was solid and it would pay off in the long run.*

Stock exchange
A forum for trading shares of corporations, also known as "stocks."

See also: American Stock Exchange, NASDAQ, New York Stock Exchange; Stock

More money can be lost on the **stock exchange** *in one day than most people make in a lifetime.*

Stock market
A forum where equities and securities can be openly traded.

See also: American Stock Exchange, NASDAQ, New York Stock Exchange

Entire fortunes have been made and lost on the American **stock market.**

Stock options
Derivative securities that give the holder the right, but not the obligation, to buy or sell specific corporate shares for a predetermined price (regardless of current market price).

See also: Corporation, Derivatives

The man was ordered by the judge to offer his ex-wife **stock options** *as they came available through his company.*

Stock screener
A program that selects stocks based on predefined criteria, such as a P/E ratio of less than 10 and an EPS of at least $0.05 per share. Many are available free on the Internet.

See also: Price-to-earnings ratio

The broker often used a sophisticated **stock screener** *to find stocks that fit his clients' specific requirements.*

Stock split
When a corporation changes its total number of shares outstanding, then adjusts the price of each share accordingly. Each shareholder maintains the same value he had before the change, but holds more individual shares.

See also: Stock

The couple was thrilled to hear of the **stock split** *because it immediately increased the number of shares in their son's college fund.*

Subsequent offering
When a corporation issues and sells additional shares directly to the public, after they've already had an IPO. Usually done when the corporation needs more money, but does not want to take on additional debt. Dilutes existing shares.
See also: Dilution, Equity financing, IPO

Lion Joe Marketing's **subsequent offering** *angered and frustrated initial investors.*

Tenbagger
A superstar stock whose value increases tenfold over its original purchase price over time. Usually starts out as a small company with a unique or innovative product, then eventually grows into a large-cap stock. Investors only capture these incredible returns when they use a buy-and-hold.
See also: Capital gains, Large-cap stock, Small-cap stock

When Jason gave his friends startup capital for their business, he had no idea he was investing in a **tenbagger** *or that they would all be millionaires before age thirty-five.*

Ticker symbol
A small group of characters (usually letters) that represents the name of a publicly traded security, used to facilitate tracking and trading of that security.
See also: Exchange

By the age of ten, Joshua could find his stock's **ticker symbol** *in the paper even though he only owned a few shares.*

Ticker tape
A strip (now computerized) that provides up-to-the-minute market information to investors. Information relays include stock symbols (also called "ticker symbols"), current market price, and trading volume.
See also: Ticker symbol, Trading volume

Many financial programs and even some news shows run a **ticker tape** *along the bottom of the television screen during trading hours.*

Tombstone
A newspaper ad placed by the investment bankers responsible for a public offering. Usually appears in financial newspapers (such as the *Wall Street Journal*). Includes information about the offering, such as the offering price and a listing of all the underwriters involved.
See also: IPO, Lead underwriter, Subsequent offering

The latest **tombstone** *about Lion Joe Inc. created so much buzz that the stocks sold in record time.*

Value stock
Corporate shares whose market price is relatively low compared to its true worth based on a fundamental analysis, and whose current pricing doesn't reflect their true worth.

See also: Growth stock

James bought **value stock** *trusting that, eventually, the price would match what the company was actually worth.*

Voting rights
A benefit that comes with shares of common stock, which allows the investor the chance to vote on important corporate matters, such as selecting a board of directors.

See also: Board of directors, Proxy

As a minimal investor in the company, the young woman rarely took advantage of her **voting rights.**

Voting stock
A class of shares that gives the owner the right to participate in corporate elections; not all kinds of shares have this right.

See also: Preferred stock

Since public policy was as important to Steve as making money, he made sure to always buy **voting stock** *so he would have a voice in the direction the companies took.*

White paper
A report put out by a company to inform the public about an upcoming event, such as a product launch.

See also: Annual report, Offering circular

The CEO made sure that the **white paper** *was delivered to all the brokers that had invested in similar stocks over the last year.*

XD
The symbol used in a newspaper to indicate a stock that's reached its ex-dividend date, commonly referred to as "going ex-dividend."

See also: Ex-dividend date, Dividend, *Wall Street Journal*

Edith never bought stocks when she saw the **XD** *marking in the paper.*

Yo-yo stock
A highly volatile corporate equity security whose share price goes up and down.

See also: Stock, Volatility

Only investors with a high tolerance for stress and risk should invest in **yo-yo stock** *because simply owning them could cause ulcers.*

TAXES

1040
The standard federal income tax form used by individuals to report their annual income and calculate the amount of federal income tax due.
See also: Income Tax, Tax preparer, Taxable income
Filling out a **1040** *is surprisingly easy if you are willing to go slowly and pay close attention to each field.*

1099
The federal form used by the payer to report nonemployee income (i.e., not salary or wages), such as interest, dividends, and other miscellaneous earnings, to the payee and the IRS.
See also: Income tax, Unearned income
Anyone who wins the lottery will receive a **1099** *stating his winnings.*

Abusive tax shelter
A financial vehicle created for the purposes of avoiding taxation in a manner which the IRS has deemed illegal.
See also: IRS, Tax shelter
Al lost a client rather than abide by her wishes that he set up an **abusive tax shelter** *for her.*

Adjusted gross income (AGI)
A federal tax calculation, where specific deductions (such as alimony payments made and some IRA contributions) are taken from total earnings to arrive at an amount on which other tax computations will be based.
See also: Alimony, IRA
Ilona's **adjusted gross income** *was significantly less than her total income due to the large alimony payments she made to her ex-husband.*

Adoption credit
A direct subtraction from income taxes due for each newly adopted child under the age of eighteen.
See also: Income tax, Tax credit
Adam and Teri were pleased to discover they were eligible for an **adoption credit** *after adopting their baby girl.*

After-tax basis
A calculation to determine the return on an investment after the effects of state and federal assessments have been accounted for. Typically used to compare the returns of corporate and municipal bonds.

See also: Corporate bonds, Municipal bond

Abby's New York state bonds returned more than her IBM bond holdings on an **after-tax basis.**

After-tax contribution
Money put into a retirement (or other) account after that money has already had income taxes taken out of it.

See also: Pretax contribution, Retirement account

Adam's Roth IRA and all of his regular investment accounts were funded with **after-tax contributions.**

After-tax return
The total earnings made on an investment minus the applicable taxes due on those earnings. Used to compare regular and tax-advantaged securities (such as corporate bonds to municipal bonds).

See also: Capital gains, Dividend

The difference in the potential **after-tax return** *helped Joan decide which bonds to purchase.*

Alimony
Money paid to an ex-spouse as ordered in a divorce settlement. Alimony is generally tax-deductible to the payer and taxable income for the receiver. Also called "spousal support."

See also: Tax-deductible, Taxable income

Alan was required to pay **alimony** *of $3,000 per month to his ex-wife.*

Alternative minimum tax (AMT)
A federal duty imposed on a recalculated income without the effect of specific "preference" items normally deductible from income calculations. Taxpayers pay whichever is greater, the AMT or their normally calculated income tax liability.

See also: Income tax, Tax deductible

In spite of the deductions she was allowed on the standard form, she still ended up paying a hefty **alternative minimum tax.**

Archer MSA (Medical savings account)
A tax-advantaged account used to pay for health-related expenses only. Interest earned on the account is tax-deferred, and may be tax-free when withdrawals are used for qualifying medical expenses. Must be used in conjunction with high-deductible health insurance plans. Though no new plans may be set up (they ended in 2007), contributions may be made to existing plans.
> See also: High-deductible health plan, Tax-deferred

When Stephanie's doctor ordered expensive tests, she was grateful she had opened an **Archer MSA** *when she signed up for her primary health insurance.*

Backup withholding
An IRS tactic to ensure tax collection on investment income by taking taxes directly out of payouts (such as dividends or interest). Similar to withholding taxes on paychecks.
> See also: IRS, Taxable income

Thanks to **backup withholding,** *Susan didn't owe any more taxes on her investments come April 15.*

Bracket creep
A phenomenon where income goes up, and is taxed at a higher rate due to inflation, even though there's no increase in actual purchasing power.
> See also: Purchasing power, Tax bracket

Jason's raise was frustrating because its only result was a **bracket creep.**

Capital gains
The excess of sale price of an investment asset over its total purchase cost.
> See also: Capital loss

The young couple was thrilled with the **capital gains** *from the sale of the Lion Joe shares they had bought only a few years earlier.*

Capital gains exclusion
A tax advantage that allows a taxpayer to avoid taxation on all or a portion of profits earned by selling an asset, most commonly in relation to the sale of a primary residence.
> See also: Capital gains, Taxable income

Before putting their house on the market, the couple researched the **capital gains exclusion** *available to them, in order to see if they'd have to put aside any money for the tax bill.*

Capital gains tax

A federal levy on profits made when the sale price of an asset exceeds the purchase price. The rate charged depends on how long the asset was held after it was purchased.

> See also: Capital gains

When Susan sold her shares of Lion Joe Textbooks Inc., she was glad to owe some **capital gains tax** *because it meant she'd made money on her first stock.*

Child tax credit

A direct deduction from income taxes due for each qualifying child in a household as listed on a tax return. Qualifying children are under seventeen years old and are U.S. citizens with their own social security numbers.

> See also: Adoption credit, Income tax

The couples' tax preparer had to remind them they no longer received the **child tax credit** *after their youngest daughter turned eighteen.*

Deductible (adjective)

An expense that may be legally subtracted from otherwise taxable income.

> See also: Expense, Taxable income

Mortgage interest and property taxes are both **deductible** *expenses for federal income tax purposes.*

Double taxation

The phenomenon where corporate earnings are taxed once by the government, and then again when they are distributed to shareholders as taxable dividends.

> See also: Corporation, Dividend, Income tax

Small corporation owners don't always realize that they'll be hit with **double taxation** *when they pay themselves dividends.*

Earned income

Compensation received as a result of intentional efforts, such as employment or self-employed business profits. Category includes such payments as salaries, wages, commissions, consulting fees, bonuses, and tips.

> See also: Adjusted gross income, Unearned income

Aisha's **earned income** *fluctuated weekly based on the number and quality of the tips she received.*

Earned income credit
A federal refundable tax break available to low-income citizens that allows eligible people to receive tax refunds even if they did not have any income taxes withheld from their paychecks.

> See also: Income tax, Tax credit

The one silver lining Jack was able to find when he had to take the pay cut was he would be eligible for the **earned income credit** *at tax time.*

Enrolled agent
A federally licensed professional who can represent taxpayers before the Internal Revenue Service.

> See also: CPA, Tax attorney

When June was notified she was being audited, she made sure to hire an **enrolled agent** *to assist her with the proceeding.*

Estate tax
A government levy on the total value of all property transferred by a decedent to his heirs and beneficiaries.

> See also: Estate

Since there was little planning before the man's death, his heirs faced hefty **estate taxes.**

Exempt income
Earnings that are not subject to taxation.

> See also: Taxable income

Child support payments are usually considered **exempt income.**

FSA (Flexible spending account)
Pretax reimbursement plans used to cover personal medical expenses that are not otherwise covered by health insurance, such as copays, deductibles and medical supplies. Money is deducted directly from paychecks on a pretax basis and placed in these funds. Any money not used within the plan year is forfeited by the employee.

> See also: Health insurance, Pretax contribution

June signed up for her company's **FSA** *because her two boys so often had to go to the doctor.*

Flat tax
An arrangement where everyone is levied at the same rate, regardless of income level.

> See also: Income tax, Tax bracket

In spite of the senator's best efforts, she couldn't get a **flat tax** *passed through Congress.*

Gains
The amount by which the sale price of an investment asset exceeds its full purchase cost. Also called "capital gains."

See also: Capital loss

The drop in the housing market kept the couple from getting the **gains** *they had hoped for.*

Gas guzzler tax
An extra sales tax charged on cars that have bad fuel efficiency.

See also: Sin tax

Many states that are concerned about their natural environments apply a **gas guzzler tax** *in an attempt to encourage people to drive more efficient cars or drive less.*

Generation-skipping tax
A federal levy imposed on inheritance assets (in excess of exempted amounts) left to grandchildren or later heirs instead of children, which allows for the avoidance of one level of the federal levy. If grandparents left money to their children, who in turn left money to their children, the estate tax would be assessed twice; by "skipping" straight to the grandchildren, the government would lose revenues, so this tax was instituted. Current law sets the levy rate at 45% on bequests exceeding $3.5 million in 2009; the tax is repealed entirely for 2010; and reverts to 45% rate on bequests exceeding $1 million in 2011.

See also: Estate tax, Gift tax

The old woman left her grandson a large inheritance, unaware that the **generation-skipping tax** *would be levied on most of it.*

Gift Tax
A federal (and sometimes state) assessment levied on anything of value given to another person in exchange for less than the item is worth. Can be as high as 45%; is only charged to the gift giver, not the recipient; and only becomes payable when the gift giver gives more than the annual gift tax deduction and has used up the lifetime exclusion. Spouses are almost always excluded from gift-tax issues.

See also: Estate tax, Gift splitting

George bought his girlfriend a $25,000 car for her birthday, and was afraid he owed **gift taxes** *on the $13,000 over the annual deduction limit until his accountant reminded him about the lifetime exclusion.*

Health savings account (HSA)
A triple-tax-advantaged savings account used only in combination with a high-deductible health plan in order to allow users to pay out-of-pocket medical expenses with pretax dollars. The employee contributes money into the account throughout the year (usually through payroll deductions). Those contributions are tax-deductible, the earnings in the account grow tax-free, and withdrawals are tax-free as long as the money is used for qualified medical expenses.

See also: Health insurance, High-deductible health plan

When Brandon had to have surgery, he was grateful he had enrolled in a **health savings account.**

High-deductible health plan (HDHP)
A health insurance policy that charges extremely low premiums in exchange for extremely high-claim deductibles (at least $1,100 for a single person). Appropriate for young, healthy people who don't need consistent medical care. Typically used in connection with a health savings account (HSA).

See also: Health insurance, Health savings account

As a healthy young man with a low income, Vern opted for a **high-deductible health plan**, *assuming he would rarely need to use it.*

Hobby loss
A businesslike loss that is not deductible for tax purposes. Based on the idea that the activity was entered into for fun, not for the purpose of earning income, and therefore the expenses cannot be deducted if they exceed any income earned. (Net income from a hobby, though, must be reported and is taxable.)

See also: Expense, Net income

Mary Anne was crushed when her homemade jams didn't sell well at the Farmers' Market, and again when she found out she couldn't deduct the **hobby loss** *on her tax return.*

Holding period
The amount of time between the purchase and sale of an investment, often used to determine how the sale will be taxed.

See also: Capital gains, Long-term, Short-term

Carol had to pay more taxes than expected when she sold her Lion Joe shares, because her **holding period** *was less than a year.*

Home office expense
A tax deduction available for self-employed individuals who work out of their houses and use Schedule C to report their business income.

See also: Tax deduction

As an independent contractor, Greg was able to deduct part of his rent as a **home office expense.**

IRS (Internal Revenue Service)
The U.S. agency responsible for the collection of taxes.

See also: Estate tax, Income tax

Every year, the **IRS** *receives millions of dollar from U.S. workers.*

Income
All monies earned, including business profits, investment earnings, wages and salaries, commissions, and winnings.

See also: Earnings, Profits

As an artist with few investments and whose paychecks were based on sales, Tabitha's **income** *varied greatly year to year.*

Income Tax
A government levy on all income, profits, and earnings.

See also: Earnings, Income, Profits

The state of Washington is one of the few states in the United States that doesn't have an **income tax.**

Itemized deductions
A listing of expenses that may be subtracted from taxable income. Includes such things as mortgage interest, state and local taxes paid, charitable donations, and medical expenses. Included in a federal income tax return on Schedule A.

See also: Income tax, Taxable income

The couple saved hundreds on their taxes thanks to their **itemized deductions.**

Kiddie tax
An assessment on unearned income transferred to children in order to take advantage of their (usually) lower assessment rates. Designed to limit this income-shifting strategy often employed by high net-worth individuals to avoid high government levies.

See also: Tax bracket, Unearned income

Deb tried to lower the tax bill on her investment earnings by transferring some investments to her son, but she ended up having to pay a **kiddie tax,** *anyway.*

Lifetime-learning credit
A tax decrease available for families with qualified tuition and related expenses for higher education. Current law allows up to $2,000 to offset total income taxes due.

See also: Income tax, Tax credit

Even though they had saved for their daughter's education, when she started college, the family was still grateful for the **lifetime learning credit** *on their taxes.*

Long-term
A period of more than one year, a critical distinction for tax purposes (especially capital gains tax).

See also: Capital gains

Instead of selling his shares on March 1, Derrick waited until March 2 so his holding period would be **long-term,** *and he'd take a smaller tax hit.*

Long-term capital gain
Profit on the sale of an investment held for longer than one year, subject (currently, but that can change) to more favorable tax rates than ordinary income.

See also: Capital gains, Income tax

Since most of the couple's income that year was **long-term capital gains** *from the sale of some blue-chip stocks, they actually did better on their taxes than the year before.*

Loss
For investors, when an asset (such as a security) is sold for less than its purchase price. In business, when total cost of goods sold and expenses exceed revenues.

See also: Capital gains, Profit

Although Olivia would take a **loss,** *once she learned about the company's unethical business practices, she felt she had to sell the stock immediately.*

Loss carryback
A tax accounting procedure that allows a company to apply a current operating loss against prior year's profits in order to get a retroactive tax refund. Losses may be carried back for up to three years.

See also: Loss carryforward

Since the prior year had been profitable, the CFO suggested using a **loss carryback** *to at least reap some tax benefit from this year's dismal performance.*

Loss carryforward
A tax rule that lets currently disallowed losses (due to caps and limits on allowable losses) to be used to offset income in future years. Typically used in regard to passive activity losses and net capital losses.

See also: Capital loss, Passive loss

The first year the real estate investor made serious money, he was very grateful for the **loss carryforward** *that helped lower his current tax bill.*

Luxury tax
An extra sales tax originally levied on the kinds of items bought only by wealthy people (such as fur coats and diamond rings). Now expanded to include sin-tax items. Used to discourage "nonessential" purchases.

See also: Gas guzzler tax, Sin tax

Brad and Janet preferred to shop at duty free stores when they traveled in order to avoid paying the **luxury tax** *on their favorite wines.*

MACRS (Modified Accelerated Cost Recovery System)
An asset depreciation method that allows for bigger expense deductions during the first few years of ownership.

See also: Depreciation

The fishing company used **MACRS** *to deduct a large portion of the purchase price of their new boat, so they sailed off without any tax worries.*

Marginal tax rate
The percentage of levy charged on the next dollar earned, based on the tax bracket schedule at the time

See also: Income tax, Tax rate

At year end, Ben always considered his **marginal tax rate** *before selling any of his profitable securities.*

Marital deduction
A provision in the federal estate tax law that allows an estate of any size to be passed directly to a spouse completely free of federal estate taxes.

See also: Estate tax

Ira knew his beloved wife wouldn't have to worry about estate taxes, thanks to the **marital deduction.**

Marriage tax penalty
A phenomenon where a legally joined couple pays more in levies on their income than they would if they were single and filing separately.

See also: Income shifting

Lorena and Marco were upset when they prepared their first joint tax return, as the **marriage tax penalty** *increased their tax bill.*

Modified adjusted gross income (MAGI)
A tax calculation upon which certain other calculations (such as the deductible portion of IRA contributions) are based. Based on adjusted gross income with certain tax-related items added back, such as college tuition deductions, student loan deductions, and foreign income.

See also: Adjusted gross income, IRA

Jan finally found a reason to be happy about her student loan payments when they helped reduce her **MAGI**.

Nontaxable income
Earnings that are not subject to a government levy. Examples include most life insurance proceeds, child support payments, and veterans' benefits.

See also: Adjusted gross income, Taxable income

Child support payments are **nontaxable income** *in order to ensure the children involved have the money they need.*

Passive activity
A money-making enterprise from which a person can earn profits without actually physically participating in the enterprise, such as merely owning (but not actively managing) rental properties. Important because of special tax treatment.

See also: Passive income, Passive loss

Since site managers had been in place for years, Thomas was able to make owning the parking lots a lucrative **passive activity**.

Passive income
Profits earned through a business activity (such as a limited partnership or a rental property) in which the investor does not physically participate.

See also: Active income, Passive activity, Portfolio income

Even though the band had broken up years before, the members still received a **passive income** *from royalties.*

Passive loss
Negative financial results (where expenses exceed revenues) sustained by a business activity in which the investor does not actively participate. For tax purposes, may only be used to offset passive income.

See also: Passive activity, Passive income

The landlord wasn't too concerned about the **passive loss** *from the one empty brownstone because the others he owned were full to capacity.*

Phantom income

A phenomenon where an investor earns taxable income even though he hasn't received any cash. This occurs with investments such as zero-coupon bonds and limited partnerships. (With zero-coupon bonds, interest is calculated and taxed annually, even though the bondholder doesn't receive annual interest payments. With limited partnerships, shareholders are taxed on their proportional share of partnership income even if that income is not distributed.)

See also: Limited partnership, Zero-coupon bond

After paying taxes on **phantom income** *for nearly five years, the man had to be convinced to stay a part of the limited partnership.*

Schedule A

The federal income tax form on which itemized deductions are detailed.

See also: Itemized deductions

The couple had made enough charitable contributions to require a **Schedule A** *on their taxes that year.*

Schedule D

The federal income tax form on which the gains and losses from asset sales are reported. Contains separate sections for short-term and long-term results.

See also: Capital gains, Capital loss

When Meryl sold her Lion Joe shares and scored her first capital gain, she filled out her first **Schedule D**.

Short term

A period of less than one year. Useful when calculating capital gains taxes.

See also: Capital gains

The economics class tracked hypothetical **short-term** *investments to see how much money they could have made in one semester.*

Sin tax

An extra state sales tax charged on "bad for you" items such as liquor and cigarettes.

See also: Gas guzzler tax

Smokers on the border of Massachusetts will often drive to New Hampshire to get cigarettes, thus avoiding the **sin tax** *levied in their home state.*

Standard deduction
A minimum subtraction from taxable income, available to all taxpayers who don't itemize their deductions.

See also: Itemized deductions

Since Raul and Tina didn't have enough deductions to itemize, they simply took the **standard deduction** *on their taxes.*

Student loan interest deduction
A special tax deduction offered to people paying off student loans, based on the amount of interest they pay. Available for loan payments made within the first five years of graduation.

See also: Income tax

Thanks to a well-paying first job and his **student loan interest deductions***, Gavin was able to pay off his student loans far earlier than he'd expected.*

Tax avoidance
A legal strategy where investments are chosen and managed to minimize taxation.

See also: Income tax

Wilhelmina worked with a tax attorney to set up a portfolio that maximized **tax avoidance** *without wandering into tax evasion.*

Tax bracket
The defined range of income subject to a specific government levy rate, where each range is subjected to a different levy percentage. Most people's incomes cross several rate tiers; this refers to the final and highest one.

See also: Income tax, Marginal tax rate

Ed's raise was enough to move the family into the next **tax bracket***.*

Tax credit
A direct reduction in the amount of government levy owed.

See also: Income tax

Nina was thrilled with the extra **tax credits** *her tax preparer was able to find for her.*

Tax-deductible
An amount that can be subtracted from total income to get to taxable income.

See also: Itemized deductions, Taxable income

The nonprofit made it clear that all donations were **tax-deductible***.*

Tax deduction

An amount that may be subtracted from taxable income before calculating the income taxes due, thereby lowering the taxes due.

See also: Itemized deductions, Standard deduction

Professional tax preparers can often find **tax deductions** *a lay person might miss.*

Tax evasion

The illegal practice where an individual or company purposely don't pay taxes that are owed.

See also: Income tax, Tax avoidance

The actor lost everything and was sentenced to three years in jail when he was found guilty of **tax evasion.**

Tax-exempt

Not subject to taxation. Can refer to a security or a taxpayer, such as a charitable organization.

See also: Municipal bond, Taxable income

The dachshund rescue organization was grateful for its **tax-exempt** *status because it ran on such a tight budget.*

Tax-free

Earnings that are not subject to taxation.

See also: Municipal bond, Triple-tax-free

Lottery winners need to remember that their winnings are not **tax-free.**

Tax planning

Arranging financial affairs to minimize government levies. Combines income, investment, and estate strategies to maximize earnings retention.

See also: Estate tax, Income tax

Many CPAs offer **tax-planning** *services to their clients.*

Tax preparer

A person who completes the paperwork necessary to report annual earnings, deductible expenses, and the levy due to a government entity. The preparer is not required to have undergone any special training or licensing to perform this task.

See also: CPA, Tax attorney

The rise of do-it-yourself tax programs has made it possible for just about anyone to claim to be a **tax preparer.**

Tax Rate
The percentage of government levy on income.
> See also: Income tax

When Madelyn moved from Massachusetts to Washington, she was pleasantly shocked at the lower **tax rate.**

Tax Shelter
An investment, a strategy, or a provision in the tax code that allows you to legally avoid or reduce your current tax liabilities. It is illegal where tax evasion is the primary goal.
> See also: IRS

For many homeowners, their home acts as a **tax shelter,** *allowing them to deduct mortgage interest and property taxes paid from their current taxable income.*

Taxable income
The net earnings upon which an annual federal and/or state levy is calculated. Taxable income equals adjusted gross income minus itemized or standard deductions.
> See also: Adjusted gross income, Itemized deductions, Net earnings, Standard deduction

When Jessica became a contractor rather than a full-time employee, her **taxable income** *dropped considerably.*

Triple-tax-free
An interest-bearing investment (typically a municipal bond) where the interest is not subject to a government tax levy at the local, state, or federal level.
> See also: Municipal bond, Tax-exempt

Since his client was looking to minimize taxes, Al advised him to invest in **triple-tax-free** *bonds.*

Unearned income
Payments received from investing or other nonemployment activities. Category includes such things as interest, dividends, capital gains, and rental income.
> See also: Adjusted gross income, Earned income

Ken was able to buy his motorcycle with the **unearned income** *brought in from the rental properties he owned with his partner.*

Wash sale
A prohibited investment strategy where a single investor buys and sells a security using two different brokers simultaneously to create the illusion of a loss transaction while not truly closing out his investment position.

See also: Wash sale rule

When the auditor looked at Greg's brokerage statements, he noticed evidence of **wash sales**, *and immediately began to assess penalties.*

Wash sale rule
An IRS regulation that forbids taxpayers to deduct losses on the sale of securities that were bought within thirty days (before or after) of the loss transaction. Also called "thirty-day wash rule."

See also: Capital loss, Wash sale

The accountant was unable to complete her client's tax return as requested because of the **wash sale rule**.

Windfall tax
A special tax charged to industries experiencing unusually high earnings rates due to economic conditions (such as oil companies that are profiting hugely on the prices paid at the pump).

See also: Luxury tax, Sin tax

When the gas prices soared, the tax attorney for Lion Joe Oil warned the CFO to expect a **windfall tax** *come April.*

INDEX

AB trust, 95
Acid-test ratio, 27
Adjustable rate, 36, 43, 44, 45, 46, 47, 48, 50, 115, 151, 177, 178, 179, 186, 211
   mortgage, 45, 47, 115, 186
Adjusted gross income, 223, 233, 237
Agricultural products, 143
Alimony, 223, 224
All or none order, 150
Amortization, 12, 63, 90, 185, 186, 190
Annuity, 90, 100, 101, 102, 114
Appraised value, 184
Articles of incorporation, 203
Asset, 2, 3, 4, 5, 6, 7, 11, 14, 19, 20, 21, 28, 29, 32, 33, 34, 36, 39, 94, 98, 99, 101, 105, 106, 107, 112, 138, 152, 185, 186, 187, 188, 191, 226, 232
   depreciation, 232
Attorney, 111
Auto insurance, 98

Bargain stocks, 19
Basis, 4, 6, 8, 14, 20, 52, 116, 224, 227
Beneficiaries, 102, 103, 105, 106, 107, 110, 112, 227
Benefits, 16, 92, 93, 95, 101, 102, 111, 114, 193, 196, 197, 198, 233
Beta, 109
Blue-chip corporation, 203, 204

Bond, 3, 5, 12, 18, 20, 22, 32, 39, 47, 51-68, 141, 165, 168, 208, 224, 234, 237
   indenture agreement, 56
   insurer, 52
   issues, 24, 158, 188
   rating, 61
Bonuses, 157, 226
Borrowed funds, 15
Brand recognition, 16
Broker, 3, 4, 8, 30, 46, 128, 140, 142, 148, 150, 151, 238. *See also* Instruction to broker
Business costs, 25
Buy-and-hold, 142, 145, 221
Buying on margin, 160
Bypass trust, 95

Call option, 143, 158, 162, 164, 172, 176
Capital, 110
   appreciation, 120, 124, 171
   gain, 20, 24, 106, 112, 115, 118, 137, 189, 225, 226, 228, 231, 234, 237
   growth, 124
   loss, 20, 112, 232
Car manufacturers, 70
Cash, 8, 15, 17, 21, 31, 39, 46, 51, 92, 105, 160, 208
   flow, 40, 63, 64
   flow gap, 36
CD, 36, 44, 49, 50, 197
Charges, 121, 122, 129

239

Charitable
  donations, 230
  organization, 91, 93, 96, 236
Check, 48
Children, 97, 99, 226, 228, 230
Child support, 223
Christmas, 86
Class of stock, 205
CMO, 64
Collateral, 20, 37, 44, 50, 55, 56, 59, 62, 142, 160, 183
Collateralized mortgage, 63, 64, 182
Commission, 116, 127, 132, 150, 151, 162, 226
Commodities, 18, 76, 145, 165, 171
  exchange, 143
Comptroller, 9
Computer quantitative analysis, 129
Consulting fees, 226
Consumer
  goods, 74
  Price Index, 71, 72, 75
Contract, 62
Controlling interest, 9, 17, 22, 75, 205
Convertible bond, 60
Copyright, 18, 29
Corporate
  charter, 218
  meeting, 218
Cost of living, 72
Costs, 13
Court, 15
Coverdell ESA, 97
Covered calls, 146, 162
Credit
  card, 48, 110
  history, 48
  rating, 38, 42
  reporting agencies, 41, 50
  risk, 60, 61
  score, 38, 41, 43
Currency, 73, 75, 76, 142, 146, 151
  values, 147

Death, 97, 101, 102, 105, 107, 112, 191
Debt, 20, 36, 37, 38, 39, 40, 41, 64, 97, 101

securities, 53, 54, 55, 56, 61, 63, 65, 79, 88, 117, 118, 127, 132
Deductions, 12, 230, 232, 233, 235, 236, 237
Default, 72, 184
Demand, 40, 44, 54, 68, 69, 75, 160, 179, 211
Derivatives, 76, 125, 127, 141, 142, 144, 148, 164, 172, 176
Dilution, 207, 215
Distribution, 193, 194, 195, 201, 207, 208
Dividends, 17, 98, 106, 119, 123, 124, 131, 205, 107, 208, 216, 218, 220, 223, 225, 226, 237
Divorce, 224
Down payment, 177, 178, 179, 182
Due diligence, 19, 149, 163
Dump, 166

Earnings, 17, 49, 60, 127, 131, 136, 167, 208, 224, 230, 236, 237
EBIT, 18, 31
Economy, 71, 79, 81, 88
Emergency fund, 107
Employer contributions, 200
Environment, 123, 130, 153
Equity, 19, 21, 183, 184, 186, 204
  securities, 60, 206, 207, 209, 216, 222
  shares, 79
ERISA, 196
ESOP, 75
Estate
  planning, 97, 103, 114
  taxes, 97, 99, 107, 232
ETFs, 125
Exam, 30, 93
Exchange, 171, 212, 214, 215, 220
Exchange-traded fund, 130, 132
Ex-date, 208
Expenses, 24, 27, 92

Fee, 122, 124, 126, 127, 128, 129, 132, 150, 163, 174, 189
Finance charges, 35, 46

Financial
  index, 74
  leverage, 11
  records and statements, 2, 4, 5, 6, 9, 14, 25, 26, 27, 28, 29, 32, 201
Fixed-income securities, 119
Fixed-rate, 177, 178
Floating interest rate, 50
FNMA, 57, 58
Food
  prices, 69
Foreclosures, 80, 182
Foreign stock markets, 81
Futures, 18, 143, 144, 165
  market, 70

Gains, 97
Gambling capital, 109
Gift, 96, 99
Goods, 136
  and services, 84
Good till cancelled order, 163
Grandchildren, 97, 99, 228
Gross domestic product, 80
Growth, 19, 115

Health
  expenses, 225, 227, 229, 230
  insurance, 94, 100, 227, 229
High-deductible health plans, 225
High-risk investments, 137
Homes, 82
Horizontal trend, 87, 155
HUD-1, 190
Hybrid fund, 116, 124

Identity theft, 110
Illness, 96
Incentives, 16
Income, 92, 97, 101, 108, 124, 171, 223, 224, 225, 230, 231, 232, 233, 234, 235, 236, 237
  shifting, 230
  tax, 223, 234, 236
Independent certified public accountant, 2

Index, 125, 162, 169, 218
  fund, 132
  futures, 86
Inflation, 66, 69, 74, 77, 78, 81, 108, 157, 225
Initial public offering, 118
Injury, 96
Insider information, 172
Installment payments, 35
Instruction to broker, 154, 155, 156, 159, 161, 171, 172, 173, 202, 203, 206
Insurance, 92, 94, 95, 96, 97, 98, 99, 100, 101, 102, 103, 106, 108, 110, 111, 113, 114, 199, 206
Intangible asset, 18, 29
Interest, 37, 40, 42, 43, 44, 55, 64, 67, 98, 106, 183, 184, 211, 223, 225, 230, 234, 237
  expense, 15
  income, 62
  payments, 18, 57, 58, 64, 66
  percentage, 44, 46, 47
  rates, 11, 35, 36, 38, 39, 42, 43, 44, 45, 48, 49, 50, 56, 57, 60, 61, 62, 63, 64, 67, 76, 78, 80, 81, 89, 127, 138, 168, 177, 178, 179, 180, 185, 187
Internet, 73, 87
Inventory
  items, 10
  purchases, 2
Investigation, 19
Investment, 3, 4
  pool, 116, 117, 118, 119, 120, 121, 122, 123, 124, 125, 126, 127, 128, 129, 130, 131, 132, 133, 134
  return, 18
  strategy, 152, 155, 157, 159, 161, 162, 169, 170, 172, 174, 238
IPOs, 158, 201, 208, 210, 211, 215, 219, 221
IRA, 95, 97, 194, 197, 198, 199, 223, 233
IRS, 88, 111, 196, 223, 225, 227, 230, 238

index

Leases, 24, 25, 29
Lessor, 185
Letter of intent, 117
Liabilities, 2, 3, 5, 6, 7, 8, 11, 20, 26, 27, 32, 33, 39, 72, 128, 237
LIBOR, 44, 47
Life
   expectancy, 194
   insurance, 97, 102, 111, 114, 195
Limit order, 171
Lipstick, 79
Liquid, 161
Living trust, 102, 103
Loan providers, 48
Loans, 48, 50, 56, 62, 90, 165, 177, 178, 179, 180, 182, 185, 186, 189, 190, 235
Loan-to-value ratio, 186
Longoria, Eva, 76
Long-term debt securities, 117
Loss, 19, 22, 231, 232, 233, 238
Low-risk investment, 145

Margin, 22, 142, 159, 160
Marital property, 94
Market
   capitalization, 202
   index, 72
   movement, 70, 203
   order, 202
   price, 31, 32, 84, 107, 138, 160, 164, 212, 216, 222
   risk, 89
   strength, 70
   trends, 146
   value, 32, 34, 73, 106, 111, 124, 213, 216, 219
Marriage, 232
Maturity, 40, 53, 54, 56, 60, 61, 62, 63, 64, 65, 68, 89, 143, 187
Medical expenses. *See* Health expenses
Merc, 82
Metal, 142, 152, 153, 174
Mid-cap stocks, 85
Minimum, 151
Minors, 113
Moody's, 61

Mortgage-backed securities, 51, 57, 58, 59, 62, 64, 67
Mortgages, 58, 59, 62, 108, 177, 178, 179, 182, 184, 185, 188, 190
Munis, 62
Mutual funds, 80, 100, 104, 115, 116, 117, 118, 119, 121, 122, 124, 125, 126, 127, 128, 129, 130, 131, 132, 133, 134, 140, 157

National gross product, 84
NAV. *See* Net asset value
Negative-equity loan, 46
Negotiable debt instrument, 52
Net
   asset value, 117, 128, 132
   profit, 12, 24, 31, 216
   worth, 7, 8, 17, 103, 136
Newspaper, 114
New Year, 212
New York State Stock Exchange (NYSE), 135, 201, 204, 212, 214, 215
Noncollateralized debt instrument, 52
Nonessential purchases, 232
Non-investment grade, 61
Normal lot, 219
Not-for-profit, 195

Oil, 83
Options, 143, 144, 145, 146, 150, 156, 162, 164, 166, 168, 169, 172, 209, 215, 220
Ownership, 219

Partner, 15, 21, 30, 97
Par value, 47, 51, 52, 60, 62, 63, 68, 209, 214, 216
Patent, 18, 29
Paycheck deductions, 196, 227
Payments, 44, 90, 98, 100, 102, 108, 113, 114, 118, 180, 183, 184, 185, 186, 189, 193, 194, 195, 199
Pension, 158
Points, 177
Ponzi, Charles, 165

index

Portfolio, 111, 150, 153, 161, 162
   diversification, 94, 122
   performance, 110
   risk, 123
Preferred stock, 98, 116, 205, 206, 216
Premium, 30, 57, 63, 92, 106, 113, 114, 161, 168
Prevailing growth trends, 127
Price, 215
   trends, 127
Price-to-earnings ratio, 213, 217
Principal, 57, 60, 61, 64, 66, 184, 186
   payments, 90
Probate, 105, 106
Profits, 3, 4, 12, 19, 22, 27, 30, 105, 226, 230, 231
Property
   taxes, 15, 186
   transfer, 181
   ownership, 184, 187, 190, 191
Prospectus, 210, 214, 217
Proxy, 211, 217
Public offering, 158
Purchase cost, 225, 228
Put options, 166

Quantitative analysis, 6, 28, 129, 167
Quarterly earnings report, 217

Redemption, 63, 66, 68, 121, 129
Refinancing, 177, 187
REMIC, 64
Rent, 15, 185
Rental
   income, 237
   property, 233
Reputation, 16
Residence, 183, 188, 225
Resistance level, 141
Retirement, 122, 192, 193, 194, 195, 196, 198, 199, 200, 224
Returns, 109, 110, 176
Reuters, 80, 108
Revenue, 2, 5, 13, 17, 27, 28, 31, 88, 210
Reverse mortgage, 179, 188

Risk, 31, 108, 109, 110, 115, 123, 155, 168, 184, 189
Run on the bank, 36

Salaries, 226
Sale(s), 17, 18, 19, 28, 29, 30, 32
   and leaseback, 19
   price, 225
   tax, 234
Scoop, 165
SEC, 18, 166, 201
Sector, 77, 86, 130
Securities, 6, 8, 17, 18, 22, 30, 31, 47, 51, 54, 55, 56, 59, 60, 67, 69, 70, 71, 75, 76, 80, 83, 84, 86, 87, 94, 95, 103, 105, 106, 113, 120, 123, 124, 130, 133, 134, 135, 137, 142, 143, 144, 148, 149, 157, 160, 162, 163, 164, 167, 170, 171, 173, 174, 175, 176, 182, 189, 207, 208, 210, 214, 215, 217, 218, 231
   Act of 1933, 136
   offering, 87
Self-employed, 195, 197, 198, 226, 230
Shareholders, 10, 31, 205, 207, 212, 217, 220, 226
Share price, 217
Shares, 203
Short-selling, 137
Short-term
   securities, 92, 127
   liabilities, 2, 3, 11, 27
Simulation, 23
Small business owners, 198
Small-cap securities, 84
Smart ETF, 125
Spouse, 94
Standard deviation, 109
Standing order, 171
Statement of Profit and Loss, 24
Stock, 26, 32, 85, 111, 116, 124, 141, 163, 164, 175, 202, 203, 205, 206, 208, 211, 215, 216, 217, 219, 220, 221. *See also* Securities
   certificate, 216
   exchanges, 75, 220. *See also* Exchange

Stock—*continued*
  market, 69, 81, 84, 88, 136
  market growth, 70
  option, 150, 156, 157. *See also*
    Option
  performance, 82
  predictor, 88
Stop order, 171, 172
Strike price, 138, 168
Student loan, 48, 233, 235
Subprime mortgage, 177, 190
Supply, 75
Swaps, 189

Takeover, 7, 15, 16, 17, 22, 25, 26, 29, 30, 31, 33, 147
Target company, 15, 22, 31, 33
Tax-advantaged, 95, 97, 128, 131, 157, 192, 194, 195, 197, 198, 199, 224, 225, 229
Tax-deferred, 65, 95, 97, 192, 194, 199, 225
Tax refunds, 227, 231
Term insurance, 114
Thirty-day wash rule, 238
TIE, 18, 32
Tips, 226
Tranche, 54, 64, 66
Transportation stocks, 74
Trend trading, 174
Trust, 93, 99, 102, 103, 107, 111, 112, 113, 120, 133
Tuition, 90, 95, 97, 231, 233

Underwriters, 158, 175, 221
Unemployment, 71, 75, 79, 81, 87, 88
Unit investment trust, 120
U.S.
  Mint, 88
  savings bond, 65, 66, 67
  tax code, 189, 192, 237

Value, 4, 6, 7, 8, 11, 14, 16, 17, 18, 19, 22, 23, 26, 28, 29, 31, 34, 41, 46, 50, 51, 61, 62, 63, 65, 70, 72, 73, 75, 76, 77, 81, 86, 90, 92, 98, 105, 106, 110, 114, 117, 126, 127, 128, 145, 146, 147, 148, 152, 154, 159, 160, 165, 166, 170, 171, 173, 175, 179, 184, 186, 207, 209, 212, 213, 214, 216, 219, 221, 222, 227, 228
Variable-rate, 177, 179
Vesting, 200
Voting stock, 26, 212, 213, 222

Wages, 3, 72, 223, 226, 230
Whole life insurance, 92
Will, 97, 102, 106, 111
Withholding, 225

Z-bond, 51
Zero-coupon bonds, 60, 68, 234
Z-tranche, 51, 68